Khonkho Wankane

Archaeological Investigations in Jesus de Machaca, Bolivia

John Wayne Janusek

Editor

Published by eScholarship, Berkeley, CA

1st edition

Ebook PDF: ISBN 978-0-9890022-9-5

POD Printed: ISBN 978-0-9982460-0-0

Available open access at: www.escholarship.org/uc/item/5hf42218

Funding of this book was made possible by Vanderbilt University Unrestricted Retention funds.

Cover image: Aerial view of the northeast section of Compound 1, highlighting the north entrance and circular Structure 6.C1. North is up.

Design: Detta Penna

Contents

Dedication

The authors dedicate this volume to Primitivo Lopez of Qhunqhu Liqi-liqi, the ritual *maestro* who consistently ensured our project's success via *wilanchas* (blood sacrifices) and *waxtas* (burned offerings), and who passed into the world of the *apus* in October, 2006.
Photograph by Wolfgang Schüler.

Preface and Acknowledgments

I first encountered Khonkho Wankane in August of 1987, during my first field season in Bolivia as a young member of Alan Kolata's ongoing archaeological research project at Lukurmata. The site, with its monumental enclosures and intriguing monoliths, struck me profoundly. Extremely little research had been conducted there. Kolata planned to initiate research later that year—a plan he realized a few months later—and he encouraged me to consider conducting my dissertation research at the site. My interest was piqued. While the course of dissertation and early post-doctoral research took me to other places, even back to Lukurmata, the idea of conducting research at Khonkho Wankane never waned for me.

I visited the site and its home community of Qhunqhu Liqiliqi nearly every year after completing my dissertation in 1994, talking to local community members, in particular the state-appointed site guardian, Alejandro Colmena, about the possibility of conducting research at Khonkho Wankane. At last, in 2000, several community members and I established the foundation for a large-scale archaeological project at the site. Funding was secured from the Vanderbilt University Discovery Program in 2001 to support two years of pilot investigation at Khonkho Wankane. Funding was secured in 2002 from the Curtiss G. and Mary G. Brennan Foundation to expand the scope of research to the site of Iruhito, on the Desaguadero River to the west. I thank the Vanderbilt Discovery Program and the Brennan Foundation for supporting this research.

This monograph summarizes the results of the first two years of archaeological research at Khonkho Wankane, in 2001 and 2002. An early, Spanish-language, and very rough version of the monograph was compiled as our project's—Proyecto Arqueológico Jach'a Machaca (with its stellar acronym, PAJAMA)—first official technical report, and it was submitted to the Bolivian Institute of Archaeology (then, INAR) and the Bolivian Viceministry of Culture in 2005 (Janusek, ed. 2005). You are reading a translated and heavily revised incarnation of that document. The report is available online, yet I decided that it merited an overhaul and official publication for two primary reasons. One, this research, which I consider Jach'a Machaca Phase One, established the foundations for larger-scale investigation. Two, later research, begun in 2004 and conducted through 2008, overshadowed many of the results of Phase One research. The upshot is that many of the archaeological details of Phase One, the details that afforded us a fundamental understanding of the spatial and temporal characteristics of Khonkho, are left out of the multiple theses and papers that are currently being published. This monograph presents archaeological data and results not found elsewhere.

Archaeological projects are fraught and unpredictable conjunctions of gathering, transaction, and production. Proyecto Jach'a Machaca Phase One was challenging, and at many times, to use Ponce's apt term for Stig Rydén's initial visit to the site (see chapter 1), *spiny*. It was initiated in the midst of a severe indigenous-speared rebellion against the then current neo-liberal government, a rebellion that the leaders of Jesus de Machaca, the canton in which Khonkho Wankane is located, are still particularly proud to have helped initiate (Albó 2012:26–87). Yet canton and community members were eager to start the project, and they supported us in every way. I am indebted to the four key project promoters in Qhunqhu Liqiliqi—Alejandro Colmena, Francisco Calle, Paulino Lifonzo, and Filomeno Limachi—who helped us secure permissions to conduct research in Qhunqhu Liqiliqi. They and their families have helped reconstruct and preserve an important part of Bolivia's pre-Hispanic history for current and future generations. Cesar Calisaya of Tiwanaku helped coordinate the project from beginning to end.

I am indebted to Alan Kolata for introducing me to Khonkho Wankane. If our interpretations differ, as detailed in chapter 1, those differences are largely due to the revitalized understanding we now have of the south-central Andean formative phases in Bolivia (Bandy 2001, 2004a; Hastorf 2003; Lémuz 2001; Janusek 2008; Janusek and Kolata 2003). Our Phase One project is indebted to numerous *apus*—animate mountain peaks that include Pukara de Khonkho to the north, Sajama to the south, Illimani to the east, and Ccapia to the west—and human persons. For 2001, key persons not included in this publication include, project co-director Pablo Rendon, conservation specialist Ludwing Cayo, and project members Oswaldo Cáceres, Nathan Clough, Margaret Andie Frey, Vianey Villegas, and Britta Watters. For 2002, key persons not represented include co-directors Ruden Plaza and Ludwing Cayo, Maria Bruno, Avery Dickens de Girón, Martin Giesso, Ashley Heaton, and Alejandra Martinez.

I extend a special thank you to Brendan Joseph McKinney Weaver, a recent Vanderbilt University Ph.D., who deftly translated several chapters of this edited monograph from the original Spanish. All images and photographs not produced by their respective chapter authors are provided courtesy of the Proyecto Jach'a Machaca archive in the Department of Anthropology at Vanderbilt University, unless otherwise noted.

Ritual specialist Primitivo Lopez of Qhunqhu Liqiliqi artfully prepared the many earth offerings (*waxta*) required to initiate the project and keep it running smoothly, often in the midst of adverse sociopolitical and climatic conditions. He passed into the realm of the *apus* in October of 2006. The authors and I dedicate this volume to his memory.

Part I

Introduction to Khonkho Wankane and Project Jach'a Machaca

Chapter 1

〜

Research at Khonkho Wankane: Antecedents, Objectives, and Initial Results of Project Jach'a Machaca

John Wayne Janusek

Research in the southern Lake Titicaca Basin during the past thirty years has established a firm foundation for understanding the Tiwanaku polity. We know that by AD 500, Tiwanaku was a prestigious ritual and political center. Its emergent political, economic, and religious networks influenced communities and productive landscapes in many regions of the south-central Andes. The ensuing 500 years witnessed the crystallization of distinctive material practices across the Lake Titicaca basin. These included multi-tiered settlement networks focused on monumental centers, platform and sunken court complexes as core ritual foci at those centers, new technologies and materials, including ceramic assemblages dedicated to novel practices of ritualized consumption, and in wetland environments, extensive systems of labor-intensive raised-field farming. Such iconic elements of Tiwanaku culture held until Tiwanaku's political-ritual networks disintegrated after AD 1000.

Still, we lack critical information regarding processes of urban concentration and polity consolidation in the region. Vast lacunae characterize specific chronological phases and geographical regions. For example, we still know very little about the critical formative phases that preceded Tiwanaku state emergence. During the long Early-Middle Formative phases (1500–200 BC), two distinct cultural complexes developed in this part of the south-central Andes: Chiripa in the southern Lake Titicaca Basin (Bandy 2001; Browman 1978; Hastorf ed. 1999; Mohr Chávez 1988; Portugal Ortiz 1988), and Wankarani further south, in Oruro (Bermann and Estevez Castillo 1995; McAndrews 1997, 2001; Ponce 1970).

The following six or seven hundred years (200 BC–AD 500), what we now call the Late Formative, has remained largely unknown until very recently. Sites such as Kallamarka, Kala Uyuni, and Tiwanaku are known to have occupations dating to this span, yet we understand sociopolitical developments in the most cursory manner. The monumental site of Khonkho Wankane in the Jesus de Machaca region south of Tiwanaku, considered by some to predate Tiwanaku expansion (Portugal Ortiz 1998; Portugal Zamora 1955), was never the focus of large-scale, systematic archaeological excavations. Yet Khonkho Wankane was the second archaeological site to be officially registered as such in the history of the Bolivian nation, only after Tiwanaku in 1919 (SNC 1997:17). Clearly, Khonkho Wankane was a major center in the past.

In addition, the Jesus de Machaca region, which comprises the Upper Desaguadero basin, is a vast geographical void in our knowledge of early pre-Hispanic cultural development in this part of the Andes. The northern side of the basin alone encompasses over 500 km, stretching from the foothills of the Corocoro range to the north and east to the Desaguadero River west and south. Khonkho Wankane occupies an inland portion of this region, just below the foothills of Corocoro and approximately 28 km directly south of Tiwanaku **(Figure 1.1)**.

Research Questions and Objectives of the Proyecto Jach'a Machaca

To help close these chronological and geographical gaps, I proposed to initiate a multidisciplinary and bi-national program of archaeological research in Khonkho Wankane and its vicinity in 2000. I designed a collaborative research program termed Proyecto Jach'a Machaca (Grand Machaca Project) that sought to investigate the chronological development and shifting character and significance of Khonkho Wankane and the Jesus de Machaca region during the Late Formative, Tiwanaku, and later periods. I sought to address several fundamental questions: What was the historical trajectory of incipient urbanism and early complexity in the region, and what were its political, economic, and ritual foundations? What was the character of local Tiwanaku influence or control, and what were its effects in local social, productive, or ritual activities and institutions? What specific productive, political, or ritual roles did Khonkho Wankane and Jesus de Machaca have as part of Tiwanaku hegemony?

Drawing on prior research at Khonkho Wankane and in the southern Lake Titicaca Basin of Bolivia, we were able to frame some of these questions in more specific terms:

- Was Khonkho Wankane the politico-religious center of a major pre-Tiwanaku polity during the Late Formative? How did the site change in significance, monumental form, ritual practices, or social composition from Late Formative through Tiwanaku periods?

- Was ritual practice a central element of local sociopolitical development? How did the character, material and iconographic expressions, or role of ritual shift over time?

- Was pastoralism the foundation of political economy in the region, and how did its role change through time? How did pastoralism intermesh with other productive pursuits, such as agriculture, fishing, or specialized craft production?

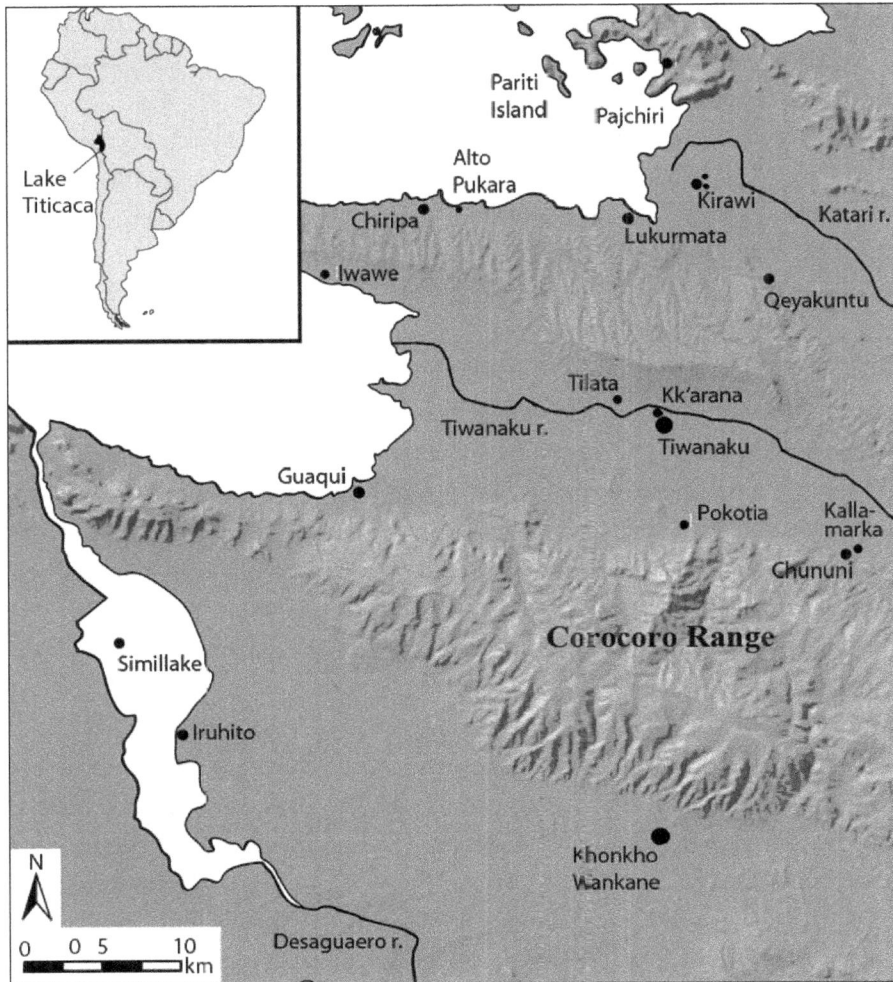

Figure 1.1 Location of Khonkho Wankane in the southern Lake Titicaca Basin.

- Was Tiwanaku influence in the region incorporative or transformative (Janusek 2008)? That is, did local sociopolitical, productive, and ritual practices or religious principles continue largely intact, or did they change substantially under Tiwanaku hegemony?

These questions guided the first phase of archaeological research in Jesus de Machaca funded by the Vanderbilt University Discovery Grant program, which I designed, in collaboration with Deborah Blom of the University of Vermont, as a two-year program of archaeological research that incorporated a diverse range of methods and specialties. Khonkho Wankane was the focus of research in 2001–2002. We defined the site as consisting of two adjacent platforms constructed over prominent, eroded mounds located 0.6 km north of the Jach'a Jawira River, a tributary of the Desaguadero. We referred to the primary platform, which supported Khonkho Wankane's central monumental complex, as Wankane, and a smaller constructed platform, some 200 meters to the northeast, as Putuni. Surrounding the platforms were several smaller mounds that comprised the site periphery.

Though Khonkho Wankane was the primary focus of research during phase 1, Proyecto Jach'a Machaca also initiated excavations at the archaeological site of Iruhito located on the east bank of the Desaguadero River and some 30 km west and slightly north of Khonkho Wankane (**Figure 1.1**). Iruhito had also been recognized as a prominent archaeological site in Jesus de Machaca (Browman 1978). Furthermore, for as long as contemporary oral narratives and written documentation can confirm, it housed one of the few Uru communities in the region (Uhle 1895). For decades, the community has been known for its mastery of riverine productive pursuits, including fishing and harvesting *totora* and constructing reed-built boats to facilitate lake and river travel. Archaeological research at Iruhito continued in later years by members of Proyecto Jach'a Machaca and its successors. These results will be published in separate volumes.

Some of the principal goals of Proyecto Jach'a Machaca in 2001–2002 included:

A) *Regional survey.* Regional analysis sought to elucidate contemporaneous settlement patterns and shifting settlement networks throughout the Formative and Tiwanaku periods, following standardized archaeological procedures of full-coverage pedestrian survey (Fish and Kowalewski 1990). Carlos Lémuz directed the survey (chapter 3). Survey entailed 3–4 people walking in straight-line transects, plotting sites on aerial photographs and topographic maps (1:25000 and 1:50000), recovering systematic samples of surface artifacts, and recording site size, components, and landscape contexts. The settlement survey covered approximately 38 km^2 and documented key sites and settlement shifts from the earliest pre-Hispanic through early Colonial occupations.

B) *Systematic mapping, geophysical prospection, and excavation at Khonkho Wankane.* Central to the project was intensive investigation at Khonkho Wankane itself. Excavations were designed to investigate the site's history of occupation, its different contemporaneous components (monumental, residential, mortuary), the diet and genetic relations of the populations it housed, and the social and ritual practices it encompassed. Excavations also sought to elucidate the relative value of crops, camelids, and non-domesticated resources in local diets and regional exchange networks. Excavations proceeded in tandem with a complete mapping of the site.

Geophysical survey—or remote sensing—directed by P. Ryan Williams (Field Museum of Natural History) and Chris Dayton (Boston University) (chapter 4) guided excavation strategy. Geophysical survey combined three

Figure 1.2 The flotation team and rig at work on the west side of Khonkho Wankane. Thanks to Maria Bruno (Dickinson College) for directing the construction of our flotation system.

complementary techniques for detecting subsurface features: ground penetrating radar (GPR), electrical resistivity, and magnetic gradiometry. Excavation strategy emphasized horizontal exposure and occupational depth. It focused on four principal site components: a) the primary monumental complex on the Wankane Platform; b) nearby residential sectors outside of the complex; c) mortuary areas west and north of the complex; and d) the east and southeast sides of the Putuni Platform to the north. Excavation units were no larger than 2 m × 2 m in area, and excavation followed cultural and natural strata. Project members recovered and curated all material artifacts found in the course of excavations, and systematically took soil, archaeobotanical, and radiocarbon samples.

C) *Laboratory and Specialized Analyses.* A particular strength of the project was its inclusion of researchers representing multiple institutions and a variety of research specialties. Analyses of ceramic, human, lithic, faunal, and other archaeological artifacts were conducted in a laboratory under construction at Khonkho Wankane. Deborah Blom (University of Vermont) and her students analyzed human remains; Martin Giesso (Northern Illinois University) analyzed lithic artifacts; Dr. James Pokines (University of Boston) analyzed micro-faunal remains; I analyzed ceramic sherds and vessels; and Maria Bruno (Dickenson College) guided the flotation process for recovering archaeobotanical remains **(Figure 1.2)**.

Figure 1.3 View of Khonkho Wankane's two principal platforms, Wankane and Putuni, facing south. Mount Sajama is in the distance to the left, and Mount Cchijccha closer to the right.

Archaeological research during Proyecto Jach'a Machaca Phase One provided a firm foundation for later research in Jesus de Machaca. In particular, it established that Khonkho Wankane was an important monumental center during the Late Formative Period (200 BC–AD 500). It confirmed that Khonkho Wankane was most influential as a regional ritual and political center during those generations. As noted below, the temporality of Khonkho's political and cultural influence had been questioned for decades. Archaeological research also confirmed that Khonkho Wankane was conscripted to the emerging Tiwanaku polity sometime after AD 500. Occupations at the site indicate that it was important to Tiwanaku regional political economy (AD 500–1000). Yet, Khonkho Wankane was relatively peripheral to Tiwanaku's coalescing ritual-political network and its emerging, panregional geopolitical mission (Janusek 2006).

Khonkho Wankane consists of two large, adjacent mounds: the Wankane mound to the south, which houses the site's monumental core, and the smaller Putuni mound (Rydén's *knoll*) to the northeast (Figures 1.3 and 1.4). Research conducted during the second phase of research at the site indicated that extensive portions of these mounds were human-built platforms (Janusek 2015, Ohnstad 2007) created by massively modifying two natural mounds located between the Corocoro foothills, to the north, and the Jach'a Jawira (Rio Grande) river, to the south. Wankane's ceremonial core comprised several monumental structures that were built over the course of the Late Formative.

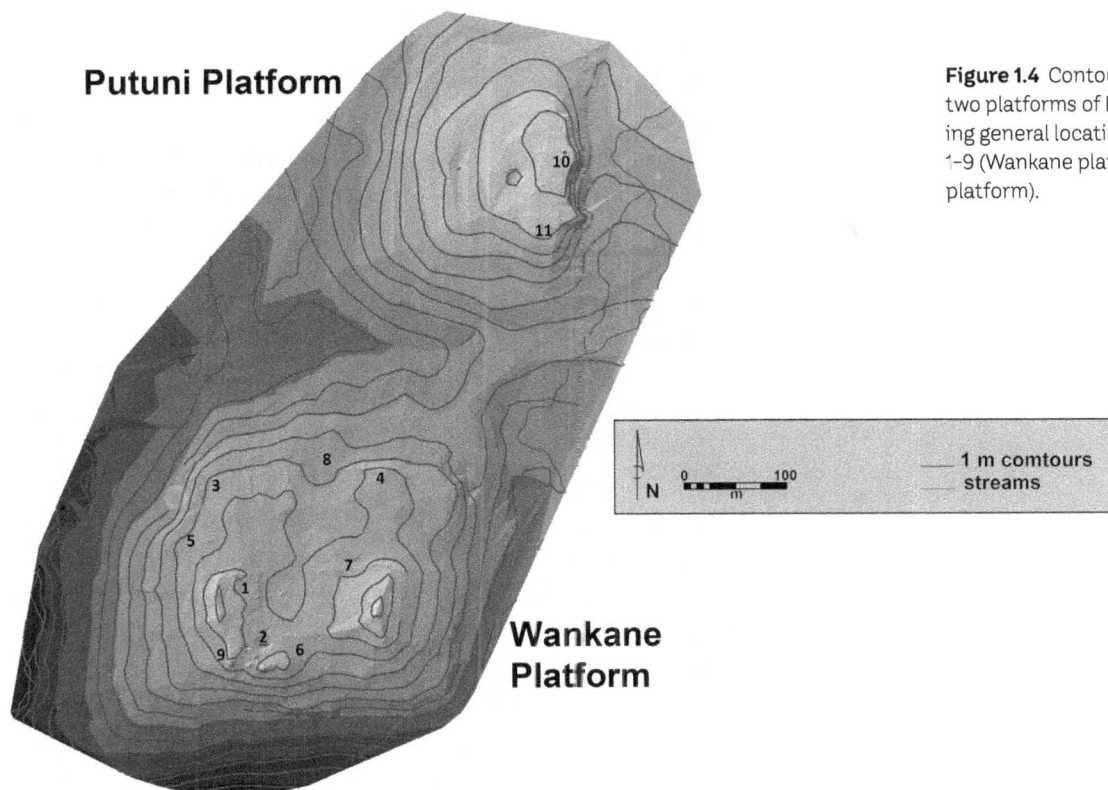

Figure 1.4 Contoured perspective of the two platforms of Khonkho Wankane showing general locations of excavation areas 1–9 (Wankane platform) and 10–11 (Putuni platform).

To clarify ensuing chapters, I describe them here drawing on results of later research (Janusek 2015; Smith 2009, 2013). They include a Main Plaza at the center of the monumental core (chapter 6), a trapezoidal Sunken Temple bounding its southwest edge (chapter 7), an extensive residential compound bounding its southeast edge (chapter 8), and a Dual-Court Complex bounding its west edge (chapter 9). Sometime toward the middle of the Late Formative, in AD 200–300, large earthen platforms were constructed on the east, south, and west edges of the monumental core. The east and south platforms were constructed inside of extensive residential compounds, while the west platform housed the Dual-Court Complex.

Our excavations employed four concrete benchmarks that an earlier team led by Alan Kolata (1987) had previously sunk into the Wankane mound (see below). Their south benchmark, located on top of the south platform, became our primary point of georeference. It is located at UTM N8141652 E534894 and at an altitude of 3889 meters above sea level. We established a grid by arbitrarily designating the benchmark as N4000 and E4000 within the global UTM coordinate system. Points at the site, as noted on the excavation unit maps of subsequent chapters, refer specifically to this primary benchmark as a point within the UTM system. Thus, a point located at N4192.90 E3937.05 is located at UTM N8141844.9 E534831.05.

The following section elaborates a history of research at Khonkho Wankane. It focuses on a chronological conundrum that has plagued interpretation of the site for decades: was Khonkho Wankane primarily a Tiwanaku regional city, as Carlos Ponce Sanginés (1981) and Alan Kolata (1993) hypothesize; or was it primarily an earlier Formative center, as Maks Portugal Zamora (1955) and his son Max Portugal Ortiz (1998), among others (Ibarra Grasso and Querejazu Lewis 1986:184), suggested?

History of Research

Very little research had been conducted at Khonkho Wankane prior to Project Jach'a Machaca's initiation in 2001. It appears that the site and its monuments had been curated and revered by inhabitants of the community of Qhuñqhu Liqiliqi, in which it is located, and perhaps the entire Jesus de Machaca macrocommunity, for centuries. Yet it is only during the first half of the twentieth century that the site came to the attention of archaeologists, the Bolivian nation, and ultimately, the world (Portugal Zamora 1955:51).

The archaeological history of the site commenced when a resident of Guaqui, a town located some 40 travel-kilometers northwest of Khonkho and *en route* to the site from Tiahuanaco, denounced ongoing excavations at Khonkho as illicit and against the interests of the state of Bolivia (Anonymous 1936). An anonymously authored and non-provenienced newspaper article that Bolivian archaeologist Jédu Sagarnaga (1987:46) located, signed October 13, 1936, names the Spaniard Valentín López del Diego and the German Tiwanaku enthusiast Fritz Buck as the key agents in these *"secret"* investigations (Portugal Ortiz 1998:117; Rydén 1947:89).[1] For his part, Fritz Buck (1937:183) relates that López *discovered* the site early in 1936. The anonymous article corroborates that López had resided for some time in Viacha, a city relatively close to Khonkho Wankane, had likely heard about the ruins, and had ultimately interested Buck in together initiating investigations at the site. After describing the sandstone monolith known as Wila Kala (chapter 5) that occupies the southeast part of the Wankane platform, the article continues that Buck, *"with an absolute lack of knowledge of such delicate matters, proceeded to extract the monolith...breaking it in two and committing a true crime"* (Anonymous 1936, paragraph 5; *my translation*). Whether or not events occurred as such, Buck nonetheless participated in the following official commission to Khonkho.

The Swedish archaeologist Stig Rydén recounts ensuing events (1947:89):

> When this became known at the National Museum in La Paz, its director, Dr. Maks Portugal, in October of that year made a journey of inspection to the ruin. Its existence was reported to the ministry

[1] I thank Jédu Sagarnaga for graciously providing a copy of this early document.

Figure 1.5 The first archaeological commission to Khonkho Wankane, in 1936, and undoubtedly the first published photo of the site. Standing in front of the Jinch'un Kala monolith, left to right, are Fritz Buck, Maks Portugal, and Guillermo Mariaca (from Buck 1937:Figure 66).

in charge at La Paz with a view to having the ruin placed under state control.

In October of that year, Maks Portugal Zamora, then Director of the National Museum of La Paz, published a brief description of the site and its monoliths in the Bolivian periodical *La Razón*. In November of 1936, then Minister of Education and Indigenous Affairs Alfredo Peñaranda, organized the first commission to investigate the site and its immediate region. Maks Portugal headed it, accompanied by Fritz Buck and Guillermo Mariaca (Anonymous 1936) **(Figure 1.5)**. This commission put Khonkho Wankane on the map of archaeological knowledge, national patrimony, and amateur speculation.

Maks Portugal: Khonkho Wankane as Pre-Tiwanaku Center

This was just the first of at least three seasons in which Portugal Zamora excavated at the site. According to Stig Rydén, who worked at Khonkho toward the end of 1938 (see below), Portugal was conducting research at the same time. In a lat-

Figure 1.6 Rydén's (1947:Fig. 29) photo (facing south) of the remnant intake of a large drainage canal under the Main Plaza of the Wankane platform.

Figure 1.7 The remnant five pieces of the Portugal monolith, located on the west slope of the Wankane platform. Photo was taken in 1987 during Kolata's investigations at the site (courtesy of Alan Kolata, Department of Anthropology, University of Chicago).

er publication, Portugal refers to a third and possibly final season of excavation in 1941 (Portugal Zamora 1955: Lamina II). Portugal Zamora summarized the results of his work in two brief articles (1941, 1955). In the first, Maks describes three sculpted sandstone monoliths that heretofore had been curated by community members: Tatakala (father or priest stone), Jinch'unkala (eared stone), and Wilakala (red stone). He describes some of the more striking elements of their sculpted iconography, including icons depicting felines, whiskered serpents, and lightning. Based on monolithic iconography, Portugal precociously concluded that Khonkho dated to a pre-Tiwanaku epoch.

Portugal excavated twelve excavation units, and the first eight "did not yield the desired results" (Portugal Zamora 1941:297). Apparently, the last four were more successful. Portugal describes the intake of a large drainage canal eight meters south of Tatakala at the center of the Wankane platform **(Figure 1.6)**. This subterranean feature drained the platform's Main Plaza and, though heavily disturbed by centuries of farming, herding, and looting, is still present further south as Wankane's primary subterranean drainage feature (chapter 6, Plaza 2007). In the twelfth unit, Portugal and colleagues located a shattered fourth monolith that our project christened, we think appropriately, the Portugal monolith (chapter 5, Ohnstad 2011, 2013) **(Figure 1.7)**.

Excavations in the Northeast Section of the Wankane Mound

In 1938, Maks Portugal initiated excavation units in the northeast sector of the Wankane Platform (Portugal Zamora 1955). There is some discrepancy regarding the precise location of these excavations: while Portugal maps them on top

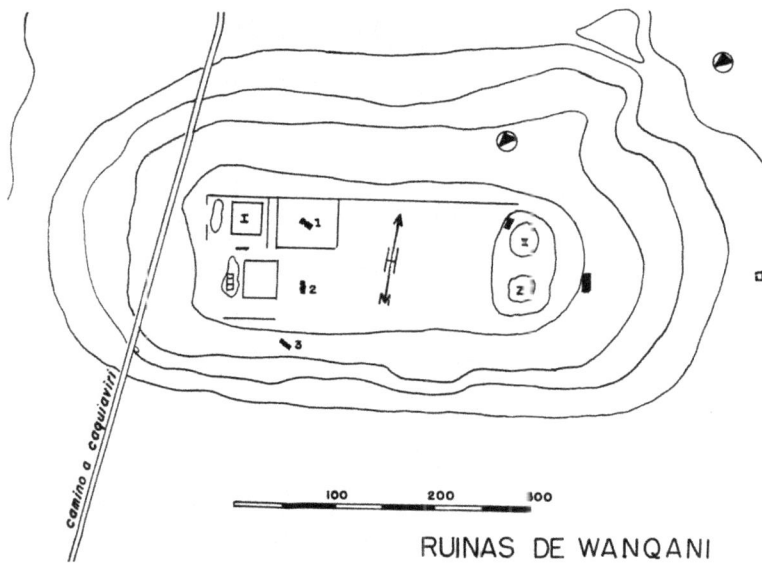

RUINAS DE WANQANI

of the Wankane East Platform (*x* and *z* in **Figure 1.8**), Rydén locates them at a significant distance to the northwest. In either case, the excavations were located in or near our Sector 12, which later revealed a large walled compound that incorporated several groups of circular structures and a stepped platform on its central east side (Janusek 2015; Marsh 2012; Smith 2009, 2013). Portugal exposed cobble wall foundations and three human burials. Rydén (1947:138–141) described two of the burials that Portugal Zamora excavated in 1938,[2] and Max Portugal Ortiz, Maks Portugal Zamora's son, published further details from his father's field notes in his own book, *Escultura Prehispanica Boliviana* (1998:129–133).

Portugal Zamora (1955) exposed three partial structure foundations **(Figure 1.9)**. Two were rectilinear and one was semi-circular. The semi-circular foundation abutted a rectilinear foundation that had been partially removed to accommodate Portugal's Tomb C. Tomb C contained Tiwanaku-affiliated material. The second rectilinear foundation supported a thick wall closely aligned to the cardinal directions and partially covering the northwest side of Tomb C. It likely also dated to the Tiwanaku period. The stratigraphically lower semi-circular and rectilinear foundations manifest a pattern that Project Jach'a Machaca found to be common in Late Formative occupations at the site. I suspect that the latter were remnant foundations of Late Formative structures. Associated with them were "disperse materials, including roughly worked stone and llama bone" (Portugal Zamora 1955:62).

[2] After describing these two burials and their offerings, Rydén writes (1947:141): "I also learnt from Max Portugal that on an earlier visit to Wancani [sic] he happened upon a grave lacking grave equipment."

Figure 1.9 Portugal's (1955: Lamina II) rendered excavation plan of structures and features excavated on the northeast portion of the Wankane platform in 1941.

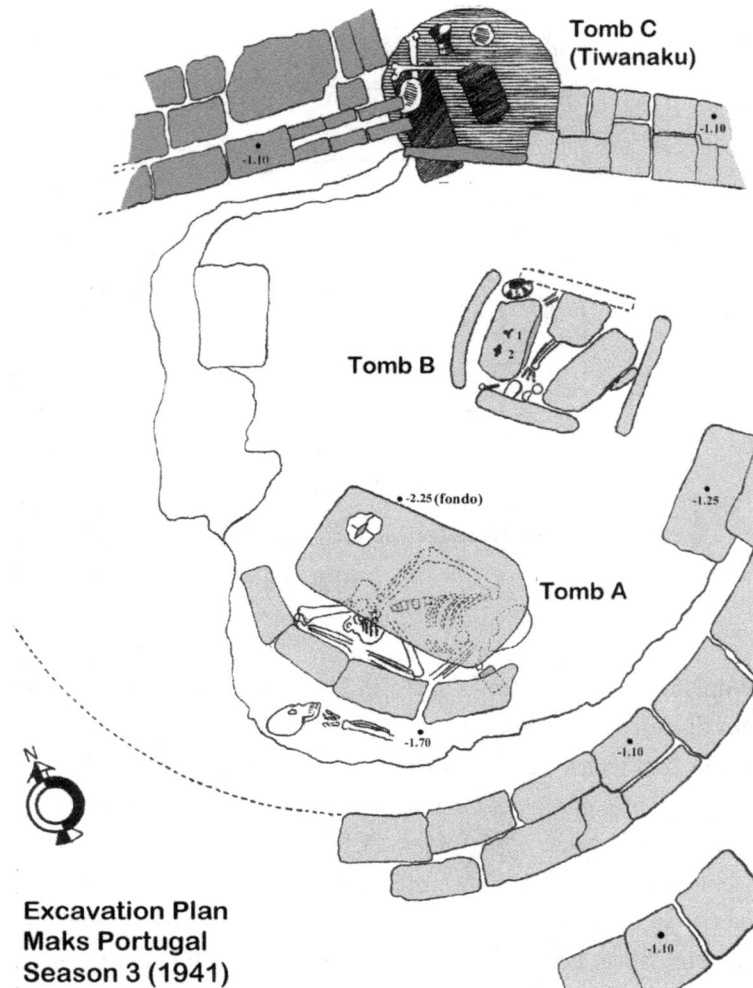

Figure 1.9 Portugal's (1955: Lamina II) rendered excavation plan of structures and features excavated on the northeast portion of the Wankane platform in 1941.

Deeper excavations exposed two cist burials under the floor of the semi-circular structure. I hypothesize that both date to the Late Formative. Because osteological analyses of the human remains were never published (and perhaps never conducted), I cannot elaborate on the sex, age, or health of the interred persons. Portugal Zamora (1955:62) considered Tomb A to contain the remains of a local authority. A large stone slab covered the cist. The person was interred wearing relatively elaborate adornments, including a necklace that incorporated four bronze stars, a bronze circular pendant, and a bronze pin. S/he also wore a chin perforation, or labrette, consisting of a terracotta core plated with gold-colored metal (and possibly gold itself, Vellard 1955:55). The person was interred with a plaster-like *masa blanca*, undoubtedly one of the plaster blocks that we now know were central to ritual practice at Khonkho Wankane (Smith and Pérez 2014). A second, poorly preserved person lay on his/her side outside of the main chamber and just outside of the semi-circular tomb collar. This person faced the tomb. Was this person interred to accompany or guard the primary person upon his/her death?

Tomb B was located less than a meter to the northwest (Portugal Zamora 1955:64–65). The cist was bounded on four sides by flat stone slabs and covered by three flat capstones. The oblique orientation of the quadrangular cist paralleled that of the slab over Tomb A. Most of the human remains had disintegrated. A remnant fragment of the cranium, part of the frontal bone, had been covered with red ochre. The individual wore a bronze labrette. His/her right arm extended toward a cache of offerings that included a circular bronze pendant and pin crafted in the same style as those found in Tomb A. The person wore a necklace with beads in multiple colors joined by a central piece of gold lamina hammered into *trilobe* form. Other offerings included a small, lens shaped dish and a long bronze pin. In addition, a stone labrette and a small obsidian arrow point had been placed carefully over the westernmost capstone, the one that covered the cranium.

Portugal excavated the burials either in 1941 (Portugal Zamora 1955) or 1942 (Vellard 1955:151). Although Portugal recovered no diagnostic Late Formative vessels in the burials, comparing them with human interments our project later excavated on the Wankane Platform, I interpret them as Late Formative burials placed under the semi-circular structure. One burial we excavated in 2005 (7W.10–13, Feature 1)—one of the few Late Formative adult interments we located at Khonkho Warkane—was located under the floor of an obsolete circular building (Structure 12.C3). Several metal adornments accompanied what was apparently a deceased adult female.

The third burial, Tomb C, and the one that intruded into the early rectilinear wall, had already been excavated in 1938, while Rydén was present. Dating to the Tiwanaku period, the burial was located just northeast of Tomb B. A flat stone slab supported the south edge of the cist. The human remains, which were in very poor condition, had been positioned on top of a large stone block at the base of the tomb (Portugal Zamora 1955:65; Rydén 1947:140). Two polychrome Tiwanaku ceramic vessels accompanied the individual: a *kero* decorated with a highly stylized serpent and front-face figure, and a *tazon* with self-contained volutes. Portugal also encountered a rectangular, perforated bone object, which Rydén (1947:140) suggests served as a "wrist guard against the slap of the bowstring" when hunting with bow and arrow.

Excavations on the East Platform

Portugal conducted excavations in at least one other area. On his crude map, he marks its location at the south end of the Wankane East Platform while Rydén locates it slightly northeast of its north end. Here, he exposed at least two other burials. They included a burial with two children that had been interred with two bronze *tupu* pins and two necklaces, one of beads and the other of snail shells. Near either this tomb or another—Portugal's description is unclear (1955:66)—was an elaborate Tiwanaku *incensario* with a modeled camelid-effigy head that contained burnt organic matter. The association of *incensarios* with Tiwanaku-period human burials was a common pattern at Lukurmata, in the Katari Valley, and other sites on the southern Lake Titicaca lake shore. Aside from one complete vessel from a burial atop Akapana at Tiwanaku (Kolata 1993:117), this is one of the few complete examples known from outside of this lacustrine region (see Bermann 1994; Janusek 2004).

A third burial just to the northeast, excavated in 1938 or 1939, also dated to the Tiwanaku period (Portugal Zamora 1955:65–66; Rydén 1947:139–140). This was a slab-lined cist tomb that contained a flexed adult accompanied by three Tiwanaku ceramic vessels[3]: a *kero* decorated with two profile feline faces, a *tazon* decorated with a profile zoomorphic face; and an undecorated, thick-walled, flaring-rim bowl with a single side handle[4] (Rydén 1947:139–140). The latter bowl type is relatively uncommon, though similar bowls characterized specific residential contexts at Lukurmata and Tiwanaku.

Portugal's Conclusions

Portugal Zamora (1955:66) concluded that the Tiwanaku burials he excavated postdated the sculpted monoliths encountered at the site. In a posthumous monograph (Portugal Zamora 1988:16), he refined his position in light of more recent research in the Lake Titicaca basin. He suggested that Khonkho Wankane was inhabited by an early society "with a clear division of social classes" that built two rectangular Kalasasaya-like platforms. The employment of red sandstone for Khonkho's monoliths and the iconographic style of those stelae, he continues, identifies the site as part of an early panregional *Pa-Ajanu* tradition. He and his son had defined this lithic sculptural style based on findings at Mocachi, Tiwanaku, Santiago de Huata, and elsewhere. Portugal Zamora considered Pa-Ajanu contemporaneous with Tiwanaku III, which Ponce (1981) had dated to approximately AD 100–400, preceding Tiwanaku state formation. Following this chronology, Maks interpreted Pa-Ajanu as part of Tiwanaku's early, pre-Classic "urban expansion." Ponce's Tiwanaku III corresponds roughly to what archaeologists now term Late Formative 2 (AD 250–500), and our research indicates that Khonkho Wankane peaked in ritual and political influence during this phase. Portugal Zamora's chronological interpretation was essentially correct, but it was all but disregarded until most recently (but see Portugal Ortiz 1998:112).

[3] Portugal Zamora notes that there were only two, though his article was published seventeen years after the excavations were conducted (see Portugal Ortiz 1998:119).
[4] This vessel appears to be of the same type encountered in specific types of structures at Lukurmata (Bermann 1994:184–186) and in specific contemporaneous contexts at Tiwanaku (Janusek 2003a)

Stig Rydén: Khonkho Wankane as "Decadent" Tiwanaku "cult centre"

The Swedish archaeologist Stig Rydén (1947:82) arrived in Jesus de Machaca at "the end of 1938," after having finished his oft-cited excavations and ceramic analyses in Tiwanaku. As he put it, "The investigations at Tiahuanacu having been completed, work was transferred to the Desaguadero district, or to be more exact, to the district surrounding the villages of Sollkatiti and Khonkho, south of Quimsachata" (Rydén 1947:81).[5] Jesus de Machaca came closer to his initial interest in studying the "Chullpa-graves" of the Bolivian highlands (1947:11). While *chullpas* are rare in both the Tiwanaku and Jesus de Machaca regions, they date to post-Tiwanaku pre-Hispanic periods that are prominently manifested in Jesus de Machaca. First, though, Rydén joined Maks Portugal in conducting excavations at Khonkho Wankane.

Rydén took photos, conducted surface collections, made impeccable artifact drawings, excavated twelve excavations units, and rendered a map that remained definitive until 2001 **(Figure 1.10)**. He was the first to conduct excavations on the "knoll" north of Wankane, what we refer to by its local toponym, Putuni. Rydén was also the first to excavate post-Tiwanaku burials at Khonkho Wankane. Once finished at Khonkho, Rydén (1947:167–476) conducted extensive archaeological research at sites in the foothills of the Corocoro range just north of Khonkho Wankane. This involved reconnaissance and excavation at sites dating largely to post–Tiwanaku Late Intermediate (Early Pacajes) and Late Horizon (Inca Pacajes) periods.

Rydén (1947:82) noted that Khonkho Wankane is bounded by two streams that descend from springs in the Corocoro foothills **(Figure 1.11)**. He considered monumental construction on Wankane "a smaller–scale counterpart of Kalasasaya at Tiahuanacu." He specified that it consisted of "three rectangular courtyards" (1947:86). The largest was the northeast courtyard, what we now term the Main Plaza. Framing its west side was the northwest courtyard, what we now term the Dual-Court Complex. Bounding the south side of both was the south courtyard, what we now term the Sunken Temple (Rydén 1947:86–89). These structures occupy the central and west portions of Wankane. Rydén never seriously considered surface topography on the east side of Wankane,

---

[5] This was, by all accounts, a harrowing journey for Rydén. As Ponce recounts (1995:157), Maks Portugal having told him the story, "el viaje de Tiwanaku hasta alli entonces resultaba espinoso, en extremo incomodo y habia que verificarlo como jinete cabalgando en lomo de especimenes criollos de caballos o mulas." Confronting volatile political conditions in 2001, our own initial journey to the site from Tiwanaku was more than a little "espinoso." Nevertheless, we trekked from Tiwanaku to Khonkho Wankane across the Corocoro range on foot rather than riding horseback, or on mules.

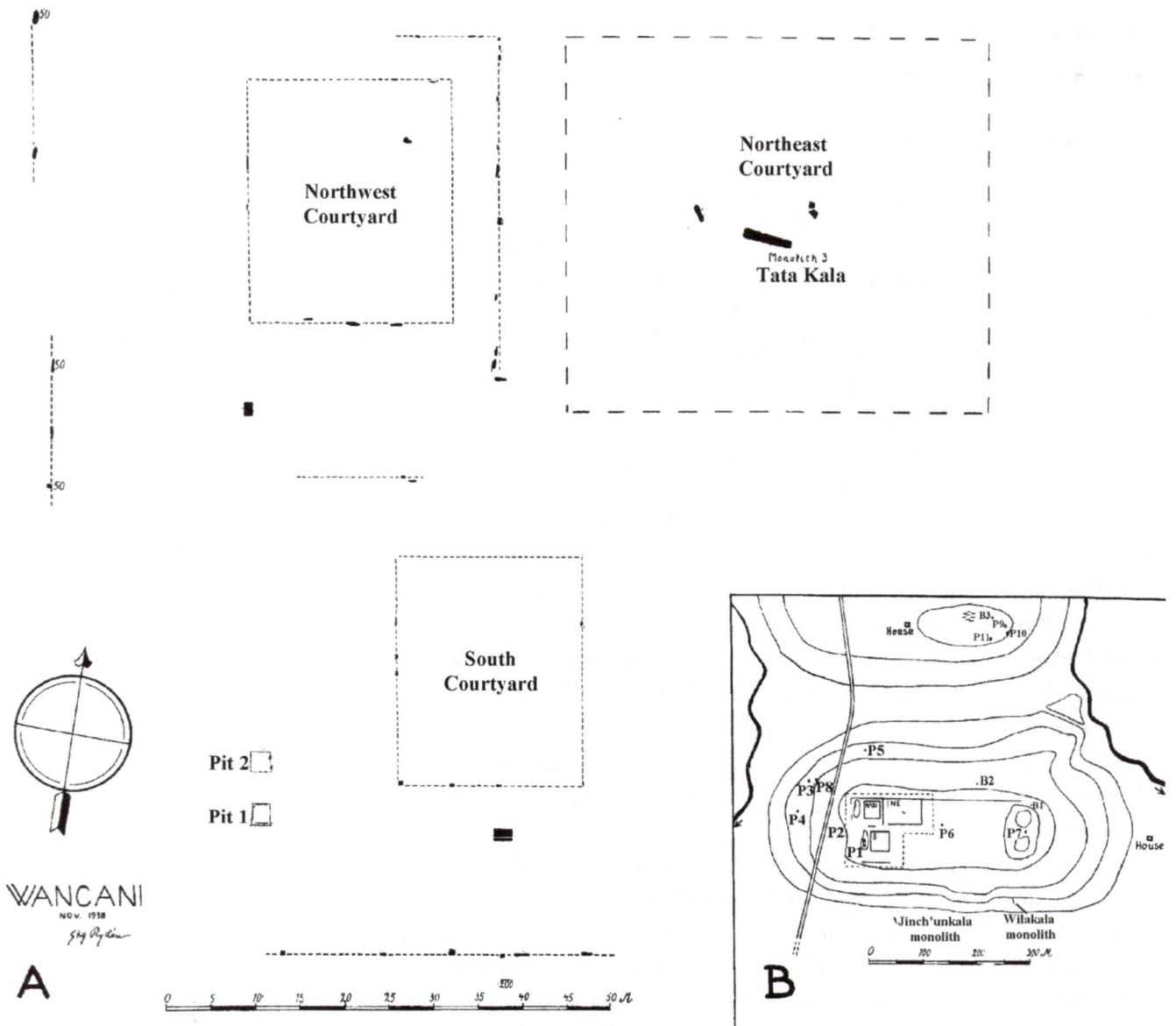

Figure 1.10 Rydén's (1947: Map 6) map of Khonkho Wankane (A), which incorporates Portugal's rendering to show the location of pits excavated at the site (P = Pit, B = Burial).

Figure 1.11 The spring-fed stream that bounds the east side of Khonkho Wankane.

where Maks Portugal simultaneously conducted excavations. Minimally, it was clear that this portion of the site incorporated a prominent east courtyard or platform (Portugal Zamora 1955).

Rydén was an impeccable archaeologist for his time. His artifact descriptions are richly detailed. He had a particular penchant for ceramic analysis. He pioneered the classification of Tiwanaku and post-Tiwanaku ceramics according to form and function, defining fundamental categories as consisting of either cooking pots, storage/fermentation jars, or *artistic* vessels. His categories provided the foundation for later, more intensive analyses of ceramic artifacts in the Lake Titicaca Basin (Alconini 1995; Janusek 2003a; Lémuz 2001). Surface finds at Khonkho Wankane included decorated ceramic sherds dating to Tiwanaku (**Figure 1.12**), Early Pacajes (his "Post Decadent" Tiwanaku), and Inca occupations, as well as numerous objects and adornments of bone, stone, and metal (most consisting of copper and tin, some with trace elements of lead, silver, or iron; see Rydén 1947:114). Rydén's published drawings include Late Formative ceramic sherds, but he was unfamiliar with those largely undecorated types.

He conducted no excavations within the *courtyards* per se, whether for lack of interest or because he was not given permission by Maks Portugal and Bolivian authorities. Nevertheless, Rydén excavated one unit inside of the Main Plaza (Pit 6), one unit in the East Platform (Pit 7), one unit on the west slope of Wankane (Pit 4), three units on the northwest slope of Wankane (Pits 3, 5, and 8), and two units on the south uppermost part of the West Platform (Pits 1 and 2).

His excavation unit in the Main Plaza (Pit 6) revealed ceramic sherds dating to Late Formative and Tiwanaku periods (Rydén 1947: Fig. 49). The unit in the East Platform (Pit 7) revealed "No finds of any kind…" (Rydén 1947:130). The unit on the west slope of the mound (Pit 4), which consisted of two adjacent trenches excavated near large surface blocks, yielded two parallel rows of stones (Rydén 1947: Map 11). The three units on Wankane's northwest slope (Pits 3, 5, and 8) revealed richer cultural stratigraphy. Collectively, they yielded ceramic sherds dating to the late Formative and Tiwanaku periods, and several sherds dating to Early Pacajes

Figure 1.12   Rydén's (1947:Figure 40) rendering of Tiwanaku style ceramic sherds from Khonkho Wankane.

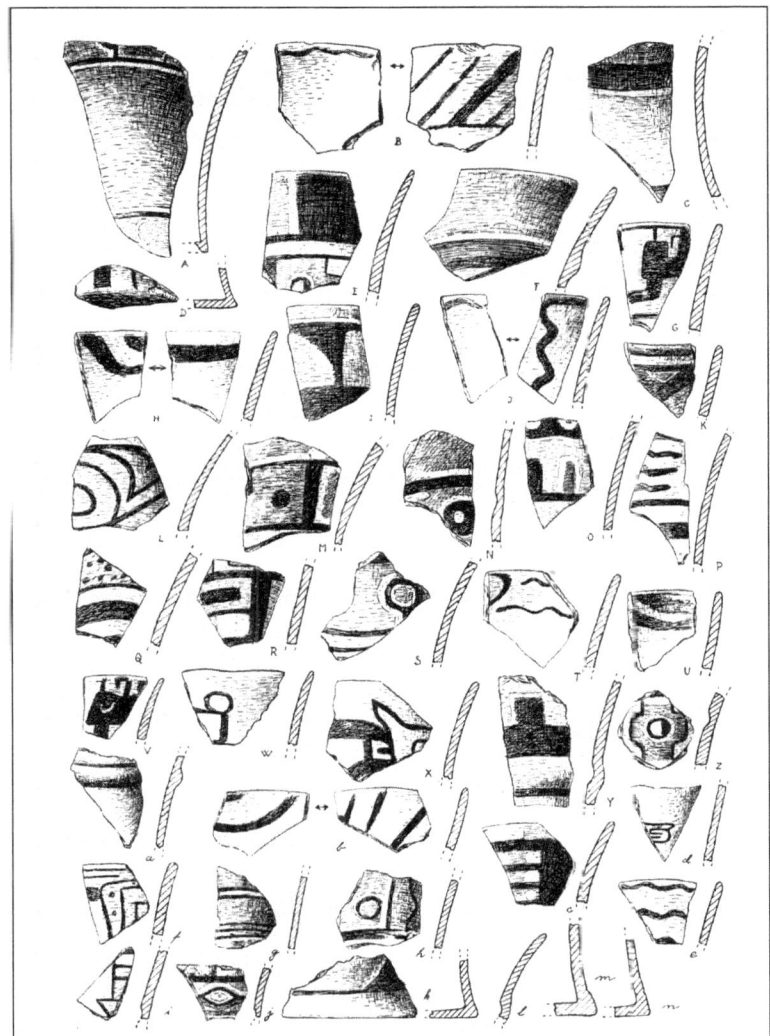

(Rydén 1947:Fig. 47–52). One unit (Pit 5) exposed the rectilinear foundations of a structure (Rydén 1947:Map 12).

The two units on the West Platform (Pits 1 and 2) exposed two adjacent, semi-subterranean slab-cist tombs that post-dated Tiwanaku occupations **(Figure 1.13)**. Rydén identified them as pre-Hispanic post-Tiwanaku (1947:119–120), though the presence of horse bones in both suggests that they were repurposed as Early Colonial burials (Late Pacajes, AD 1535–1570). The tombs are still present on the crest of the south edge of the West platform, and both are rectangular in form. The burials have been looted or otherwise disturbed, and their human remains were highly disturbed. The northernmost tomb (Pit 1) contained "three or four adults and one child" (Rydén 1947:118), while the other (Pit 2) contained "at least thirteen people…including five children" (ibid.:120).

Rydén was the first to systematically investigate the Putuni mound to the north. Surface ceramics from Putuni were similar to those from Wankane, except local Inca style ceramics were absent in his collection (1947:141). He recovered several lithic objects, including two arrow points, a *trompo*, fragmented hoes, and retouched flakes. He excavated three units on the east side of the mound (Pits 9, 10, 11, and Burial 3), all on the east side of a large reservoir near its center. Pit 11 yielded Tiwanaku ceramic sherds and several lithic hoe fragments down to 50 cm, below which the soil was sterile. The other three pits, all near the east edge of the mound, yielded substantial osteological remains. Pit 9 exposed a possible offering consisting of camelid cranial bones placed under two juxtaposed stone slabs 75 cm below the surface. The four sherds recovered from the context were undecorated, and in light of his descriptions (Rydén 1947:148) and our later research on the mound, may date to the Late Formative. Pits 10 and 12 both revealed human remains. Pit 10 revealed a small cist burial with highly degraded human remains without any clear offerings or adornments. Associated sherds dated to Tiwanaku. Pit 12 was a slab-cist grave that contained the remains of at least three individuals, including one child (Rydén 1947:152). A sherd from the tomb presented a modeled effigy handle dating to the Pacajes phases.

Despite Rydén's meticulous descriptions and superb eye for detail, he (1947:154) concluded that Khonkho Wankane was first occupied during "the Decadent Tiahuanaco period," what Ponce Sanginés later termed Tiwanaku V (AD 800–1000). He came to a conclusion very different from his Bolivian colleague Maks Portugal, who dated Khonkho's initial occupation to a pre-Tiwanaku era. Rydén (1947:153) based his chronological conclusion on Khonkho's "architectural style, the excavated finds, the monoliths adjoining the ruins, and, to some extent, the character of the graves." Rydén (1947:154) noted that Wankane's monumental courtyards mimicked those of the *Kalasa-saya* at Tiwanaku, but that at Khonkho, architectural stones were smaller and the structures "impress one as being poorer and more degenerate."

Similarly, Rydén interpreted the two best preserved monoliths at Khonkho Wankane—Jinch'unkala and Wilakala—as relatively "Decadent" in style and chronological age (1947:164). This later interpretation was perhaps influenced by that of his colleague from the American Museum of Natural History, Wendell Bennett, who had conducted archaeological research at Tiwanaku in 1932 and at nearby sites in 1933–1934. Bennett (1934:467–468) had inter-

Figure 1.13 View and plan of Rydén's (1947:Fig. 46) excavation (Pit 2) in an Early Pacajes slab-cist burial on the Wankane platform. Rydén suggests that it incorporated thirteen individuals.

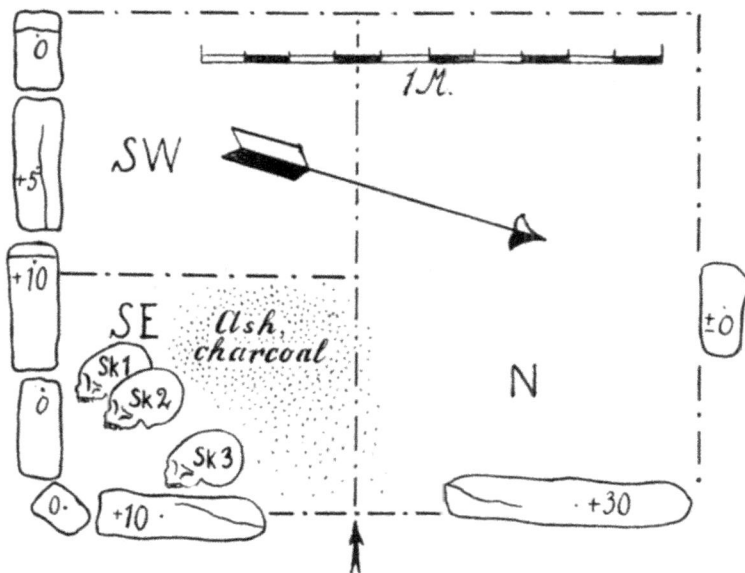

preted the *Bearded Stela* of Tiwanaku's Sunken Temple *(Templete)* as a late stylistic innovation dating to Tiwanaku's "Decadent" phase. Tiwanaku's Bearded and Khonkho's Jinch'unkala and Wilakala monoliths share multiple material, technical, and stylistic affinities that Portugal considered elements of a formative material complex.

Primarily ceramic evidence drove Rydén to interpret Khonkho Wankane as a late, "Decadent" Tiahuanaco site (1947:157–158). Based on his excavations at Tiwanaku, Bennett (1934) precociously deduced three successive chronological phases; Early, Classic, and Decadent Tiahuanaco. His Early Tiahuanaco corresponds roughly to our Late Formative, and his Classic and Decadent Tiahuanaco to Ponce's Tiwanaku IV and V (my Tiwanaku 1 and 2, Janusek 2008). Rydén recovered none of the decorated Early Tiahuanaco sherds that Bennett recovered in deep strata under Tiwanaku's monumental core. Later research at Tiwanaku and across the southern Lake Titicaca Basin—including Khonkho Wankane—indicate that decorated *Early Tiahuanaco* vessels are uncommon overall (Bandy 2001; Bermann 1994; Lémuz 2001). In most contexts, 95–100% of sherds are from undecorated cooking *ollas*, storage jars, serving bowls, or small pitchers (Janusek 2003a, b). Neither Bennett nor Rydén was attuned to the finer details and distinctions of undecorated Late Formative and Tiwanaku ceramic vessels. Rydén recovered plenty of decorated Tiwanaku and post-Tiwanaku Early Pacajes and Pacajes-Inca style ceramic sherds, noting that Khonkho's Tiwanaku "artistic pottery" is geometrical and late. "Early Tiahuanaco culture," he surmised (1947:154), "is altogether unrepresented."

For Rydén, Khonkho Wankane was a center of "secondary and local importance" that dated primarily to late or "Decadent" Tiwanaku. Ponce would later characterize this phase as that of Tiwanaku imperial expansion. Yet Rydén's skill with ceramics led him to make another precocious insight. He noted that at both Tiwanaku and Khonkho, "pottery finds preponderantly consist of fragments of drinking vessels and of water and fermentation containers…" Furthermore, he noted that few "profane buildings" had been recovered at either site, but that "beds of ashes have been observed, and bones that were the residue of meals have been recovered…". (1947:158–159). Based on these observations, Rydén interpreted Tiwanaku and Khonkho Wankane more as "centres of culture than of settlement," and the archaeological remains recovered the residues of "ritual meals" rather than "permanent settlement on the spot" (1947:159). Without jumping to the conclusion that either was an *empty* ceremonial center, he made the important point that ritual practices involving commensal events were central at Tiwanaku and Khonkho Wankane. Our research corroborated this conclusion.

Khonkho as Bolivian Cultural Patrimony and Tiwanaku City

After the early work of Portugal Zamora and Rydén, Khonkho Wankane fell off the radar as assuredly as it had appeared. Research at the site occurred over the following half-century, but little aside from Portugal's second and last article on the site (1955) was published. Despite Maks Portugal's precocious insights to the contrary, Stig Rydén's interpretation of Khonkho as a secondary Tiwanaku-period center would hold until Project Jach'a Machaca initiated research in 2001 (Janusek 2011, 2013; Janusek, Ohnstad, and Roddick 2003). During this time, based on countless meta-citations and quick visits to the site, Khonkho Wankane crystalized in academic and popular consciousness as a regional Tiwanaku center and, ultimately, Tiwanaku's *second city*.

On the heels of Rydén's belated publication, Bennett published a synthesis on Lake Titicaca Basin chronology in *American Anthropologist*. In this influential journal he summarized his Swedish colleague's findings (1950:93). Citing Rydén's ceramic analyses and site interpretations, Bennett proposed reformulating his original three phase chronology for Tiwanaku and the southern Lake Titicaca basin. He suggested recasting Khonkho Wankane as the type site for *Decadent Tiahuanaco* and post-Tiwanaku, pre-Inca occupations. He thus suggested renaming Decadent Tiahuanaco "Wankani" and the immediate post-Tiwanaku occupations "Khonkho." These names failed to outlive their initial publication, and Ponce (1980:71) later noted with characteristic bluntness that "the suggestion had no resonance whatsoever." Yet the publication demonstrates how entrenched this chronology had become, and the impact its distribution had on readership across the discipline.

The French naturalist Jean Vellard served as director of the Museum of Archaeology in 1941–1942, directly following Maks Portugal (Ponce 1995:133). He (1955) published a brief article on Khonkho Wankane that focuses on Khonkho's monoliths. He mentions several other monolith fragments similar to those at the site. For example, he notes that one fragment presents iconography that reproduces *exactly* the frontal iconography of the Wila Kala. He notes the "same stylization of the face, the identical position of the arms and hands, and similar serpent figures as pectorals." He never clarifies whether or not these fragments were found at Khonkho or were part of the collections at the Museum in La Paz that he directed. Tiwanaku incorporates several monoliths similar in style to those at Khonkho, and I suspect that the fragments Vellard describes were from there. In addition, Vellard conducted Khonkho's first bioarchaeological study. He analyzed twelve crania from Khonkho Wankane collected by local community members. Ten demonstrated clear cranial modification; nine in the annular or *conical* style, and one in the tabular or *flattened* style.

Like most others of his era, Vellard assumed that Khonkho Wankane was a local Tiwanaku site. Yet he inferred that understanding Khonkho Wankane was important to understanding the pre-Hispanic history of its region. He concluded that, "systematic investigations will be necessary for establishing with precision the characteristics of the successive cultures that occupied Khonkho Wankane. For this reason it appears necessary to draw attention to a little known archaeological locality that may offer very attractive perspectives for archaeological investigation, and that one day will expand our knowledge regarding Tiwanaku culture" (Vellard 1955:154).

The formation of the *Centro de Investigaciones Arqueológicas de Tiwanaku* (CIAT) in 1958 instituted a brave new world of Bolivian archaeology founded on nationalist principles and dedicated to a scientific—and at times, *scientistic*—archaeological agenda (Ponce 1995:211–226). The human juggernaut behind the agenda was Carlos Ponce Sanginés, and two of his star associates were Maks Portugal Zamora and Gregorio Cordero Miranda. Following a swift and effective state agrarian reform and political revolution, Ponce's archaeological revolution cast Tiwanaku as Bolivia's primary cultural heritage. In his view, nearly all Bolivian sites of significance were in some way linked to Tiwanaku state development or military-political control. Khonkho Wankane was no exception. In an exhaustive history of Tiwanaku research, Ponce notes: "as archaeologist, Maks Portugal Zamora (1906–1984) represents the transition between the 'preceding' and the 'institutional' stages of Bolivian archaeology" (Ponce 1995:280). Not surprisingly, Rydén's chronology, rather than Portugal's—Ponce's transitional personage in Bolivian archaeological history—meshed better with this nationalist agenda.

Ponce concentrated his decadal archaeological efforts in Tiwanaku's monumental core. He never excavated at Khonkho Wankane. In an early publication (1990), he compared the iconography of Khonkho's monoliths with that of Tiwanaku's Bearded Stela in his analysis of the "Semi-subterranean Temple." Following Portugal Zamora, he noted that Khonkho's monoliths resonate stylistically with an early monolithic style found in this Tiwanaku structure. Yet in thousands of pages of later publications and forceful, charismatic lectures, Ponce appropriated Khonkho Wankane to Tiwanaku. For him, Khonkho was an urban center, and its urban character was directly linked to Tiwanaku political expansion (Ponce 1980, 1981). As he put it (1995:157), the site "pertains to Tiwanaku culture." He elaborated (1980:36), "the urban regime concentrated exclusively in Tiwanaku's cultural nucleus, and encompassed the cities of Tiwanaku as well as [Khonkho] Wankane, Lukurmata, and Pajchiri." Ponce considered Tiwanaku an urban society, a civilization in V. Gordon Childe's sense of the term, even if it was limited to a few urban centers located within the "heart of the culture in question" (Ponce 1980:36). In his classic synthesis (1981:83), Ponce notes that Tiwanaku's key urban centers constitute a rough north-south axis in the southern Lake Titicaca basin.

Alan Kolata adopted a parallel Tiwanaku-centric view of Khonkho Wankane in the 1980s. Kolata's research began as a relatively small-scale study of Katari basin raised fields and settlement patterns (Kolata 1986). In 1986, Kolata initiated large-scale excavations at Lukurmata, one of Ponce's proposed urban centers (Kolata ed. 1989; Ponce 1989). Intensive archaeological and paleoecological research indicated that Lukurmata was a major Tiwanaku urban settlement (Bermann 1994; Janusek 2004; Stanish 1989). It remained to do the same for the other sites that Ponce considered Tiwanaku urban centers. Kolata directed excavations at Khonkho Wankane in November of 1987. Taking an extensive page from Ponce's interpretive framework, Kolata (1987:264) investigated Khonkho Wankane in order to understand Tiwanaku's "Regional Settlement System." He conceptualized the 1987 field season as one that would investigate the "Tiwanaku sustaining area" (1987:265). Following Ponce, for Kolata Khonkho was one of three principal secondary urban centers, along with Lukurmata and Pajchiri. Kolata writes of his proposed research (Kolata 1987: 267–268):

> One important component of [1987 field] research relating explicitly to the regional settlement system will involve intensive mapping, surface collection, and excavation operations at the most important Tiwanaku secondary center in the southern component of the sustaining area: Khonkho Wancane [*sic*].

> Khonkho Wancane, like its northern counterparts, Lukurmata and Pajchiri, possesses an impressive core of civic-ceremonial architecture. In the case of Khonkho Wankane, this architecture takes the form of massive, terraced platform mounds surmounted by an ensemble of cut stone constructions. The principal elements of this ensemble are a sunken, semi-subterranean temple similar in concept, if not in scale, to the semisubterranean temple at Tiwanaku itself, and of course, to the virtually identical sunken temple at Lukurmata, and a large rectangular structure demarcated by lines of vertical stones which replicates in design and scale of construction the Kalasasaya at Tiwanaku. An intact… subterranean network of stone-covered drainage canals… runs throughout Khonkho Wancane's artificial platform mound. Preliminary, qualitative assessment suggests that the labor investment in public construction at Khonkho Wankane surpasses that at either Lukurmata or Pajchiri.

> A systematic program of surface collection as well as test excavations will be initiated at Khonkho Wankane during the latter half of the 1987 season. The research will be directed explicitly toward defining internal site organization, and toward intensively exploring presumptive

domestic contexts. I anticipate that this program of research, which will be expanded during the 1988 season, will provide invaluable comparative data with which we may begin to reconstruct a general portrait of Tiwanaku administrative settlements in the *altiplano*.

Project Wila Jawira members conducted test excavations at Khonkho Wankane in November of 1987 **(Figure 1.14)**. Excavations focused on what we now term the Sunken Temple and Dual-Court Complex. Five units were excavated in the Sunken Temple: three in the south stairway and its antechamber, one in its southwest corner, and one in its west stairway. One additional unit was excavated in the courtyard of the northernmost of the two courts comprising the Dual-Court Complex.

Finessing Ponce's hypothesis, Kolata (1993:103) interprets Khonkho Wankane as one of Tiwanaku's *satellite cities*. For him (1993:174), Khonkho housed nearly 10,000 inhabitants and most people lived in outlying villages herding, farming, and fishing. For Kolata, the physical and symbolic trappings of urbanism were transferred from Tiwanaku to Pajchiri, Lukurmata, and Khonkho (Kolata 1993:131). In Tiwanaku, according to Kolata (1993:131), a moat carved "the urban landscape into a ceremonial core of temples and elite residences within an island enceinte counterpoised against extensive sectors of vernacular architecture." This "symbolically dense architectural arrangement was extended to regional Tiwanaku capitals such as Lukurmata, Pajchiri, and Khonkho Wancane [*sic*] as a self-conscious emblem of Tiwanaku dominion and legitimacy" (Kolata 1993:131). In this line, Kolata thoroughly assimilates Khonkho Wankane to Tiwanaku cultural and political hegemony.

Still, Khonkho's monoliths remained a conundrum. Like Maks Portugal, Argentinian archaeologist Dick Ibarra Grasso considered Khonkho Wankane part of an early 'Tiwanaku III' culture contemporaneous with the Sunken Temple at Tiwanaku and the site of Kallamarka in the Tiwanaku Valley (Ibarra and Querejazu 1986:184). Early in his career, Max Portugal Ortiz (1988:112), Maks' son, conducted regional reconnaissance near Khonkho and collected surface materials at the site. He acknowledged that his father considered Khonkho's monoliths pre-Tiwanaku, but noted that his own research revealed Classic Tiwanaku ceramic sherds at the site. By the time Max had finished his magnum opus on pre-Hispanic Bolivian stone sculpture (1998:117–131), his position had coalesced. He interpreted Khonkho Wankane's monoliths as key manifestations of an early Pa-Ajanu monolithic style horizon that included similar representatives at Tiwanaku, just to the north, and at Arapa, Peru, in the northern Lake Titicaca basin. For him, this sculptural style pre-dated Classic Tiwanaku urban expansion in the region.

Khonkho Wankane played a critical role in the pre-Hispanic southern Lake

Figure 1.14 View of the south entrance to Khonkho's Sunken Temple, taken in the course of Kolata's excavations at the site in 1987 (courtesy of Alan Kolata, Department of Anthropology University of Chicago).

Titicaca basin. An official 1997 Bolivian publication that sought to formalize the procedures for conducting archaeological research in Bolivia listed Khonkho Wankane as a Class I National Monument. The publication defined Bolivian national monuments based on the quality of architectural structures and other objects of artistic or scientific importance (SNC 1997:17). By then it was already apparent that understanding pre-Hispanic cultural development at Khonkho Wankane would require intensive, long-term, multidisciplinary research. Project Jach'a Machaca launched such an initiative in 2001.

Organization of the Monograph

This monograph presents the results of archaeological investigations at and around Khonkho Wankane in 2001 and 2002 by members of the Proyecto Jach'a Machaca. Pilot research during this phase provided a robust database to articulate more specific objectives and define more pointed questions for future research. After a brief season of geophysical survey and laboratory analysis in 2003, intensive research resumed in 2004 funded by a host of public and private foundations.

In the next chapter I discuss results of our project's chronological analyses based on investigations initiated during Phase One. I present the results of sixteen carbon samples submitted for radiometric analysis at University of Arizona's Accelerator Mass Spectrometry (AMS) Laboratory. I then present some of the fundamental results of ceramic analyses at the site based on our Phase One research.

In chapter 3, Carlos Lémuz presents preliminary results of our settlement survey in the area of Khonkho Wankane, which covered an area of approximately 38 km². Lémuz directed this portion of the project. The survey demonstrates that occupation in the region began no later than the Middle Formative period—and more likely, during the preceding Late Archaic period (5,000–1,500 BC)— and continued through the Early Spanish Colonial Period. Indeed, there is no clear evidence for any hiatus in occupation up through today. Lémuz' ongoing survey and surface collection promises to reveal much about long-term changes in pre-Hispanic settlement organization in the region.

In chapter 4, Arik Ohnstad and I analyze the monumental objects that have singularly rendered Khonkho Wankane a relatively famous site since 1936: its carved monoliths. To date, we know of four carved monoliths at the site. We articulate a brief history of knowledge about the monoliths and previous interpretations of their iconography. We then present our interpretations of their iconography and original significance. Ongoing iconographic research in collaboration with David Browman, of Washington University, will help clarify the meaning of Khonkho's lithic iconography in relation to that of contemporaneous sites in the Lake Titicaca Basin.

Chapter 5 summarizes the goals, methods, and results of geophysical survey at Khonkho Wankane. Chris Dayton and colleagues discuss the three different techniques that we combined in order to detect sub-surface archaeological features and test the relative merits of the techniques themselves. Techniques included ground-penetrating radar (GPR), magnetic gradiometry, and electrical resistivity. Overall, this combined methodology proved highly effective in locating certain subsurface features—in particular, stone wall foundations that were 60–80 cm below the surface. Especially productive was the combined use of GPR and electrical resistivity.

Chapters 6 through 9 summarize the results of excavations in various components of Wankane's monumental architecture (**Figure 1.15**). In chapter 6 I discuss the Wankane Main Plaza (Sector 7), Rydén's Northeast courtyard, where the massive Tatakala monolith lies slumped over and lying face up. Of

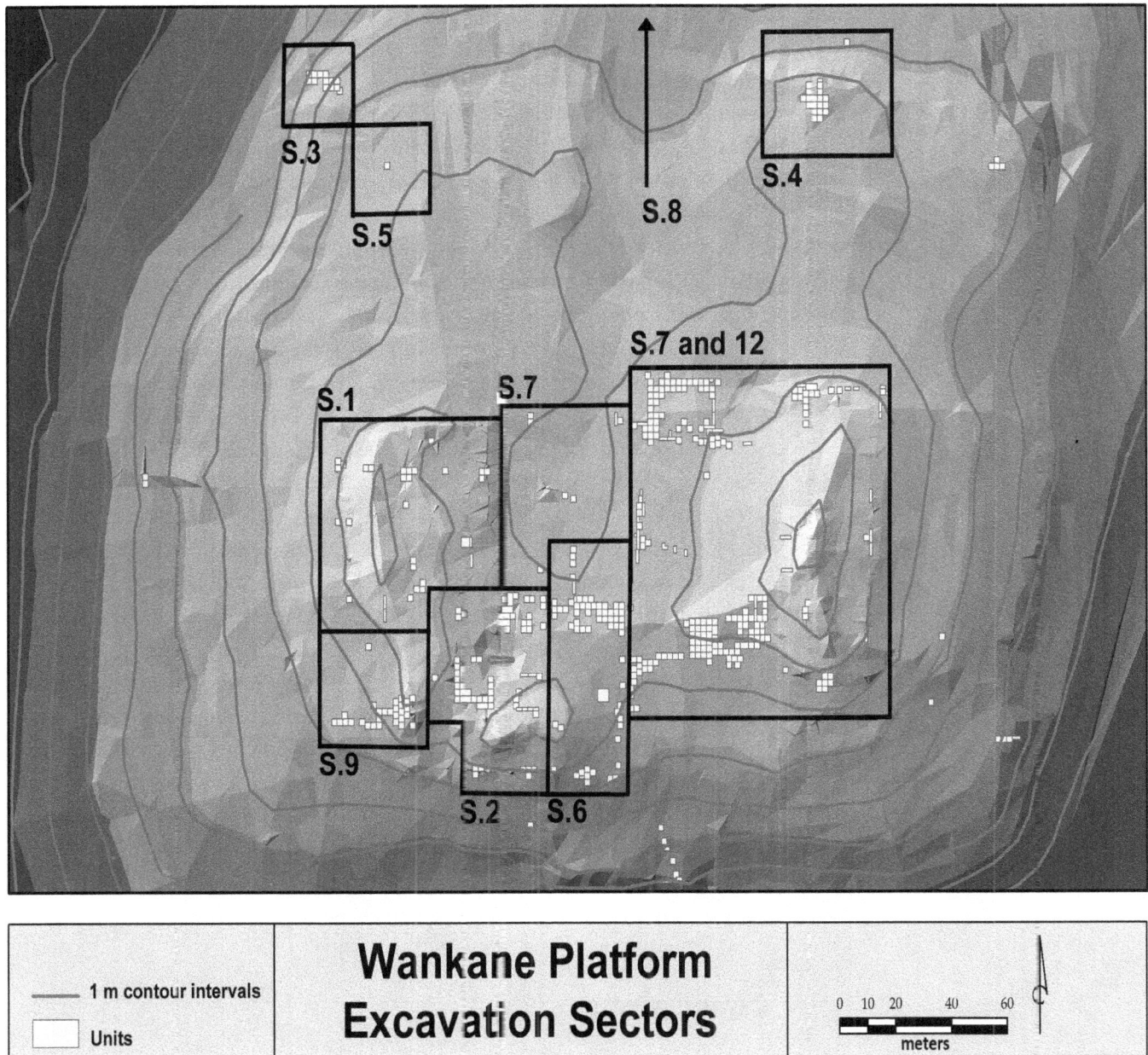

Wankane Platform Excavation Sectors

1 m contour intervals
Units

0 10 20 40 60
meters

note here is a massive subterranean drainage canal that appears to date much earlier than previously considered. In chapter 7 Adolfo Pérez and I discuss our ongoing research on and near Khonkho's Sunken Temple (Sector 2), what Rydén considered the South courtyard. We spent a great deal of time and effort in 2001–2002 excavating and analyzing this semi-subterranean structure. In chapter 8, Maribel Pérez and I summarize our research in the Dual-Court Complex of the West Platform (Sector 1), what Rydén termed the

Figure 1.15 Plan of excavations units Proyecto Jach'a Machaca opened on the Wankane platform, divided by sector.

Northwest Courtyard, and we present our ideas about its chronology, form, and significance. In chapter 9, Andy Roddick, Maribel Pérez, and I discuss our excavations in Compound 1, located in the south portion of the Wankane mound and adjacent to the Sunken Temple. This was the first of three such compounds that we later identified through geophysical survey and excavation by the end of 2004. Of note is a circular structure and its associated features in the compound's northeast corner.

Chapters 10 through 12 present the results of research in residential, mortuary, and midden sectors of the Wankane mound. In chapter 10, Deborah Blom and I present results of research in an excavation block in a sector of the site just off the main platform, where we located substantial evidence for Tiwanaku mortuary activity. In chapter 11, Denisse Rodas, Arik Ohnstad, and I present the results of excavation on the north edge of the Wankane platform and one of the most complex occupations at the site (Sector 4). Here we appear to have located an area of specialized production that dated to the Tiwanaku Period as well as the earlier Late Formative. Jose Luis Paz completes this section by detailing the results of his soil cores at Khonkho, his test unit in Sector Five, and his test unit and other excavations in Sector Eight, which yielded stratified midden as well as mortuary and residential contexts dating to Late Formative and Tiwanaku periods.

In chapter 13, Jake Fox presents the results of his excavations on the Putuni mound, the northernmost component of Khonkho Wankane. Excavations in Sector Ten yielded features and middens associated with Tiwanaku Period residential and mortuary activity. Excavations in Sector Eleven yielded more complicated results. Here, excavations units yielded thick strata of sterile construction fill over thin surfaces of Late Formative occupations. These strata formed the base of a massive platform covering the east side of Putuni. It remains to determine its significance and chronology.

Conclusions

In the final chapter I synthesize some of the key results of Phase One Proyecto Jach'a Machaca investigations. Our research confirmed many long-suspected ideas and challenged others. Khonkho Wankane, we find, reached its apogee during the Lake Titicaca basin Late Formative (200 BC–AD 500) (Janusek 2013, 2015) **(Figure 1.16)**. While small quantities of diagnostic Middle Formative ceramics (800–200 BC) appear on the eroded south slope of the site, to date no such occupations have been recovered *in situ*. Nevertheless, they have been recovered at several nearby sites, the largest of them located near the Jach'a Jawira River south of Khonkho. The site continued to be occupied—or

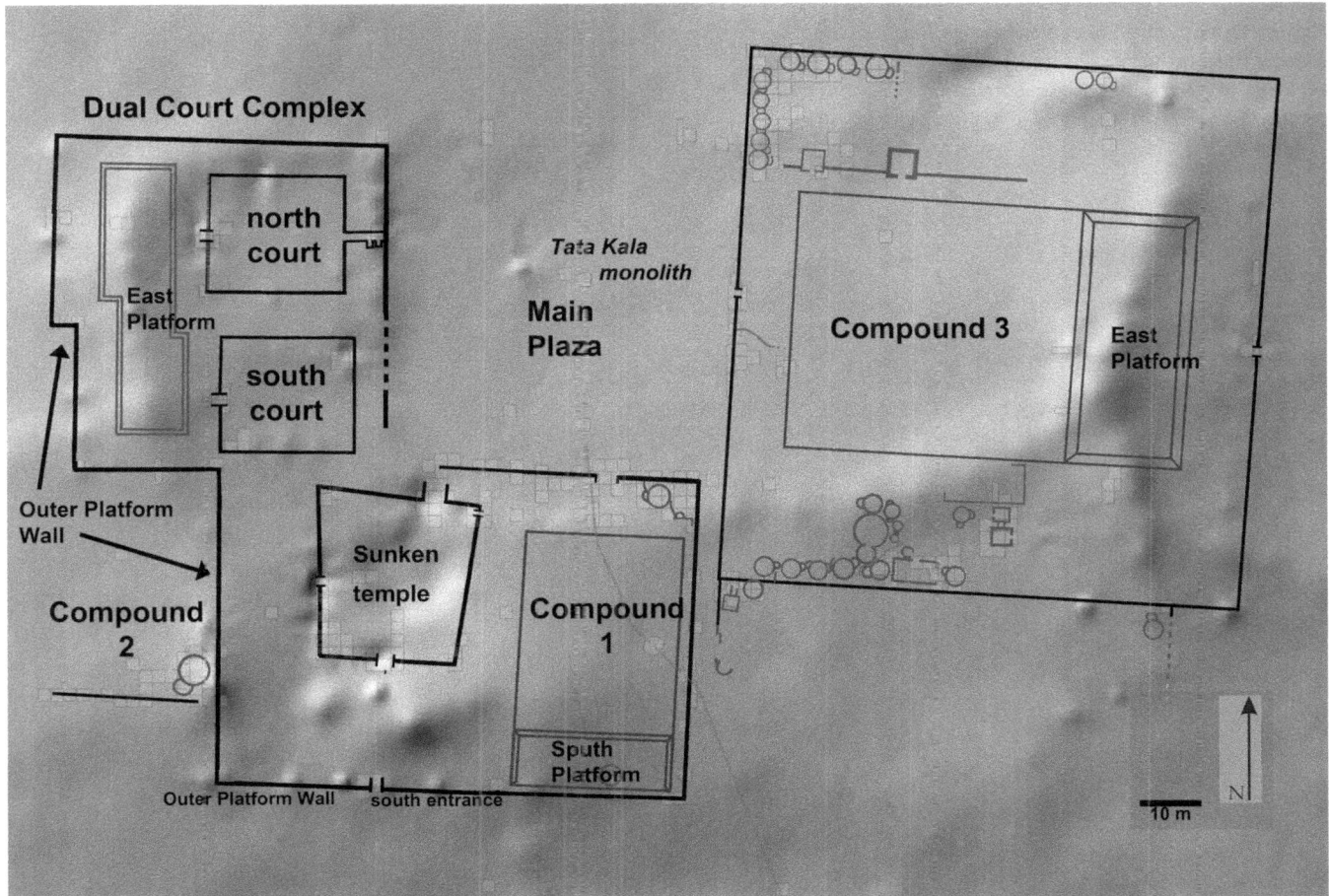

Figure 1.16 Plan rendering of major Late Formative structures on the Wankane platform.

was reoccupied—in the Tiwanaku period (AD 500–1000), though the site's ceremonial complex was mostly abandoned and its regional sociopolitical significance diminished during this period. Surface artifacts, human interments, sunken reservoirs (*qochas*), and other features indicate that the site continued to be visited and employed during the Early Pacajes period (AD 1100–1450). However, as at many other Early Pacajes sites in the basin (Janusek and Kolata 2003), we have yet to identify clear *in situ* occupations. By the Pacajes Inca phase, the focus of human settlement had shifted to the foothills of the Corocoro range north of Khonkho.

Khonkho Wankane thrived as an incipient urban center during the south-central Andean Late Formative (**Figure 1.17**). I employ the term to decouple the entrenched coterminal status of the adjective *urban* and the noun *city*. Despite Ponce's and Kolata's preliminary claims, Khonkho Wankane was not a city. During the Late Formative, Khonkho was one of several transacting ritual-political centers that thrived in the Andean altiplano. Tiwanaku, the panregional center that Khonkho and its interlocutors ultimately produced,

Figure 1.17 Map of the Lake Titicaca Basin showing the locations of selected major sites with Late Formative occupations.

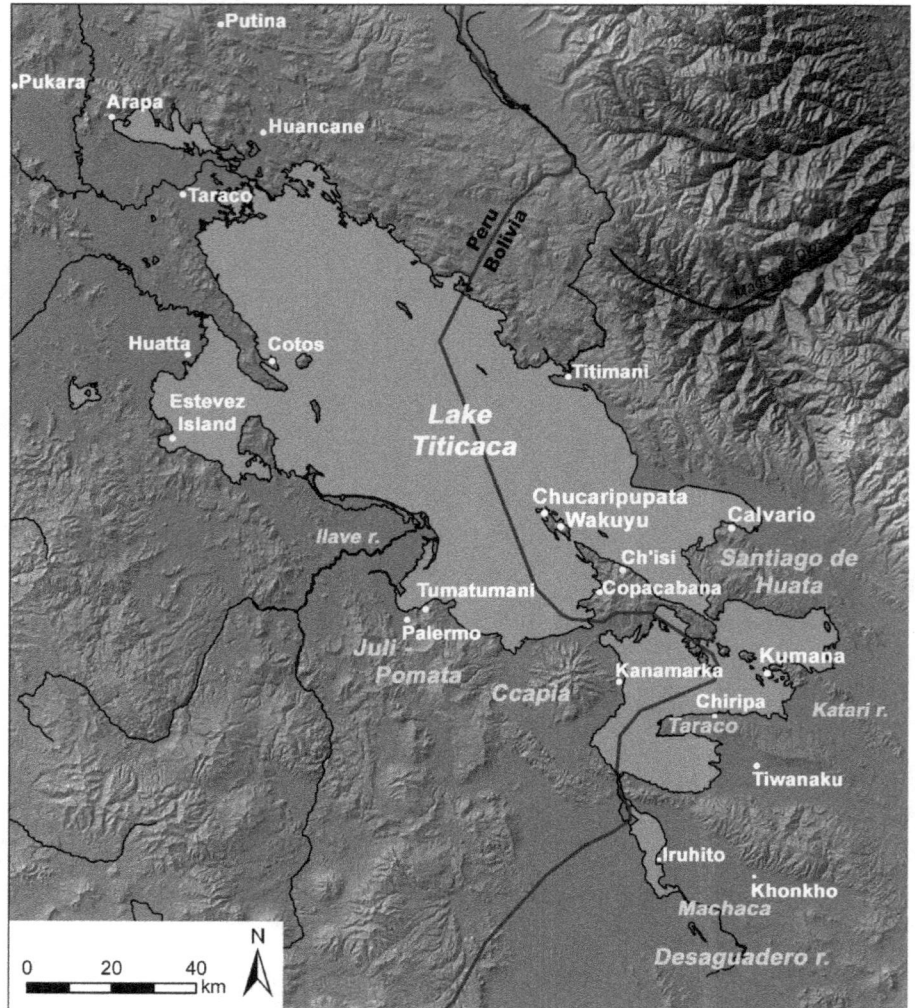

became a city. I consider the recurring formative practices that constituted Khonkho and its interlocutors *incipient urban* practices (the term *proto-urban* is also apt). Thus, I consider the *urban* a more encompassing set of processes, geographically and temporally, relative to the manifestation of a particular locale as a *city*. Urban practices and processes characterize but also transcend and in some cases produced cities.

Chapter 2

〰

Khonkho's Chronology: Radiocarbon and Ceramic Evidence

John Wayne Janusek

The urgent question of Khonkho Wankane's chronology rendered specific analyses paramount. Members of Proyecto Jach'a Machaca prioritized specific archaeological practices in order to address Khonkho's pre-Hispanic history. These included, first, the careful recovery of carbon samples to construct what is typically termed an *absolute* chronology of the site. Although radiometric measurements are in no true sense absolute, all come with calculated percentages of error, their basis in the known half-life deterioration of C14 means that archaeologists can provide a date range that is *rigorous* in regard to linear timekeeping. A second practice included the comparative analysis of time-sensitive artifacts. As in most Andean contexts, this meant most importantly ceramic vessels and sherds. Ceramic technical styles were relatively variable and subject to change in the pre-Hispanic altiplano. Yet other artifacts and even feature types helped us to construct an early chronology for Khonkho.

This chapter summarizes evidence for Khonkho Wankane's chronology based primarily on radiocarbon and ceramic evidence drawn from excavation sectors initiated in 2001–2002. I do this to create some coherence for the volume. I submitted a first group of radiocarbon samples for radiometric processing in 2005, once the project was funded by the National Science Foundation ((BNS-902198). Samples were submitted for Accelerator Mass Spectrometry (AMS) dating at the NSF-subsidized Arizona AMS laboratory (http://www. physics.arizona.edu/ams/about_us/history.htm). Here I consider only samples that derived from excavation sectors initiated in 2001–2002; others are published elsewhere (Janusek 2011, 2013) and several remain to be published.

Like radiocarbon samples, the ceramic evidence I present derives from excavation sectors initiated in 2001–2002. I initiated the ceramic analysis in 2002 by focusing on the specific attributes that characterized the pastes, inclusions, surface treatments, surface finish, decoration (painted, incised, or punctate), and form of individual sherds. This was not a hyper-rigorous *attribute analysis* in the sense that Lee Steadman (1995) defined it in the western Lake Titicaca basin, but it transcended its form-focused predecessors in the south-central

Andes (my own included, Janusek 2003a). Conjoined with radiometric results, it allowed us to construct a broad but solid chronology for Khonkho Wankane.

Khonkho's Chronology: Initial Radiocarbon Evidence

Sixteen AMS measurements collected from a variety of occupational contexts in Sectors 1–10 revealed a bimodal distribution of measurements (**Table 2.1**). By far, most (n = 13) dated securely to the Late Formative period. Further, each carbon sample that was predicted to date to the Late Formative based on stratigraphic position, associated ceramic sherds, or other evidence, produced a date securely centered in the Late Formative period (200 BC–AD 500). The three samples predicted to date to the subsequent Tiwanaku period turned out to date securely to that period (AD 500–1100).

The sixteen Late Formative dates were secured from carbon samples collected from Sectors 1, 2, 3, 6, 7, and 10. I describe them following the order of the chapters that describe those sectors. Sample KW-030 consisted of a chunk of carbonized wood from a pebble surface approximately 70 cm below the current surface of the Main Plaza (chapter 6) and just south of the Tata Kala monolith (see chapter 5). The sample was collected in the course of deep excavations near the center of the plaza in 2007 (Ohnstad 2008). An earlier clay floor and layer of construction fill predate the pebble surface. The date and its prior layers indicate that the Main Plaza was first built early in Khonkho's history, and specifically in Late Formative 1.

Samples KW-005 and KW-006 consisted of carbonized wood from 2002 excavations in the southeast corner of the Sunken Temple (chapter 7). The samples were recovered from superimposed contexts, one (KW-006) from its latest documented surface and the other (KW-005) from occupational debris resting over this surface. The samples date to AD 80–400, firmly in Late Formative 1 and continuing into Late Formative 2, indicating that the Temple was last fully employed during these phases.

Samples KW-002 and KW-003 consisted of wood charcoal recovered from the south court of the Dual-Court Complex (chapter 9). We recovered sample KW-002 from an early prepared pebble floor in the south court, and sample KW-003 from a later surface located approximately 15 cm above the floor. The samples date firmly to AD 250–550, indicating that the south court of the Dual-Court Complex was employed during Late Formative 2.

Samples KW-001, KW-004, KW0-15, KW-018, KW-019, and KW-031 all derived from excavations in Sector 6, either within or in the vicinity of Compound 1 (chapter 8). Collected between 2002 and 2007, they provide a rela-

Table 2.1 Results of sixteen AMS measurements selected from contexts first excavated during Proyecto Jach'a Machaca Phase One. Samples were processed at the University of Arizona Accelerator Mass Spectrometry (AMS) laboratory, and calibrations were processed using OxCal Version 4.0 (compare with Janusek 2013:Table 2.1). Note: 'Context' designations refer to site sector, followed by unit, followed by stratigraphic level (so, 6.61.14 refers to Sector 6, Unit 61, Level 14); F refers to a cultural feature number, and L to a level within a feature.

U AZ. AMS Lab #	Project #	Material	Context	13C	Uncalibrated RCYBP	Calibrated Date (95.4%)	Predicted phase	Stratigraphic Context
AA74199	KW-019	wood	6.61.14	-26.5	1,950+-33	37 BC – AD 126	LF	
AA74198	KW-018	wood	6.92.10	-21.8	1,877+-38	AD 58-234	LF	Wankane platform construction fill
AA66946	KW-001	wood	6.61.10	-23.9	1,845+-44	AD 60-260	LF1	Occupation zone over early platform construction
AA74203	KW-023	dung	10.6.7	-24.1	1,836+-38	AD 78-255	LF1	Final sub-Putuni occupation
AA66950	KW-005	wood	2.43.F2	-26.9	1,800+-52	AD 80-350	LF1	Occupation above latest surface of Sunken Temple
AA66951	KW-006	wood	2.43.F23	-24.4	1,781+-66	AD 80-410	LF	Latest surface of Sunken Temple
AA80806	KW-030	wood	1.29.10	-23.0	1799+-41	AD 125-340	LF	Pebble floor under Main Plaza
AA80807	KW-031	wood	6.34.4.R1	-23.0	1792+-36	AD 130-336	LF	Floor associated with truncated west wall of Compound
AA66949	KW-004	wood	6.37.6	-25.0	1,765+-38	AD 130-390	LF	Early floor between Compound 1 and Sunken Temple
AA66960	KW-015	wood	6.47.4	-23.6	1,738+-37	AD 210-410	LF1	Occupation Zone in Compound 1
AA66955	KW-011	wood	3.11.7	-24.0	1,719+-38	AD 230-410	LF1	Occupation zone in northwest sector of Wankane Platform
AA66947	KW-002	wood	1.25.5	-25.5	1,696+-37	AD 250-420	LF2	Pebble floor of south court of Dual Court Complex
AA66948	KW-003	wood	1.10.3	-25.2	1,560+-37	AD 410-580	LF2	Surface 15 cm above floor of south court of Dual Courts
AA66952	KW-007	wood	4.18.F6.L2	-23.0	1,279+-37	AD 650-860	Early Tiw	Tiwanaku period ash pit
AA66961	KW-016	dung	4.4.2.R1	-23.5	1,261+-36	AD 660 – 870	Tiw	Tiwanaku period hearth
AA66953	KW-009	wood	3.18.3.F1	-22.1	1,157+-37	AD 770-980	Early Tiw	Tiwanaku period area of intensive burning

tively robust summary of the Wankane platform's Late Formative history. Deep excavations in Sector 6 in 2005–6, sunk under Compound 1, revealed Wankane platform construction fill and some of Khonkho Wankane's earliest occupations. Sample KW-018, taken directly from this fill, indicated that it dated to Late Formative 1 (AD 58–234). Carbon samples collected from occupation zones just over this fill (KW-001, KW-019) likewise dated firmly to Late Formative 1 (37BC–AD 260). Samples taken from occupations associated with Compound 1 itself (KW-004, KW-015, and KW-031) date firmly to later Late Formative 1 and early Late Formative 2 (collectively, AD 130–410). Clearly, Sector 6 experienced a long and dynamic history within Khonkho Wankane.

Carbon sample KW-011 was taken to date the Late Formative structure excavated in Sector 3, on the sloping northwest portion of the Wankane mound (chapter 10). While human interments in the sector contained Tiwanaku style ceramics, remnant portions of this structure yielded Late Formative ceramics. Carefully isolated and removed from a remnant portion of the floor, the charcoal fragment securely dated the structure to Late Formative 2 (AD 230–410). Also associated with the floor of this structure was the greater section of a Kalasasaya bowl. Conjoined evidence indicates that Kalasasaya ceramic bowls continued to be made and used during Late Formative 2.

Sample KW-023 was a camelid dung pellet collected from a deep excavation on the east side of the Putuni Platform in 2007. It derived from a final, ephemeral occupation that pre-dated the complex construction fill strata that Jake Fox documents in chapter 13. This date (AD 78–255) indicates that early activities—however ephemeral or temporary (Janusek 2015)—occupied the east side of the Putuni area just before the Putuni Platform was constructed or expanded. It also indicates that platform construction in Sector 10 likely took place during or toward the end of Late Formative 1.

Carbon samples KW-007, KW-009, and KW-016 were collected in sectors 3 and 4 (chapters 10 and 11). Located north of the Main Plaza, Sector 4 was intensively occupied during the Tiwanaku period. The three samples—two charcoal, one camelid dung—derived from contexts with associated Tiwanaku style artifacts, and unsurprisingly, all dated firmly to the Tiwanaku period (AD 650–980). Sample KW-016 came from a hearth (Unit 4.2, R1) nestled into the northeast corner of a kitchen in the southwest portion of Structure 4.1. Sample KW-007 came from a shallow ash pit in the northwest section of Sector 4, south of the specialized oven, and KW-009 derived from an extensive area of burning and gray ash in Sector 3 to the west. The only surprise was that KW-009, predicted to date to Early Tiwanaku (AD 500–800), dated to Late Tiwanaku (AD 770–980).

Khonkho Wankane radiocarbon results exceeded expectations. They collectively define a site that was built in Late Formative 1, reached its apogee as a center in Late Formative 1–2, and was occupied on a smaller scale during the Tiwanaku period. Later excavations and AMS dates corroborated these conclusions. Predicting temporal phases relied on a concurrent analysis of ceramic sherds from Khonkho Wankane. Ceramic analysis followed protocols already established for the Lake Titicaca Basin (Bandy 2001; Janusek 2003a; Lémuz 2001; Stanish et al. 1997). Felicitously, our radiocarbon analysis reciprocally corroborated the conclusions of multiple ceramic analyses in the Lake Titicaca Basin. These analyses have established a foundation for identifying and distinguishing Late Formative and Tiwanaku ceramic assemblages.

Khonkho's Chronology: Ceramic Evidence

Broadly speaking, ceramic assemblages followed the temporal changes outlined in Janusek 2003a. Still, Khonkho Wankane presented certain unique material patterns and furthermore, ceramic assemblages varied significantly across sectors.

Late Formative Ceramic Assemblages

The most common Late Formative ceramic forms included *ollas*, jars, small jars, and bowls (**Figure 2.1**). Most *ollas* had at one time or another served as cooking vessels, and most jars had served as storage vessels. Nevertheless, the form, paste, and surface finish of these vessels were highly variable, and so their functions likely shifted in the course of their lives. Many *ollas* were at some point used as storage vessels, and many jars as cooking vessels. If function did not strictly delineate form, neither did form strictly delineate function. Yet relatively large jars dedicated to storage or fermentation commonly presented modelled or punctate neck decoration (Figure 2.2)

Late Formative assemblages also included smaller ceramic vessels, what I gloss here as *serving wares*. Most common were small jars (*vasijas*) and bowls. Most small jars served as *dippers* or pitchers (**Figure 2.3**). They likely served to transfer drink from a large *olla* or jar to the smaller bowls that directly served consumption. Most of them had side handles that perfectly suited this purpose. Some were simply hand-molded and wiped, while others were elaborately burnished. A small proportion (~5%) were decorated with a red band around

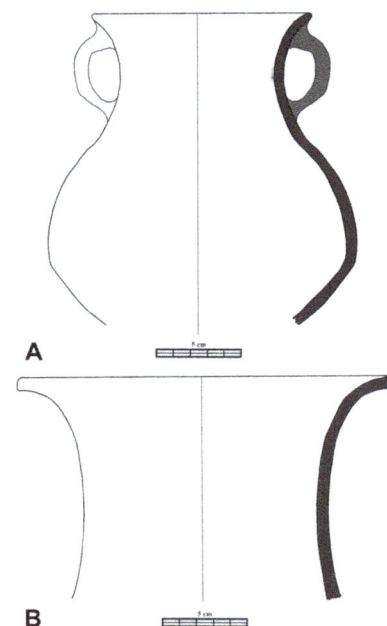

Figure 2.1   Late Formative *olla* (A, U7.40, L2) and jar (B, U7.19, L2) fragments from Khonkho Wankane. The *olla* presents an unburnished surface, and light brown paste with mica inclusions; the jar (*tinaja*) presents a combed surface, and brown paste with dense mica inclusions.

Figure 2.2   Late Formative jar rim with punctate neck decoration (U. 12.17, L3). Scraped and roughly smoothed surface, burnt orange paste with carbon core and sand, fiber, and fine mica inclusions.

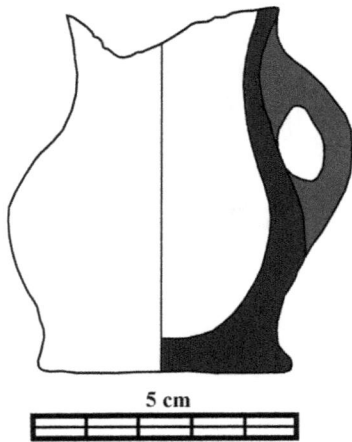

Figure 2.3 Late Formative small jar (*vasija*) from Khonkho Wankane (U12.25, F1). Fugitive red paint and dull orange slip on unsmoothed surface, beige paste with feldspar inclusions.

Figure 2.4 Two Late Formative bowls (*cuencos*) from Khonkho Wankane. A) U1.27, L3, F1, burnished interior, orange paint on beige paste; B) U6.76, L5; burnished interior, heavily sooted dark brown paste with fine dense mica inclusions.

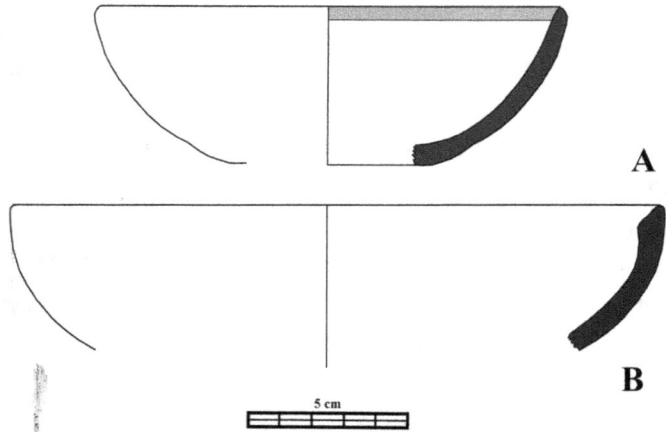

Figure 2.5 Late Formative *Kalasasaya* style bowl from Khonkho Wankane (U3.11, L7). Burnished interior and exterior, red paint on chestnut slip, dull orange paste with sparse mica inclusions.

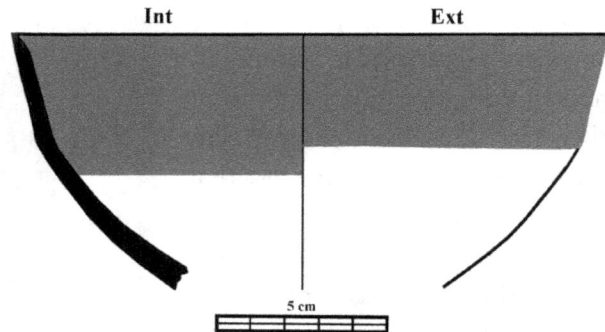

the outer rim, rendering them part of the Kalasasaya ceramic tradition that characterized the southern Lake Titicaca basin Late Formative.

Bowls (*cuencos*) were nearly invariably ellipsoid in form, unlike their Tiwanaku period successors (**Figure 2.4**). Most were burnished but undecorated. Some 5% of bowl sherds were decorated with a red or reddish-brown band along the exterior or interior rim, a classic Kalasasaya flourish (**Figures 2.5 and 2.6**). This style has been pegged as a strictly Late Formative 1 style. At Khonkho we found that this bowl style continues into Late Formative 2, if not precisely in the same material manner (also Marsh 2012). Late Formative 1 incarnations include small ellipsoid bowls consisting of fine, light beige paste with sparse feldspar and fine crushed red mineral inclusions. Late Formative 1 contexts included small shallow bowls with horizontal side handles (**Figure 2.7**). Late Formative 2 contexts included larger bowls with coarse dark pastes and variable inclusions.

Other Late Formative forms were less commonly represented. They included ritual bowls with short annular bases and, at least in some cases, scalloped rims (**Figure 2.8**). These were most commonly found in the Sunken Temple, (Sector 2, chapter 7), and they tended to incorporate soot-covered interiors and porous pastes amenable to the expansion and contraction that repeated heating and cooling demand (Janusek 2003a:42). These were most likely employed as *sahumerios*—that is, incense or animal fat burners employed to ritually purify a place—in the Sunken Temple. An even less common form included incised ceramic trumpets. Only two fragmentary examples are known from Khonkho Wankane, one from the east entrance of the north court of the Dual-Court Complex (Sector 1, chapter 9), and one from a later excavation in Compound 3. The fragment from Sector 1 was heavily eroded but consisted of a fine, dense beige paste with crushed red mineral inclusions (**Figure 2.9**).

Figure 2.6   Image of the Kalasasaya bowl rendered in Figure 2.5.

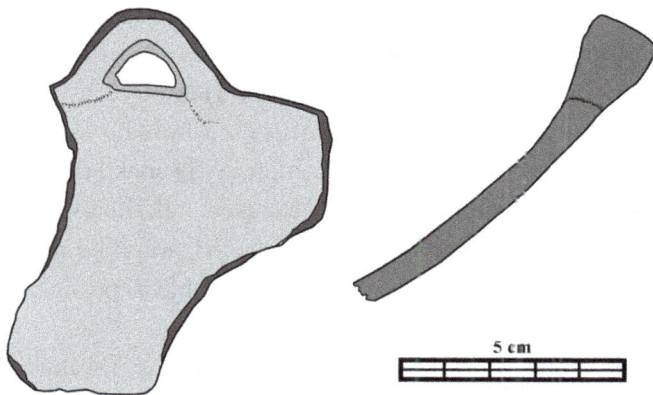

Figure 2.7   Late Formative shallow bowl with horizontal handle from Khonkho Wankane (U1.25, L3). Combed interior and smoothed exterior, brown paste with fine mica inclusions.

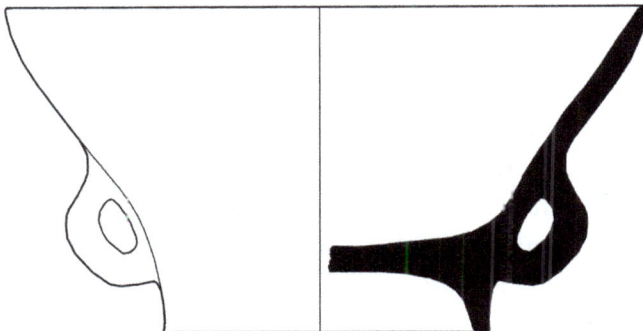

Figure 2.8   Late Formative *sahumerio* from Khonkho Wankane (U12.25, F1). Dull orange wash on orange paste, smoothed exterior and combed interior, light and dark mineral inclusions.

Figure 2.9 Eroded Late Formative ceramic trumpet from Khonkho Wankane (U1.13, F1, L2). Light brown paste with coarse mineral or grog inclusions.

5 cm

Tiwanaku Ceramic Assemblages

Forms dating to the Tiwanaku period included a specific sample of forms known from the global *oeuvre* of Tiwanaku culture (Janusek 2003a). A variety of *ollas* dedicated to various cooking and food preparation tasks were, of course, most common across the site. These vessels tended to be larger than Late Formative *ollas*—at least 3–6 cm higher on average—and more clearly distinguished in form, paste, and surface finish from jars (*tinajas*). Tiwanaku jars were designed for liquid storage and fermentation (Janusek 2003a:58–60). While these were not nearly as frequent or diverse at Khonkho Wankane as they were at Tiwanaku, they were far more common in Tiwanaku than in Late Formative occupations at the site. Tiwanaku *tinajas* were tall, their walls thick, their pastes dense and fully oxidized or partially reduced, and their inclusions were finely crushed. They were made to be as impermeable as possible to ferment and store valuable beverages.

Tiwanaku style serving-ceremonial wares were abundant in Tiwanaku period contexts, in particular in the specialized production area of Tiwanaku 4 and as burial offerings in Sectors 3, 4, and 8. The formal repetoire of vessels was substantially limited in relation to the broader repertoire of vessels documented at Tiwanaku, Lukurmata, and on some islands in Lake Titicaca (Alconini 1995; Bermann 1994; Janusek 2003a; Korpisaari and Pärssinen 2011). They were primarily limited to *keros*, or drinking vessels; *tazons*, or generalized eating/ consumption bowls; and *vasijas*, or pitchers (**Figures 2.10**). This ceramic triad comprises the most fundamental assemblage of Tiwanaku serving-ceremonial forms known for the south-central Andes. *Sahumador* lamps and elegant *escduillas* were altogether absent at Khonkho (Janusek 2003a). Nevertheless, we located sherds of modelled *incensarios* in the north court of the Dual-Court

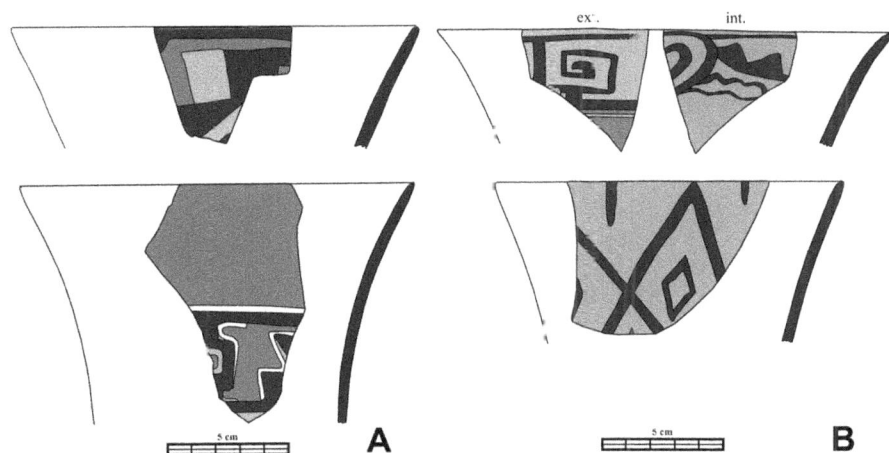

Figure 2.10   Tiwanaku style *kero* (A) and *tazon* (B) sherds from Khonkho Wankane. All are from Tiwanaku occupation contexts on the Putuni mound.

Complex and a llama effigy vessel on the Putuni platform in Sector 11, Feature 1 (chapter 13).

Conclusions

Radiocarbon and ceramic evidence corroborate the conclusion that Khonkho Wankane was an important Late Formative center that continued to be inhabited—or was inhabited once again—during the Tiwanaku period. Carbon samples and ceramic sherds indicate that the site, construed as the conjoined Wankane and Putuni platforms, was a major center of ritual activity and monumental transformation during the Late Formative. These same data indicate that Khonkho Wankane served as a regional settlement during the ensuing Tiwanaku period. While Khonkho Wankane was reconfigured as an important place for contemporaneous settlement, specialized production, and mortuary ritual, it was no longer the monumental ritual center it had been during the preceding Late Formative period.

Part II

Survey and Stone Sculpture

∽

Chapter 3

Initial Results of Surface Survey around Khonkho Wankane

Carlos Lémuz Aguirre

The first phase of regional survey in 2001–2002 covered an area of 38 km² in the vicinity of Khonkho Wankane, covering lands in the contemporary communities of Qhunqhu Likiliki and Qhunqhu Milluni. This survey followed full-coverage protocols and covered terrain bounded by geographical features and political boundaries: the mountainous slope of the Corocoro range to the north, the Jach'a Jawira River to the south, the Llinqui Jawira River to the west, and the boundary separating the communities of Qhunqhu Likiliki and Kuypa to the east. The survey covered terrain ranging from 3,850 to 4,300 meters above sea level, and produced substantial settlement pattern results as summarized in the conclusion to this chapter.

Chronology and Geography

This survey employs a regional chronology conjointly developed by multiple archaeological projects in the Lake Titicaca Basin (Albarracín-Jordan 1996; Bandy and Hastorf, 2005; Hastorf ed. 1999, Janusek 2003a, 2008; Lémuz 2001, 2005; Stanish 2003; Stanish et al. 1997). Earliest evidence for human occupation in the southern Lake Titicaca basin dates to the Late Archaic period (5,000–1,500 BC). Earliest complexity dates to the subsequent Early-Middle Formative (1,500–200 BC). The Middle Formative—locally represented by Chiripa material culture—dates to 400–200 BC. The Late Formative period, corresponding roughly with the Central Andean Early Intermediate Period, dates to 200 BC–AD 500 and can be usefully separated into Late Formative 1 (200 BC–AD 300) and Late Formative 2 (AD 300–500). Following is the local Tiwanaku Period (AD 500–1000), corresponding to the Central Andean Middle Horizon. Tiwanaku is followed by Early Pacajes (AD 1000–1450), which corresponds to the Late Intermediate Period. Inca Pacajes (AD 1450–1535) corresponds to the Late Horizon, and Colonial (or Late) Pacajes (AD 1535–1575) is a local manifestation of early, pre-Toledan Spanish Colonial occupation.

Khonkho Wankane occupies two hills on a relatively flat and marshy plain (*pampa*) between the foothills of the Corocoro range, to the north, and the Jach'a Jawira River, to the south (**Figure 1.1**). Two tributary streams of the Jach'a Jawira River define the east and west extremes of the site's two mounds.

Both descend from springs located on the slopes of Corocoro's south flanks. Full-coverage survey defined three ecological zones of human settlement: an upper colluvium, a lower colluvium, and a springs and grass zone (Albarracín-Jordan and Mathews 1990). The upper colluvium comprised hill slopes between 3950 and 4300 m.a.s.l. on the south flanks of the Corocoro range. The zone was minimally occupied in this particular geographical region until the second half of Early Pacajes. The lower colluvium, at 3900–3950 m.a.s.l., includes both low alluvial fans of the north Corocoro foothills and a series of low hills overlooking the north shore of Jach'a Jawira. The springs and grass zone, at 3840–3900 m.a.s.l. and characterized by soils rich in clay and surfaces dense with grasses and marsh, constituted most of the lower plain (*pampa*) and low hills between the Corocoro colluvium and Rio Jach'a Jawira. Khonkho Wankane and its satellite sites occupy a cluster of natural hills in this springs and grass zone.

Settlement Patterns

Although the first settlements in the Machaca region probably date to the Late Archaic period (5,000–1,500 BC), the area sampled in the first phase of survey provides no evidence for Late Archaic settlement. However, it is likely that most Archaic communities chose to settle on the banks of the Desaguadero River rather than along the saline tributaries of the Jach'a Jawira River, where nutritional potential is comparatively low. Our ongoing analysis of lithic materials, especially materials from the lithic workshops identified in this phase of survey, will ultimately provide the evidence to accept or reject this hypothesis.

Middle Formative Occupation (800–200 B.C.)

The Middle Formative occupation consisted of six sites and comprised a total area of 6.66 ha (**Figure 3.1**). Just over half of the total occupied area of this phase (53%) centered at a single site, JM-110, while the rest was distributed among five smaller sites, each less than 1 ha in area. Two small sites occupied the lower colluvium in the Corocoro foothills (JM 6 and 67), each settled along one of the perennial tributaries of the Jach'a Jawira. Most sites were located further south, in the springs and grass zone below 3900 m.a.s.l. and on the south slopes of low hills facing Jach'a Jawira (**Figure 3.2**). Most of these sites were habitation settlements, and some yielded evidence for the production of projectile points. While the inhabitants of these sites likely farmed nearby fields, our survey revealed no agricultural tools and this absence is

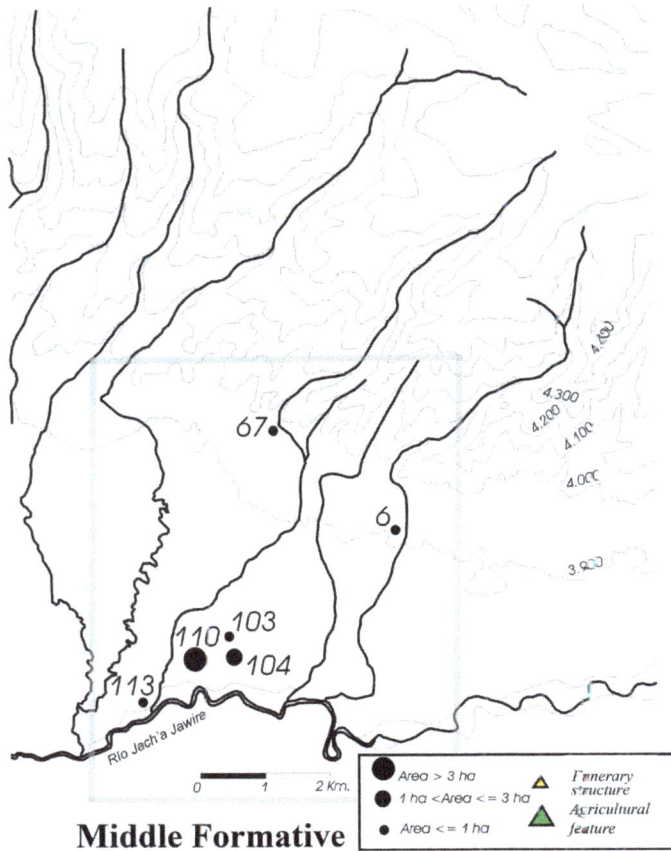

Figure 3.1 Middle Formative settlement patterns in the vicinity of Khonkho Wankane.

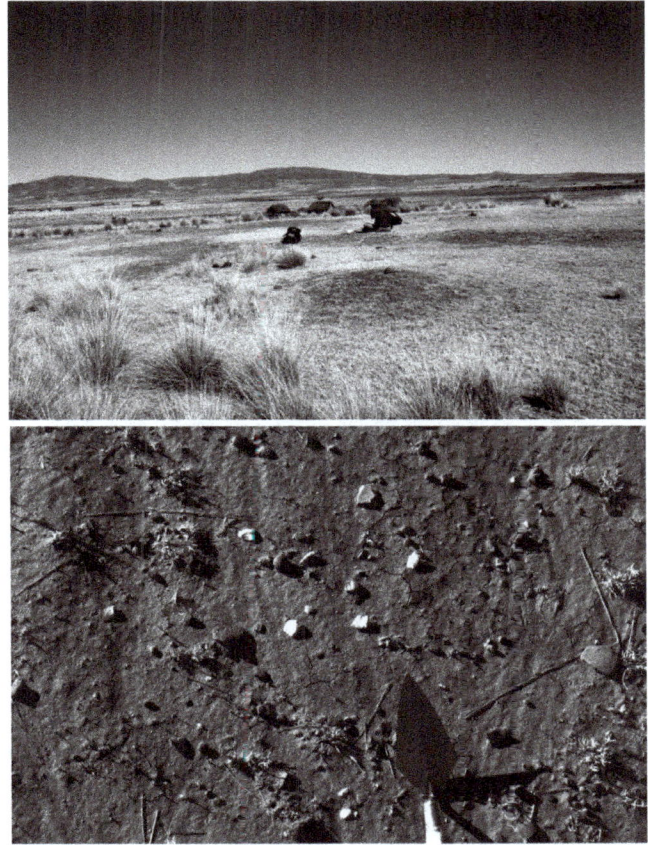

Figure 3.2 The Middle Formative site of JM-113, which yielded high quantities of lithic debitage.

surprising. Many Middle Formative sites located closer to Lake Titicaca—including sites on the Taraco Peninsula, in the lower Katari valley, and on the Santiago de Huata Peninsula—revealed abundant agricultural hoes and spades (Bandy 2004b; Janusek and Kolata 2003; Lémuz 2001).

Late Formative 1 Occupation (200 B.C.–A.D. 300)

Eight sites revealed surface artifacts characteristic of the Late Formative 1 phase **(Figure 3.3)**. Combined occupation covered an area of 4.9 ha, or some 25% less than the combined occupied area recorded for the Middle Formative. Late Formative 1 witnessed a dramatic shift in settlement focus approximately 2.35 kilometers to the east. Most sites occupied a series of low natural hills in a marshy springs and grass zone near two tributary streams of the Jach'a Jawira that originate as springs in the Corocoro slopes to the north. However, more than 80% of the total occupied area concentrated at the site of Khonk-

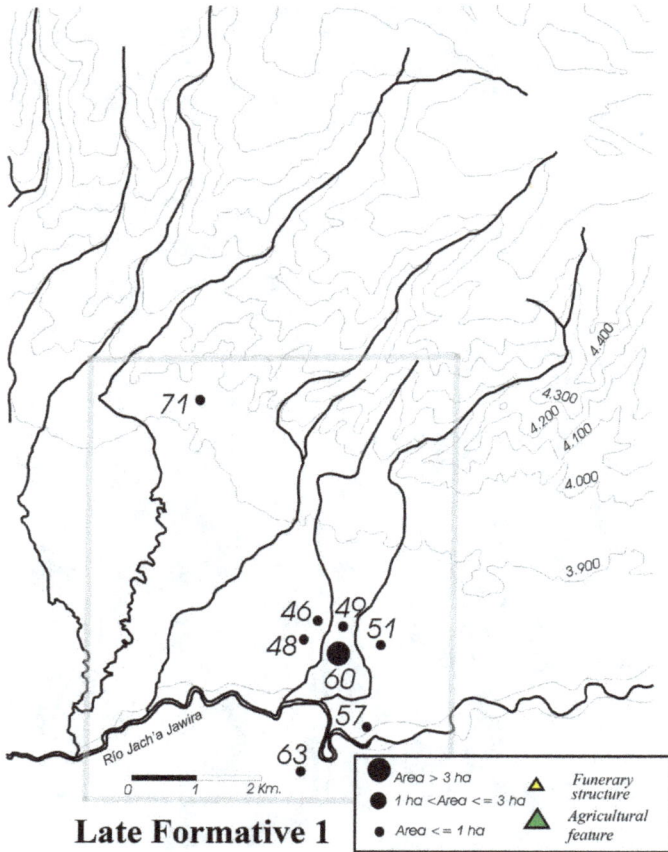

Figure 3.4   The Late Formative 1 site of JM-71, located in the lower colluvial zone northwest of Khonkho Wankane.

Figure 3.3   Late Formative 1 settlement patterns in the vicinity of Khonkho Wankane.

ho Wankane. Khonkho comprised the Wankane (JM 60) and Putuni (JM 49) mounds. Further north, only the site of JM-71 demonstrates that people inhabited the lower Corocoro colluvium **(Figure 3.4)**. In light of the new settlement pattern, it is clear that local resource exploitation and sociopolitical organization had changed substantially from the Middle Formative.

Late Formative 2 Occupation (A.D. 300–500)

The number of sites dating to Late Formative 2 is nearly double that dating to Late Formative 1 **(Figure 3.5)**. We located fifteen sites that covered a total area of 15.77 ha, more than three times the area covered by Late Formative 1 occupations. Some 91% of the total occupied area is below 3,900 m.a.s.l. Occupations occur in pasture lands, near springs, or in lower colluvial zones. Nearly 60% of the total occupied an area clustered near the two major mounds of Khonkho Wankane (JM-49 and JM- 60) **(Figure 3.6)**. Other occupations either clustered near Wila Nayrani (JM 110) or were distributed among the grazing lands of the grassy *pampa*. The presence of Late Formative 2 occupa-

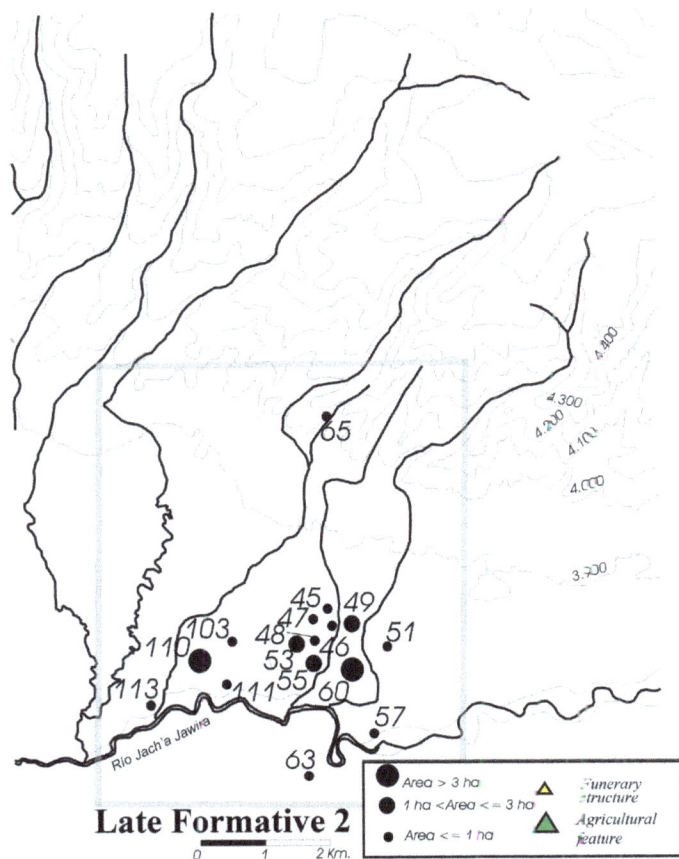

Figure 3.6   The Late Formative 2 site of JM-48, located just west of Khonkho Wankane. It is one of a cluster of mounds that were occupied during the Late Formative. (Photo by John W. Janusek.)

Figure 3.5   Late Formative 2 settlement patterns in the vicinity of Khonkho Wankane.

tions in areas of high agricultural productivity, for example on the colluvial slopes of Corocoro to the north, is remarkably low. I hypothesize that the substantially increased occupation area during this phase, which may mark increasing population in the region, is likely linked to the increasing importance of pastoralism as a regional productive economy.

Khonkho Wankane became an important site during Late Formative 1, and its occupation area and relative centrality intensified during Late Formative 2. Throughout the Late Formative, it remained the largest ritual, economic, and demographic center in the immediate region. Monumental architecture has not been located in the smaller settlements that clustered near the site. The geographical location of Khonkho Wankane, and the surface material evidence identified at it and at smaller nearby sites, suggest that its productive economy was grounded in camelid husbandry. It was likely a hub for llama caravan traffic and exchange linking populations to the north, in the Tiwanaku Valley and along Lake Titicaca's shores, with populations further to the south and east of Lake Titicaca, toward the Wankarani region near present-day Oruro.

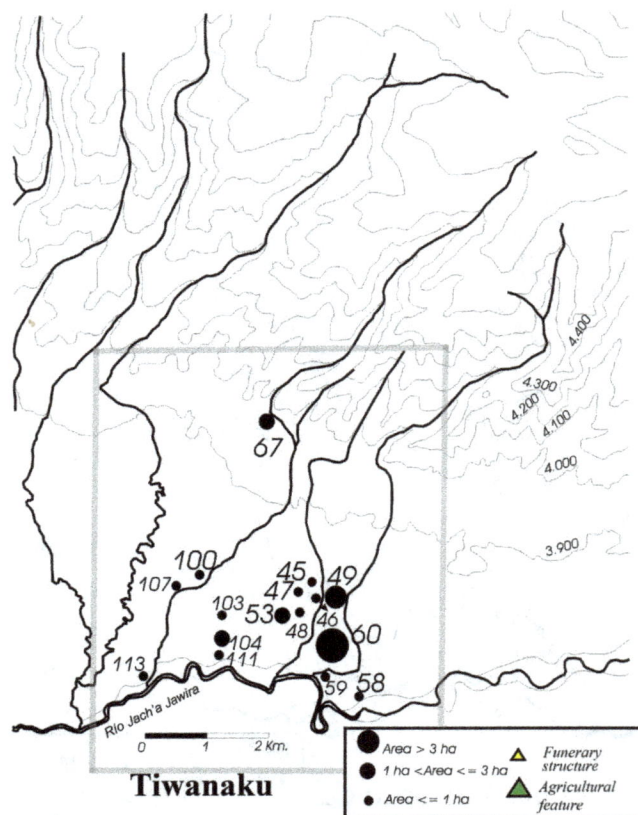

Figure 3.7   Tiwanaku settlement patterns in the vicinity of Khonkho Wankane.

Tiwanaku Occupation (A.D. 500–1100)

Our survey registered sixteen Tiwanaku sites, fifteen of which are habitation settlements **(Figure 3.7)**. Although the number of sites did not increase from Late Formative 2, the total occupied area increased substantially: Tiwanaku occupation covered 25.6 ha, 54% greater than the total Late Formative 2 occupation area. Further, the Formative pattern of occupations concentrating at and near large centers intensified during the Tiwanaku phase. Khonkho Wankane, sites JM-49 and JM- 60, continued to maintain a significant occupation during the Tiwanaku period. Assuming occupation area corresponded roughly to population, Khonkho Wankane was home to 73% of the local population. In any case, human occupation clearly concentrated in the springs and grass zone rather than colluvial zones. The frequency of lithic agricultural implements at Tiwanaku period sites was much greater than it had been during Late Formative phases.

Figure 3.9   Circular habitation structures on a terrace of Pukara de Khonkho (JM-61).

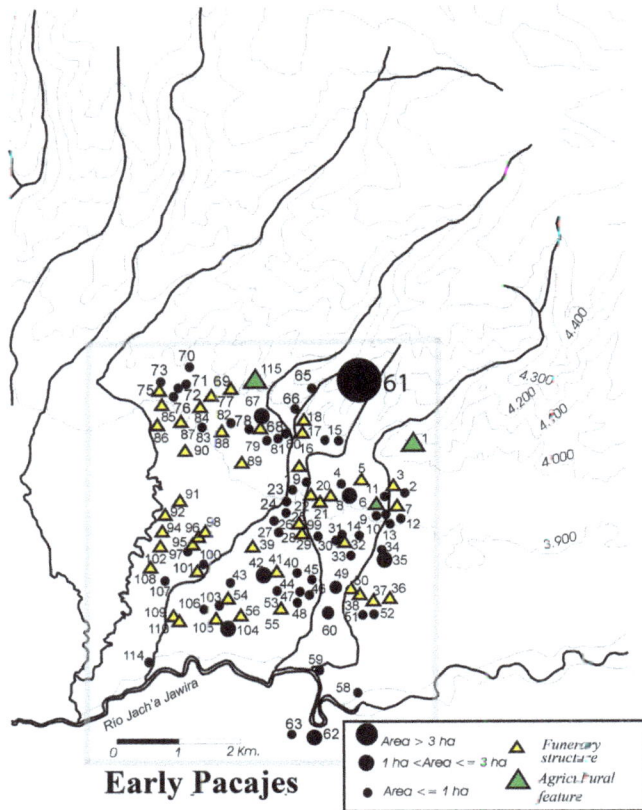

Figure 3.8   Early Pacajes settlement patterns in the vicinity of Khonkho Wankane.

Early Pacajes Occupation (A.D. 1100–1450)

The onset of Early Pacajes marked an abrupt shift in regional economy and political organization. Many of the settlement tendencies that prevailed during the Late Formative and Tiwanaku periods were dramatically ruptured. We identified 108 sites dating to this period, 62 of them habitations and 46 funerary sites or agricultural features (**Figure 3.8**). Total occupied area increased by 43% in relation to the Tiwanaku period, including a substantial increase in occupation of lands above 3,900 m.a.s.l., a striking break from prior trends. A large portion of the population shifted its activity to the colluvial slopes of the Corocoro range, which were now turned into residential terraces. Stretched across the slopes of a mountain due south of Khonkho Wankane, Pukara de Khonkho (JM-61) became the major demographic center in the region during the latter half of this period (AD 1300–1450, see Zovar 2012) (**Figure 3.9**).

Of the 62 sites located in our survey, 52 are less than one hectare in area and those comprise only 33.8% of the total occupation area. Drawing on work

Figure 3.10　Pacajes–Inca settlement patterns in the vicinity of Khonkho Wankane.

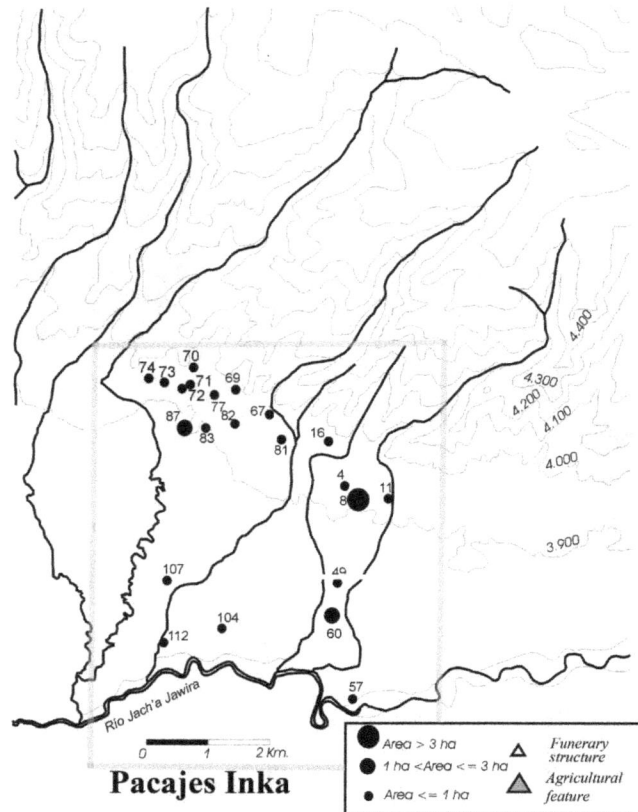

Pacajes Inka

●	Area > 3 ha	▲	*Funerary structure*
●	*1 ha <Area <= 3 ha*	▲	*Agricultural feature*
•	*Area <= 1 ha*		

in adjacent regions, it is likely that many of these small sites were short-term habitations or even periodic encampments (Janusek and Kolata 2003). Overall, it appears that while agriculture remained important and may have even increased in importance, camelid husbandry became an even more central focus of the regional economy during Early Pacajes. The hydrology of the region continued to play an important role in Early Pacajes settlement choices, influencing the location of settlements near the primary tributaries of the Jach'a Jawira River. Local hydrology even influenced the location of above-ground funerary cists. Those tended to be located on hills near the ravines that traversed the springs and grass and colluvial zones.

Pacajes-Inka Occupation (A.D. 1450–1535)

Survey revealed 23 settlements dating to the Late Horizon, known locally as the Pacajes-Inka period (**Figure 3.10**). Inka presence in the region was focused on the Corocoro lower colluvial zone. The distribution of Pacajes-Inka ceramic sherds on the surface is not an accurate indicator of contemporaneous occupation in the area. In the short time that the Inka settled the region, they left no sign of having directly influenced all households, and it is likely that many settlements did not acquire the pottery or other artifacts diagnostic of this phase. Still, it appears that local Inka administrators established an intimate relationship with Early Pacajes communities and their affiliated areas of agricultural and pastoral exploitation (also Choque Canqui 2003).

Settlement distribution analyses indicate that 85% of the Inka and their local, ethnically affiliated allies lived above 3,900 m.a.s.l. Furthermore, 76.07% of the Inka occupation was distributed over four relatively large settlements, which included the relatively large sites of Ch'auch'a de K'ula Marka (JM-8) and Palli Marka (Rydén 1947:184–225, 232–282). I hypothesize that the Inka sought to control local Pacajes communities from such concentrated colluvial settlements. Settlement survey in the adjacent Tiwanaku and Katari basins, to the north (Albarracín-Jordan and Mathews 1990; Janusek and Kolata 2003), and on the Santiago de Huata Peninsula, to the northeast (Lémuz 2001), revealed similar patterns of occupation during the Late Horizon.

Colonial Pacajes Occupation (1535–1575)

Spanish arrival and conquest abruptly transformed local political, ritual, and economic practices. Among other things, Spanish hegemony intensified local labor requirements for mining activities. We identified 18 sites corresponding to this phase, 13 of which were habitation settlements. They comprised a total occupied area of 4.42 ha. Sites included an early Colonial chapel built over Inca occupations in Ch'auch'a de K'ula Marka (JM-8) **(Figure 3.11)**. Yet the number of Colonial Pacajes occupations identified

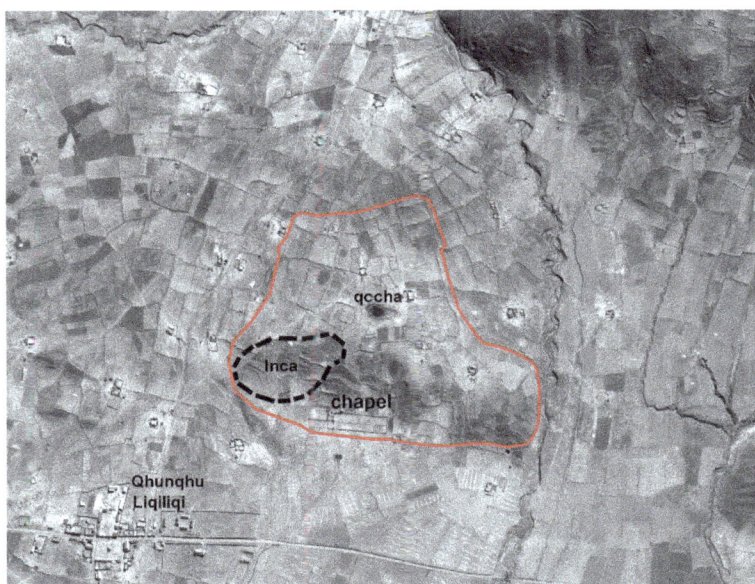

Figure 3.11   The Late Horizon and Early Colonial site of Ch'auch'a de K'ula Marka (bounded by red line). The dashed lines bound an area of dense Late Horizon surface artifacts, and marks an area that Rydén excavated in the 1930s.

near Khonkho Wankane pales in relation to the substantial numbers of Early Colonial sites identified in the Tiwanaku and Katari valleys (Albarracín-Jordan and Mathews 1990; Janusek and Kolata 2003). Clearly, we require a better understanding of artifacts diagnostic of the Early Colonial Period on a regional scale to more fully understand early Spanish Colonial occupation and settlement transformations.

Conclusions

Archaeological survey in the vicinity of Khonkho Wankane revealed human occupations dating to all phases of pre-Hispanic human occupation post-dating the Archaic period and continuing through the Early Spanish Colonial period (Table 3.1). They indicate a long-term, increasing intensification of occupation in the surveyed region over the course of the pre-Hispanic and early Colonial periods. Notable patterns include evidence for the production of projectile points at Middle Formative sites, and the increasing concentration of artifactual debris and activity at Khonkho Wankane and nearby sites in the Springs and Grass Zone (sites JM-49 and JM-60) throughout the Late Formative. This pattern continued through the Tiwanaku period, even though, as later chapters clarify, the character and regional significance of Khonkho shifted dramatically.

Early Pacajes brought dramatic changes to the region, as it did to the nearby

Table 3.1 Results of settlement survey in 2001–2002, divided by chronological phase, and types of sites (habitation sites, other types of sites, e.g., burial sites, churches), and other features (e.g., agricultural features such as terraces and sunken basins, or qochas) classified by number of sites and collective area (in ha) covered by those sites.

Phase	Habitation sites Nº	Habitation sites Area (ha)	Other sites Nº	Other sites Area (ha)	Other features	Total Nº	Total Area (ha)
Colonial Pacajes	13	4.42	5	25.281	1	18	29.701
Inka Pacajes	23	14.975			2	23	14.975
Early Pacajes	62	36.6	46	36.62		108	73.22
Tiwanaku	15	25.606	1	0.06	3	16	25.666
Late Formative 2	15	15.777	1	0.84	3	16	16.617
Late Formative 1	8	4.9807			1	8	4.9807
Middle Formative	6	6.665			1	6	6.665

Tiwanaku and Katari valleys to the north. The number of Early Pacajes sites and total Early Pacajes occupation area exploded, and this explosion correlates with a substantial decrease in overall site size in conjunction with the increasing ephemerality of settlements and the corresponding mobility of their peripatetic inhabitants. By 1350, the site of Pukara de Khonkho, centered on a mountain just north of Khonkho Wankane in the upper colluvial zone, emerged as a spectacular new regional center (Zovar 2012). The rise of Pukara de Khonkho was the local manifestation of an emergent panregional Andean centrality that ultimately produced the early Inca polity and its multiple interlocutors across the highland Andes.

Inca presence promoted a new world of imperial control in the region. More than three quarters of Inca period occupation was focused on four relatively large settlements, all centered in the lower colluvial zone at the base of the Corocoro range. Undoubtedly, establishing these centers was part of an imperial program of transferring populations from remote and dispersed hilltops such as Pukara de Khonkho to lower foothill places such as Ch'auch'a and nearby Palli Marka. Early Spanish Colonial occupations continued this trend, punctuated by the construction of a chapel at the Inca site of Ch'auch'a de K'ula Marka, at the foot of Pukara de Khonkho. Contemporary Qhunqhu residents tell us that the low plain it occupies is where men gathered and were accounted before they headed south for their *mit'a* services in the mines of Oruro and Potosi.

Chapter 4

〜

Geophysical Investigations at Khonkho Wankane

Christopher P. Dayton, Patrick Ryan Williams,
Benjamin R. Vining, and Scott C. Smith

Geophysical prospection is integral to archaeology. Some suggest that geophysical prospection has the potential to eventually replace the inherently destructive practice of excavation, preserving subsurface remains for future investigators (Kvamme 2001). Yet most archaeological research questions demand details not obtainable by geophysical means: subtle lithic scatters, faint differences in soils and sediments, ceramics sherds in each stratum, morphologies of bone fragments, and so on. We cannot "see beneath the soil" (Clark 1990). More realistically, geophysical prospection can complement excavations by offering subsoil locational information regarding archaeological features of interest, thereby minimizing their cost and spatial extent. Furthermore, it can provide a broad subsurface perspective that may include the layout of buried buildings, paths, open ritual spaces, and other pronounced spatial features.

Geophysical research at Khonkho Wankane exemplified this approach. In 2001–2004, geophysical prospection guided and complemented the excavation of ritual and residential architecture on the Wankane platform mound (JM-60). In this chapter we briefly describe our geophysical research, the survey methods and data-processing procedures employed, and the relative usefulness of those methods, and then summarize key results of excavation-based *ground-truthing* of the geophysical results.

Geophysical Survey Methods

Geophysical prospection is not the search for objects or structures per se, but the search for contrasts between materials (Kvamme 2001:356). Different instruments react to different types of contrasts. Three geophysical methods were employed at Khonkho: ground-penetrating radar, magnetometry, and earth resistance survey.

Ground-Penetrating Radar

The first subsurface remote-sensing survey at Khonkho utilized ground-penetrating radar (GPR), which involves transmitting electromagnetic waves into the ground and plotting reflections that result from interfaces between different materials; for instance, between wet and dry strata, stone and soil, or soil and air **(Figure 4.1)**. Radar works best in dry, nonconductive media. Wet soils, especially if they contain clays or salts, can carry electromagnetic energy away from the survey area, leaving an insufficient amount of energy to generate readable reflections (Gaffney and Gater 2003:49–50).

In 2001 a geophysical survey team from the Bolivian National Unit of Archaeology and Anthropology (UNAR) collected ground-penetrating radar (GPR) data with a Geophysical Survey Systems SIR-2000 digital controller and a 400 MHz antenna, under the guidance of Patrick Ryan Williams. Fifteen grids of alternating transects separated by one-meter intervals were laid out based on visible architectural remains in the monumental core. Collection parameters included the following: a range of 40 ns two-way travel time, a pulse rate of 32 scans per second or about 1 scan every 3 cm, automatic gains set by experimentation, and low and high pass filters set respectively at 1110 and 70 MHz. Distance marks were manually entered every meter on each transect.

Figure 4.1 Ground Penetrating Radar survey at Khonkho Wankane (photo by John W. Janusek).

All GPR data were examined and processed using Radan NT, provided by Geophysical Survey Systems. Initially, the data were analyzed as individual profiles, the traditional format for radar interpretation. After tentative identification of walls and other features along each transect, the profiles were digitally assembled into interpolated three-dimensional *blocks* of data. The blocks were sliced at various depths to produce map views of anomalies extending across multiple transects. After considerable trial and error with the multiple grids—filtering, slicing at different depths, repeated examination and comparison, re-filtering, re-slicing, etc.—we chose to concentrate on one slicing depth that seemed the most informative: from 9 to 21 ns, or approximately 25–57 cm beneath the surface based on an estimated relative dielectric permittivity of 30. Although this is quite thick for a time slice, we were primarily interested in the areal extent of major architecture rather than resolving features at different depths. In other words, we were comfortable with the prospect of averaging some elements of the architectural palimpsest together. Slices from the core of the Wankane site representing the 9–21 ns depth range in all grids were exported to Adobe Illustrator and arranged into a composite map of radar reflections (**Figure 4.2**). This image, in which numerous courts, plazas, and

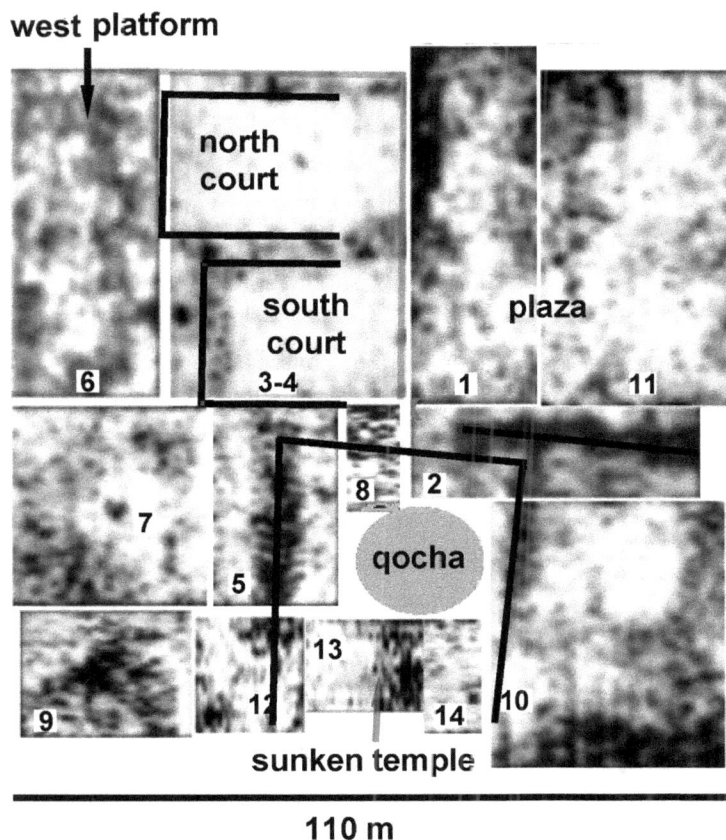

Figure 4.2   Plotted results of ground-penetrating radar survey in the monumental core of Khonkho Wankane. The numbers refer to discrete geophysical grids.

110 m

small enclosures are visible, served as a geophysical base map on which data from subsequent surveys were plotted for comparison.

The most striking physical features visible in the initial radar data were the linear gray (highly reflective) areas surrounding white (low reflection) in grids 6 and 3/4, which excavations indicate were two (north and south) courts of a Dual-Court complex (Chapter 9; Janusek 2015, Janusek et al. 2003). In addition, grids 1 and 11 revealed a large diffuse area of moderately low reflections. Excavations revealed that this was a large plaza with no internal architectural walls, an interpretation supported by the presence on the surface of a fallen monolith near its center (Chapter 6). There were also extremely heavy reflections in the smaller grids in the bottom half of the image, on either side of a known trapezoidal sunken court complex corresponding to grids 2, 5, 8, 12, 13, and 14 (Chapter 7). These data, however, were likely to include false signals or artifacts of inconsistencies in the data collection process. Therefore, we were particularly interested in carrying out more logistically coherent surveys of that area.

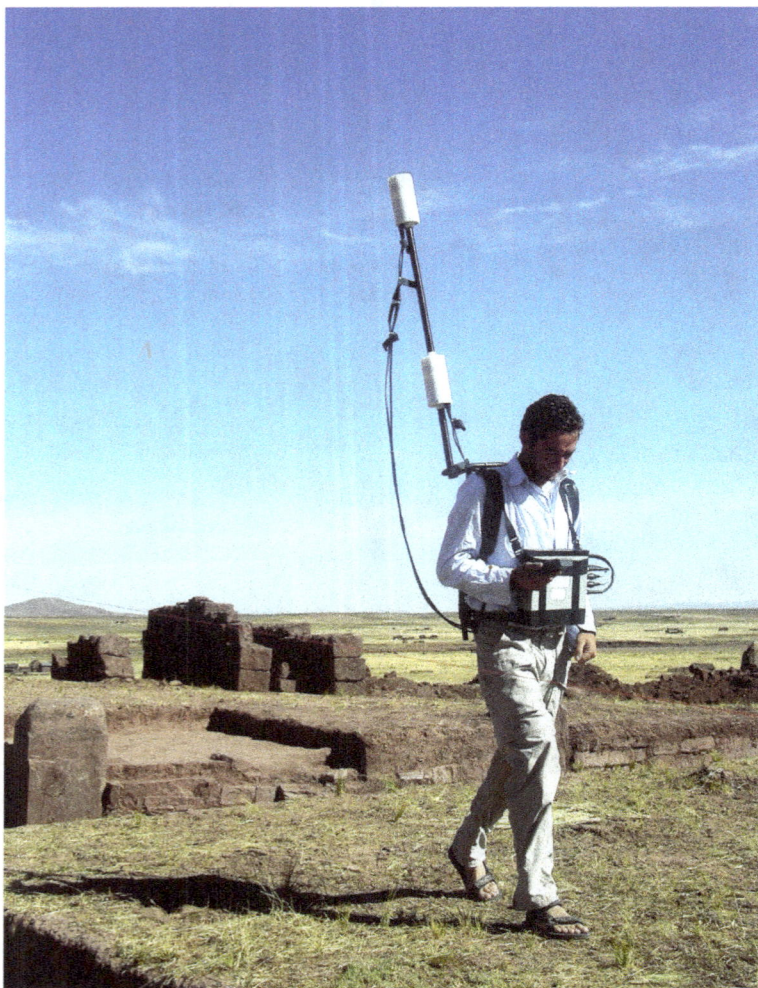

Figure 4.3 Magnetometry survey at Khonkho Wankane (photo by John W. Janusek).

Magnetometry

Magnetic data were also collected at Khonkho Wankane. This avenue of prospection was prompted by successful results from a residential sector at Tiwanaku. Accordingly, in 2002 and 2003, Ryan Williams, Ben Vining, and colleagues used a GEM Systems GSM-19 Overhauser gradiometer provided by the Field Museum to measure magnetic field variations over an area of Khonkho Wankane much larger than that represented by the radar base map (**Figure 4.3**). Unfortunately, few clear magnetic anomalies of interest or major patterns were identified. The only clear anomalies consisted of several large, semi-carved stones of green andesite that occupy the surface of the southeast quadrant of the monumental complex (**Figure 4.4**). It is possible there was simply too much surface noise, even though the area was repeatedly foot-surveyed to clean magnetic trash. Each year, thousands of bottle caps are discarded at the site during a winter solstice celebration on June 21, just before the archaeological season begins. Despite our best efforts, we likely failed to pick all of them up.

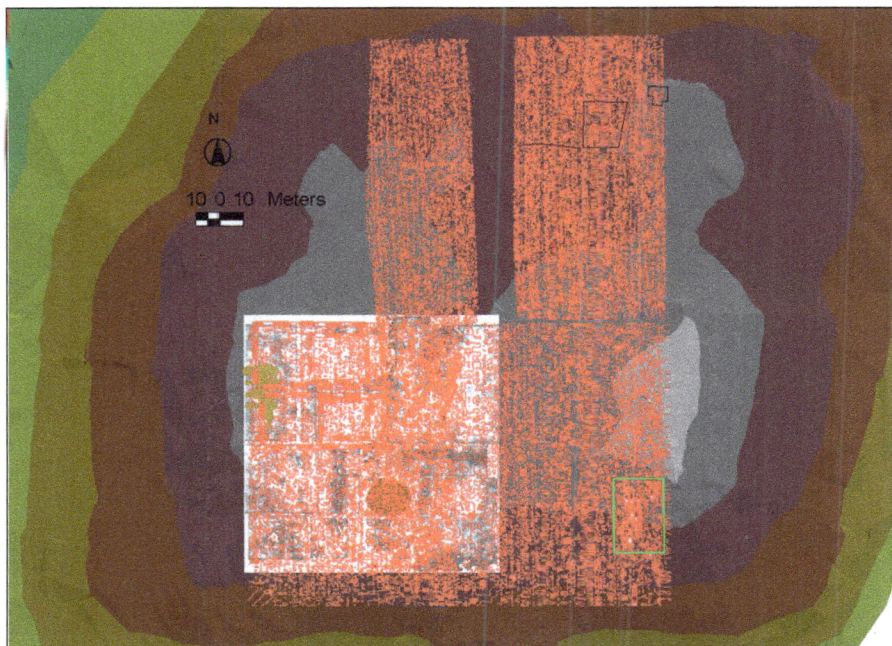

Figure 4.4   Plotted results of magnetometry survey at Khonkho. The box encompasses the few anomalies located, which included several partially carved volcanic stones.

Magnetometry has yielded useful results elsewhere in the *altiplano*. For instance, in the Mollo Kontu residential sector at Tiwanaku, Williams documented extremely high magnetic readings that may indicate a buried andesite monolith. However, at Khonkho we have found that GPR and earth resistance data better capture the subtle contrasts in density and moisture retention that illuminate the overall architectural layout of the site. We still recommend magnetometer survey for others working in similar situations, and will likely do more of this type of survey at Khonkho as well. Magnetic data can be collected more rapidly than other data, and it is worth having different kinds of data on hand for later processing and analysis.

Earth Resistance

In 2004, we carried out earth resistance survey at Khonkho. Our expectations were low because the resistance meter we used was a much simpler instrument and nearly an order of magnitude less costly than the radar and magnetic units. Resistance survey proved us wrong by yielding extraordinarily useful data, and we encourage other Andeanists to attempt this relatively inexpensive, uncomplicated method.

Like ground-penetrating radar, resistance survey actively transmits electromagnetic energy into the soil. Resistance survey differs from radar, however, in that its measurements are aided by electrically conductive materials. In other words, if resistance to a current is to be measured, the current has to be able to flow in the first place. Although the terms *resistance* and *resistivity* are often

Figure 4.5 Resistivity survey at Khonkho Wankane (photo by John W. Janusek).

used interchangeably, resistivity is a more sophisticated property that allows precise comparisons among strata, materials, or entire sites (Gaffney and Gater 2003:28; Kvamme 2001:361).

Chris Dayton, Ben Vining, and Scott Smith conducted the 2004 earth resistance survey using equipment provided by Patrick Ryan Williams at the Field Museum **(Figure 4.5)**. This survey built on 2003 work by Patrick Ryan Williams and Ben Vining that indicated resistance measurements were feasible at the site (Williams et al. 2003). Furthermore, like magnetometry, the resistance survey was motivated by intriguing results from the aforementioned pilot study at Tiwanaku (Williams et al. 2004). Fortunately, one of the obstacles encountered in the Tiwanaku pilot study was not encountered at Khonkho. While the hard, clay-rich surface crust at Tiwanaku required shallow plowing to allow sufficient penetration of the resistance probes, the sandier soils of Khonkho Wankane did not present this problem.

We used a TR Systems resistance meter in the twin-probe configuration, with two mobile probes within the survey grid and two stationary probes some distance from the data collection grid. Other probe configurations—for instance, the Wenner arrays commonly used in Europe—are more sensitive to subtle contrasts and can be more easily converted to true resistivity. Yet they have other drawbacks, such as non-intuitive representations of anomalies (Gater and Gaffney 2003). We judged the twin-probe array sufficient for our purposes, since we did not intend to create tomographic sections or convert the measurements from resistance to resistivity. Instead, we focused on areal coverage of near-surface deposits and immediate, intuitive displays of the results.

At Khonkho we collected resistance measurements every meter along transects spaced one meter apart, covering approximately one hectare of the monumental core. Twenty-one grids were surveyed, most measuring 20 × 20 m, with several extending to 20 × 30 m to include architectural remains noted on the ground surface during data collection. The mobile probes were fixed at a separation of 0.5 m, while the distance between the stationary probes varied from 0.2 m to 2 m, depending on what was needed to calibrate the meter from one grid to the next. Each data point was taken manually, after the meter indicated sufficient penetration of the soil and the readout had stabilized.

Although it helps to have one or two assistants to hold cords and move tapes, a single operator can efficiently handle these tasks alone and cover five to seven 20 by 20 m grids in a day. The speed of each reading—and by extension, the entire survey—depends on ground conditions. While the resistance survey took considerably more time than the ground-penetrating radar or magnetic prospection, its advantages were soon apparent. We experimented with complex filters and processing techniques, but the simplest strategies yielded the best results. First, we compiled all measurements into a single data table and calculated the mean and standard deviation for the entire dataset. Next, following Jones (2001), we manually removed measurements falling more than two standard deviations from the mean in order to remove extreme values and highlight subtle variations in the values displayed (although Jones used a three standard deviation cutoff). The resulting data range was 20–80 ohms of relative resistance. Finally, we used Golden Software's Surfer plotting program to smoothly interpolate among the remaining values and display all of the survey grids as simple grayscale plots, with low resistance in black and high resistance in white.

Improvements on the earlier radar plot are immediately apparent. The interior courtyard and exterior platform walls of the Dual-Court Complex were much better defined, as was the Main Plaza's northeast corner (**Figures 4.6 and 4.7**). More exciting, resistance survey revealed an anomaly in the southwest sector of the monumental complex characterized by a semi-circle of higher resistance surrounded by a circle of lower resistance (**Figure 4.6**). Excavations by Jennifer Zovar (2006) revealed that this anomaly constituted the west side of a large circular structure (Structure 9.C1, the east side of which was buried deeper under soil eroding from the monumental platform). Unlike the plaza and other monumental features recovered by radar, this structure had no prior surface expression.

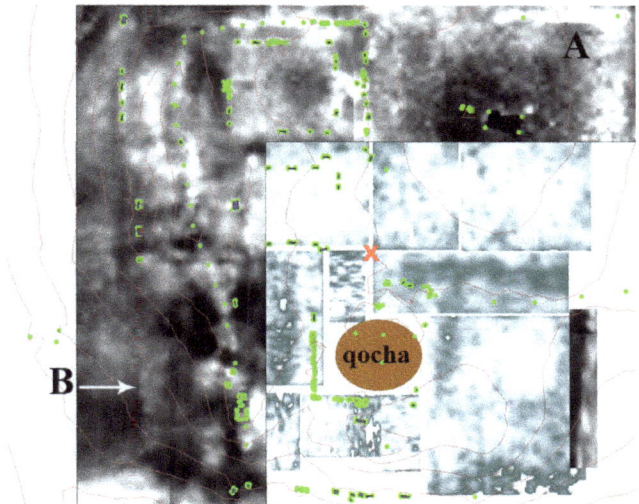

Figure 4.6   Plotted results of resistivity survey plotted over results of Ground Penetrating Radar at Khonkho, highlighting wall foundations of the Dual-Court Complex, A) the northeast corner of the Main Plaza, and B) the west edge of a circular structure that turned out to be Structure 9.C1.

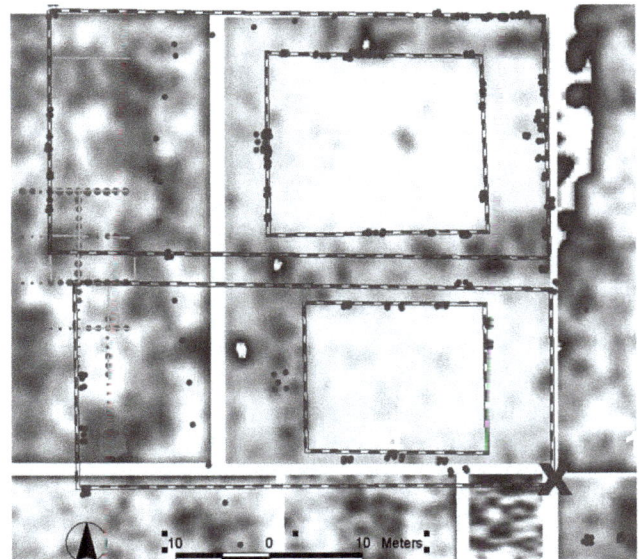

Figure 4.7   Detail of the Dual-Court Complex as plotted based on combined geophysical surveys.

Conclusions

We employed three geophysical methods at Khonkho Wankane: ground-penetrating radar (GPR), gradient magnetometry, and earth resistance. Ground-penetrating radar and earth resistance proved the most effective methods. Resistance data were the most precise and aided the identification of previously unknown architectural features confirmed by excavations. Although the collection of earth resistance data tends to require more time than GPR or magnetic surveys, the benefits are considerable, given appropriate environmental conditions and research questions. Archaeological projects rarely have superfluous funding, so cost is an important issue; a resistance meter can be purchased for a fraction of the price of a GPR unit or gradient magnetometer. In addition, the data we collected at Khonkho Wankane required very little processing to be useful. We simply cut off the extreme values, normalized the results across grids, examined the resulting plots, and commenced excavations.

〜

Chapter 5

The Stone Sculpture of Khonkho Wankane

Arik Ohnstad and John Wayne Janusek

Ever since Khonkho Wankane was first revealed to the world in 1936 (Portugal Ortiz 1981:149), its stone monoliths have been the focus of published discussions of the site. Their size and evocative imagery have made them intriguing to scholars even as Khonkho itself has languished in relative obscurity, overshadowed by its more famous neighbor to the north. Indeed, most scholars have taken as their primary subject the elucidation of Khonkho's temporal and cultural relations with Tiwanaku, while others have focused on broader culture historical questions.

In this chapter, we summarize our coalescing perspectives on the chronology, culture history, and significance of the monoliths. We then present detailed descriptions of Khonkho's monoliths and other stone sculptures. In the course of this discussion we summarize key elements of our emergent ideas regarding the iconographic significance of Khonkho's four sculpted monoliths.

Prior Research on Khonkho Wankane's Stone Sculpture

Perhaps the first scholarly publication to mention Khonkho's monoliths is Fritz Buck's *El Calendario Maya en la Cultura de Tiahuanacu* (1937). He published drawings of several iconographic elements from Monoliths 1 and 2 (Wilakala and Jinch'unkala) (**Figure 5.1**) and a photograph of Jinch'unkala (**Figure 1.5**). Buck considered these monuments to be "the clearest and most irrefutable evidence of a direct Central American influence over a cultural group of ancient Peru" (1937:183). Making far-fetched connections between Khonkho's sculptural iconography and Maya glyphic writing, Buck dated the site to A.D. 500 and, like Maks Portugal Zamora, considered its monoliths to antedate Classic Tiwanaku sculptural styles (1937:187).

Maks Portugal Zamora came to similar conclusions about the chronology of the site (see chapter 1). In 1941, he published photographs of the monoliths in the *Revista Geográfica Americana*. In this article Portugal characterized a number of motifs on the Khonkho monoliths as "primitive" versions of motifs seen

Figure 5.1 Iconography of the Wila Kala (A) and Jinch'un Kala (B) monoliths according to Buck (1937:Figs. 47, 64a, and 65).

Figure 5.2 Iconography of the Wila Kala and Jinch'un Kala monoliths according to Maks Portugal Zamora (1936, cited in Rydén 1947: Fig. 33).

on Classic Tiwanaku sculpture (Portugal Zamora 1941, 1955). These included the zigzag streamers descending from the eyes of the central Wilakala personage, the "condors" on Monolith 4, the winged camelid on the lower back of Jinch'unkala, and the bicephalic serpents on all of them (**Figure 5.2**). Portugal suggested that the winged camelid was the prototype for an ethnographically known *demigod* recognized by modern Aymara in certain constellations near the Milky Way (Portugal Zamora 1941:300, 1955:55).

In a 1972 conference paper, David Browman broadened the cultural context for understanding Khonkho monoliths. He proposed four pre-Tiwanaku stylistic monolithic traditions (further refined in Browman 1995, 1997). He placed Khonkho Wankane monoliths in the third of these, what he called the Pajano style. Browman took the name from the term Pa-Ajanu, first employed by Posnansky in 1945, and derived from the Aymara term for "two-faced," in reference to two anthropomorphic beings depicted on opposing sides of some stone sculptures. Chávez and Chávez (1975) later employed the same double-faced pattern to define the "Yayamama" style.

Max Portugal Ortiz (1981, 1998) situated Khonkho monoliths in a broad context. He employed the term Pa-Ajanu to refer to a long but coherent tradition of religious art centered geographically on Lake Titicaca. According to Ortiz, this tradition began in Tiwanaku III (our Late Formative 2). Later, he (1998) extended the origins of the Pa-Ajanu tradition back to the Middle Formative Chiripa period. Altogether, Portugal Ortiz followed his father's chronological placement of Khonkho's monuments. He saw them as marking a transition from Tiwanaku III to Classic Tiwanaku styles, which we designate the Late Formative 2–Early Tiwanaku (or Tiwanaku 1) transition.

Jach'a Machaca Stone Sculpture Research

Our interpretation of the monoliths is informed by their iconographic content and our excavations at Khonkho Wankane (**Figure 5.3**). We follow Browman, Maks and Max Portugal, and others in dating the monuments to the Late Formative period and broadly to the basin-wide Pajano/Yamamama sculptural tradition.

We note that Khonkho's monoliths manifest particularly strong stylistic and iconographic relations with Pukara style sculptures, centered at sites such as Taraco, Pukara, and Arapa in the northwest Lake Titicaca basin, and sculptures located in the Tiwanaku Valley just north of Khonkho Wankane, especially Tiwanaku (**Figure 1.17**). We find further iconographic relations between Khonkho's monoliths and Pucara style textiles and ceramic vessels as well as textiles associated with Paracas, a formative cultural complex that flourished on the Andean south coast of Peru.

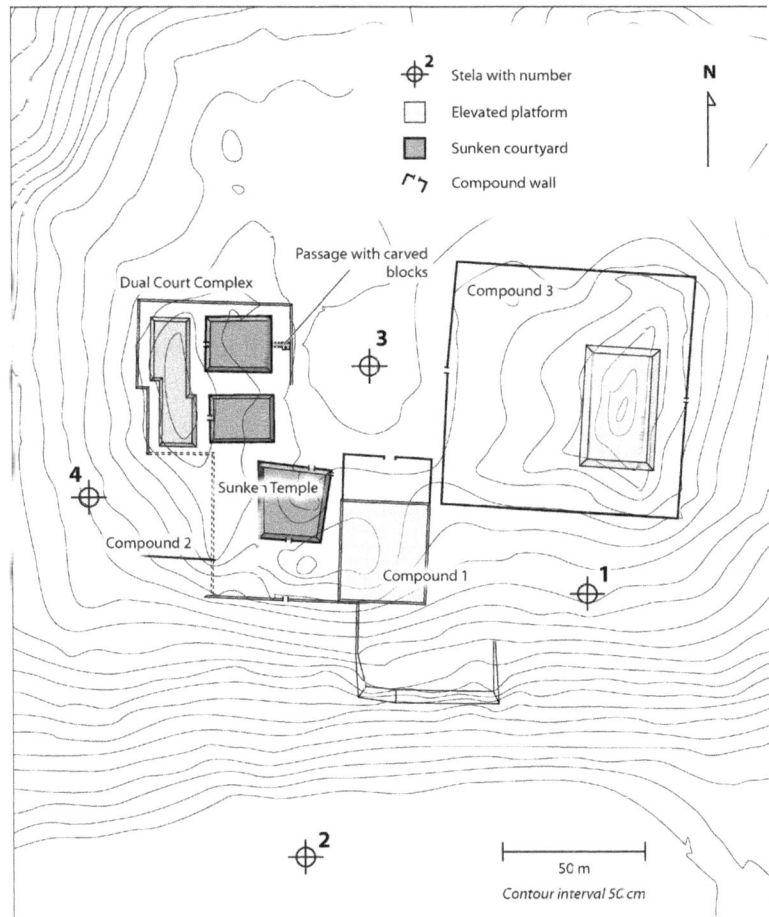

Figure 5.3   Plan map of Khonkho Wankane showing the found location of Khonkho's four monoliths: 1) Wila Kala, 2) Jinch'un Kala, 3) Tata Kala, 4) Portugal.

Excavations in the Sunken Court and Dual-Court Complex (see chapters 7 and 9) suggest that the former antedates the latter and that neither is later than Late Formative 2/Tiwanaku III (approximately A.D. 300–500). If, as seems likely, the monoliths from Khonkho were related to or at the least contemporaneous with ritual activities in these courts, cross-dating based on iconographic ties to Pukara ceramics and Paracas/Nasca textiles, together with other stylistic attributes, suggests a probable date no earlier than the onset of Late Formative 1.

We view this phase as one of local stylistic divergence across the basin, rather than as an epoch unified by a single Pajano or Yayamama style. Indeed, either term would be something of a misnomer when applied to the monolithic sculptures from Khonkho Wankane, for unlike other monuments grouped under the Pajano style, there is little reason to think that Khonkho Monoliths 1 and 2 originally had two faces. The wide variety of monolithic styles present in the Titicaca Basin during the Late Formative (Portugal Ortiz 1998)—Pajano, early Tiwanaku, Pukara/Pokotía—suggests that, despite many commonalities in visual culture, there was likely substantial competition and conscious attempts at differentiation between ritual-political centers (Bandy 2001).

We are actively exploring the iconography, materiality, and spatial contexts of Khonkho Wankane's stone sculpture. We argue that the anthropomorphic monolithic beings depict apical, mythical ancestors who likely also embody critical elements and prominent features in surrounding landscapes. Through comparison with other Formative period sculpture and ceramic iconography, Paracas/Nasca textiles, and historic and ethnographic materials, we are investigating the cosmological content and practical contexts of these monuments, including their roles in ongoing sociopolitical changes.

Renderings and Descriptions of the Sculptures

Khonkho's monoliths have been described in numerous publications (e.g., Browman 1972; Portugal Zamora 1941, 1955; Portugal Ortiz 1998 Rydén 1947; Vellard 1955). However, because the few drawings that have been published have generally been incomplete and at times incorrect, the monoliths have never been fully accessible to scholars. We attempt to rectify this situation by presenting complete drawings of each piece of stone sculpture available to us. We have compiled them from photos, rubbings, and detailed observations made by Proyecto Jach'a Machaca members, with reference to older photos from the investigations led by Maks Portugal. While our renderings remain subject to further revision, they are the most accurate and detailed images of the monoliths yet published (see also Janusek 2015 and Ohnstad 2013).

All of the monoliths from Khonkho Wankane consist of red-hued sandstone, despite Vellard's assertion (1955:152) that some are of andesite. Each is executed in low relief, though in rare instances simple incision is used to inscribe details, for example the folds of the clothing of the small frontal figure on Monolith 4 or Portugal. The numbering of the monoliths in the descriptions below follows that assigned by Rydén (1947). First, however, we describe two related sculptural stones that project members found at the site.

Architectural stones

Two small sculpted stone blocks were recovered from the Late Formative Dual-Court Complex, where they appear to have been incorporated as architectural elements (see Chapter 9). Both of these architectural stones depict themes that are echoed in the monumental sculptures on the site.

The first of the blocks measures approximately 30 cm × 35 cm and depicts a winged camelid (**Figure 5.4A**). The camelid's teeth are bared, and it has a large round eye with a small dependent *tear* marking and a simple dorsal wing (see also the description of Monolith 2, below). The other stone is larger and more eroded than the first. It measures 25 cm × 47 cm and depicts a human head in profile, and possibly a trophy head **(Figure 5.4B)**. A zigzag streamer descends from the eye (compare it to those on monoliths described below).

Monolith 1 (Wila Kala)

Three faces of the quadrangular Wila Kala are preserved **(Figure 5.5)**. Wila Kala is the tallest of Khonkho's monoliths, and was broken in two soon after its initial discovery (see Chapter 1) **(Figure 5.6)**. Portugal gives its measurements as 5.38 m × 60 cm × 38 cm (Portugal Zamora 1941:294); the monolith has since been erected and its base buried, so it is not possible to check the accuracy of its height.

Monolith 1 depicts an anthropomorphic figure with a T-shaped nose connected to a well-defined brow, a mouth in the shape of a squared oval, and

20 cm

Figure 5.4   Rendering of the iconography of the two architectural stones recovered from the east entrance of the North Court of the Dual-Court Complex.

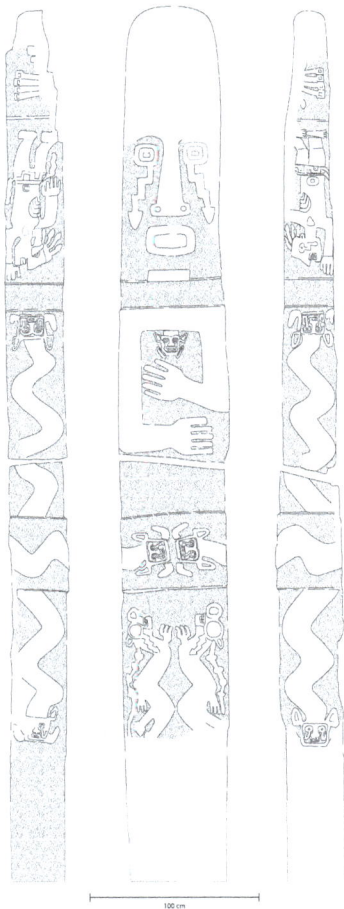

100 cm

Figure 5.5   Iconographic rendering of the Wila Kala monolith.

Figure 5.6   View of the Wila Kala monolith. Photo by Wolfgang Schüler.

ringlike eyes with zigzag eye streamers. The figure appears to wear a headdress, perhaps depicting solar rays, though only the sides of the headdress, which wrap around the lateral faces of the stela, are still visible. The neck of the figure is depicted as a recessed panel, above which is a small rectangle, perhaps depicting the chin or a chin ornament.

The arms are crossed over the chest in a manner typical of many monuments in the Yayamama/Pajano style (see, e.g., Browman 1972; S. Chávez and K. M. Chávez 1975). They wrap around the collar area to mark out a formalized boxlike shape, identical to that of a monolith from the site of Wakullani on the Taraco Peninsula (see Portugal Ortiz 1998:Fig. 90). The figure's belt is represented by a raised panel around which has been depicted a bicephalic serpentlike creature, whose heads meet on the front of the monolith.

The same creature appears to be depicted both as a simple head in the pectoral region, and on sides of the monolith, stretching from the bottom of the monolith to the neck panel, interrupted by the belt panel and its horizontal bicephalic creature. These serpent beings, like those on Monoliths 2 and 4, as well as an early Tiwanaku monolith (see Portugal Ortiz 1998:Figs. 111, 112), have heads marked by feline ears, catfish (*suche*) whiskers, and eyes with zigzag or recurved eye streamers.

Just above these serpents on each lateral face of the monolith are two mirrored profile figures, with bared teeth, distinctive headdresses/hairstyles, zigzag breechcloths, semicircular neck ornaments, exposed ribs, one leading and one trailing arm, and large, ringlike navels. These figures have very specific iconographic cross-ties with the "Falling Man" or "Backbent Figure" motif of Pucara textiles and ceramics (see, e.g., Browman 1972; Frame 2001), as well as with Pukara and Pokotía style statuary. Vellard (1955:152) viewed these figures as trophies of war hung up by their feet for display. In any case, these "Falling Men" reappear in the same position on the sides of Monolith 2.

The two falling figures are balanced compositionally by two felines rampant at the bottom front of the monolith. Both likely served as mutually indexical signs. These creatures are more or less exact mirror images of one another, though it is interesting that the one on the right's nose and eye are about 40% larger than the one on the left. They have feline forelimbs, but human feet, which led Rydén (1947:163) to suggest that they represent human beings wearing animal costumes. Zigzag, probably serpent-headed tear streamers emerge from these beings' eyes. Trailing from the back of each feline's head is a ball-and-collar motif identical to one that recurs on camelids in Pukara ceramic iconography. An iconographically similar motif is found on felines in Recuay ceramic styles (Buck 1937:Fig. 61).

Photos taken before the monolith's base was sealed in concrete seem to indicate a lack of carving below these figures.

Monolith 2 (Jinch'un Kala)

The Jinch'un Kala is very similar in form and iconographic content to the Wila Kala **(Figure 5.7)**. Like the Wila Kala, it is a long, quadrangular slab of reddish sandstone, with recessed and raised panels accentuating certain features of anatomy and costume. Portugal Zamora (1941:294) gives its dimensions as 4.54 m long by a maximum of 70 cm wide. Monolith 2 has been raised and a significant portion of its base is set in concrete, so that it is not currently visible.

The Jinch'un Kala depicts a large, anthropomorphic figure similar to that depicted on the Wila Kala and on Monolith 4, though only three faces of the monolith are preserved, the rear and the flanks **(Figure 5.8)**. The flanks of the monolith are substantially the same as those of the Wila Kala—twin bicephalic serpentlike creatures with the distinctive set of Khonkho attributes (eye markings, feline ears, and *suche* whiskers) are depicted below paired profile representations of a "Falling Man" with bared teeth, zigzag breechcloth, exposed ribs, semicircular neck ornament, and zigzag eye markings. On the Jinch'un Kala, the representation of the "Falling Man" has three streamers trailing from its chin similar to those on certain figures seen in Pukara ceramics (e.g., Rowe and Brandel 1969–1970:Fig. 20; S. Chávez 1992:204, 205, etc.).

The front of the monolith, and thus the face of the anthropomorphic being has been heavily eroded, but its hair appears to be depicted on the preserved rear face, in a style similar to that used on certain Tiwanaku monoliths, such as the Ponce monolith: long, straight streamers terminating in downward facing fish heads. In the case of the Jinch'unkala, there are eight of these streamers, divided into symmetrical groups; four of the fish heads face left while the other four face right.

The hair streamers descend from a raised panel that appears to represent a kind of turban headdress. On this is depicted an intriguing scene centered on a prone humanoid figure with an incised spoon-like shape emerging from its mouth. Out of this figure's back emerges a strange creature with a large squared head, open mouth, and three tightly scrolled dorsal appendages. Three similar scrolls oriented in the opposite direction are seen just above the prone figure's head. Another scroll terminates at the top of a *bean pod* that emerges from the prone figure's forehead. Six round shapes—perhaps representing seeds or legumes—are arrayed between the square-headed creature's limb-like appendage and the hand (or a foot with an opposable fifth toe) of the prone figure.

The lateral faces of this panel depict the profile bodies of felines with tightly curled tails. The heads of these felines would surely have appeared frontally on the eroded side of the monolith, in the same manner as the felines at the bottom of the Bearded Monolith (Monolith 15) in the Semisubterranean Temple at Tiwanaku.

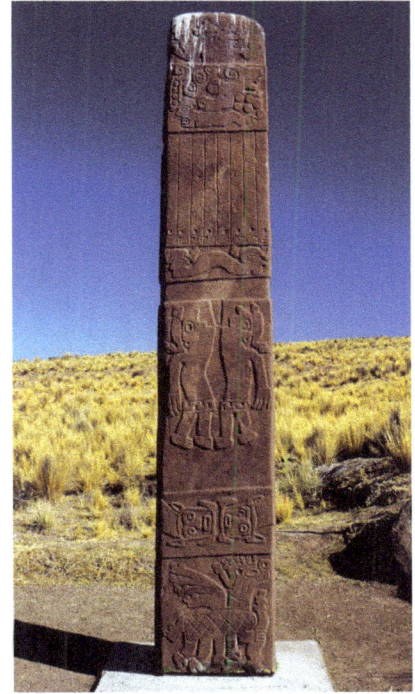

Figure 5.7   View of the rear of Jinch'un Kala. Photo by John Janusek.

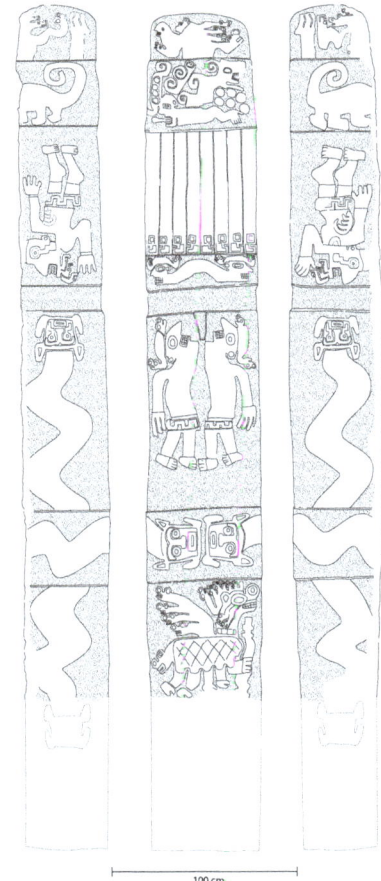

Figure 5.8   Iconographic rendering of the Jinch'un Kala monolith.

On the uppermost back panel of the monolith is an amorphous shape with a vaguely humanoid head and a number of appendages or rays terminating in feline heads. The sides of this panel depict a now eroded shape with streamers terminating in feline and fish heads, paired with a three-feathered motif similar to one that commonly appears on Pukara ceramics associated with headdresses, staffs, and trophy head streamers; a similar motif also commonly appears on depictions of Tiwanaku and Wari headdresses.

In the middle section of the back of the stela appear twin humanoid figures, similar in composition to the paired felines on the front of the Wila Kala. Like those felines, these humanoids raise their faces upward. They also bare their teeth and wear the same zigzag-patterned breechcloth as do the "Falling Man" figures. This suggests that these "Rising Man" figures represent the same character as the "Falling Man," though in a different state. It is interesting to note that each "Rising Man" also has one raised and one lowered arm, though the raised arms are merely suggested by a recessed triangular zone between the two figures. The line drawn to separate the toes from the rest of the foot is common in Pukara ceramic representations. Likewise, the bicephalic feline headdress seen on these figures is commonly seen in Pukara and in Tiwanaku style ceramics.

Above the recessed panel that marks the neck of the main figure is what seems to be another representation of the "Rising Man" motif. Here, the profile humanoid heads face outward, connected by a serpentine body. Each head wears the same bicephalic feline headdress that the "Rising Man" below wears. This representation may mark a transition in narrative flow to the sides of the monolith, as the two heads of the "Rising Man" here point outward to the downward-turned faces of the paired "Falling Men."

Below the raised panel that marks the main figure's belt is a representation of a camelid with bared teeth. The basic iconographic elements of the camelid are shared with Pukara ceramics and stone sculpture (see illustrations in, e.g., S. Chávez 1988, 1992): the dual-perspective style for depicting cloven hooves, the colored (here, cross-hatched) coat serrated along its lower boundary, the round nose, the mane on the crown of the head, and the lozenge on the neck. However, this camelid also has bared teeth, a common trait of profile heads—whatever the species—at Khonkho, as well as feline-headed streamers trailing from its eyes (Both of these features are also found on a Pukara sculpture from Livitaca; see S. Chávez 1988:Fig. 12.) The Jich'unkala camelid is, furthermore, winged, and the wing, mane, and tail terminate in feline heads (Vellard misinterpreted these as condor heads; see Vellard 1955:153). Finally, the camelid has a fifth limb, with humanoid fingers and elbow joint, shown gripping a notched staff nearly identical to that carried by a number of representations of the Camelid Woman on Pukara ceramics (e.g., S. Chávez 1992:Figs. 142–145). While a number of publications (e.g., Rydén 1947:Fig. 33; Browman 1972:Fig.

9; Portugal Ortiz 1998:Fig. 107) have depicted a feline head terminator on the bottom of this staff, early photos (e.g. Portugal 1941:297) and one early drawing (Buck 1937:Fig. 65) suggest that no such element was ever in fact visible. The bottom of the staff appears to have widened abruptly at the bottom.

Monolith 3 (Tata Kala)

The Tata Kala is the largest of the known monoliths from Khonkho Wankane, measuring 5.1 m long by 95 cm wide at its widest point (Portugal Zamora 1941) **(Figure 5.9)**. It lies prone in Khonkho's Main Plaza and likely stood in that space during the Late Formative. Tata Kala, translated by Portugal as the "stone monk," is today the most revered of the monoliths and a centerpiece of contemporary ritual for the Jesus de Machaca region.

The monolith is, however, highly eroded, and few carvings are visible on its surface (see Ohnstad 2011:131–134 and 2013:58–60 for its definitive iconographic reconstruction). Portugal Zamora reports that during his 1937 investigations at the site, serpent-like beings similar to those on Monoliths 1 and 2 were barely visible near where the monolith meets the ground, notably in the belt region (Portugal 1941:293, 1955:60). He also reports "relief faces in circular form, positioned in the same manner as those of the Bennett Monolith [at Tiwanaku], that is on the skirt [or tunic]" (1941:296). Only after 2002 did we explore in greater detail Tatakala's remnant iconography.

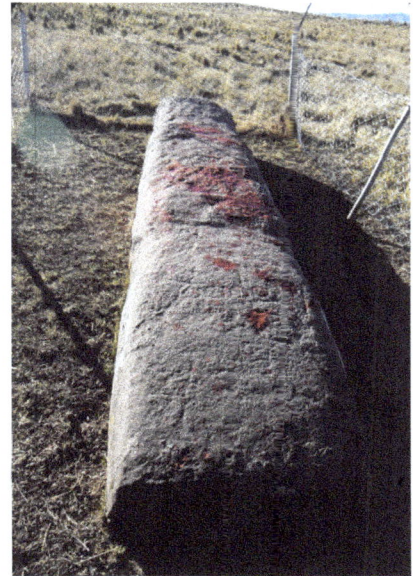

Figure 5.9   View of the Tata Kala monolith at sunrise, June 21, 2002, showing blood offered and remnant iconography (photo by John W. Janusek).

Monolith 4 (Portugal)

The incomplete fourth monolith was recovered by Portugal Zamora—during either his 1937 or 1941 excavations—some 10–20 cm beneath the surface on the west side of the Wankane platform (Portugal 1941:297, 1955:Fig. 10) **(Figure 5.10)**. He described two large fragments, the larger (4-1) approximately 1.8 m long and 53 cm at its widest point and the smaller (4-2) about 1.44 m × 32 cm. Cleaning the area of the remnant monolith in 1987, in the course of Kolata's excavations, revealed three smaller fragments that had been curated by the local community (4-3, 4-4, and 4-5, **Figure 1.7**).

Figure 5.10   Maks Portugal's (1955:Fig. 10) photo of the ritually destroyed Portugal Monolith, found interred on the west side of the Wankane platform.

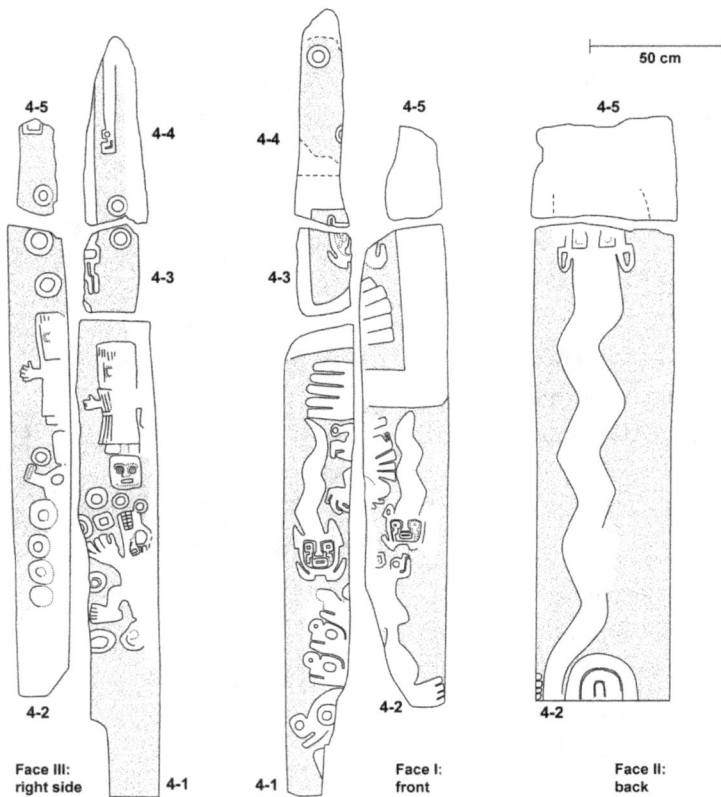

Figure 5.11 Provisional reconstruction of the Portugal Monolith.

Together, the five stones constitute most of a monolith that had been broken along both vertical and the horizontal axes (**Figures 1.7 and 5.11**). Portugal assumed that the two large fragments he recovered were from the same stela, and his conclusion is reasonable. We refit all five stones to reveal the crossed arms of an anthropomorphic being similar to that of Wila Kala and Jinch'un Kala. In this scenario, the three small fragments exposed in 1987 constitute remnants of the being's quartered, incomplete head. Altogether, the designs on our hypothesized front face line up well. However, the reconstructed Face III (right side) presents difficulties. While the imagery on each side of Face III is nearly identical, the two designs do not fit together well, and seem to represent different *versions* of the same theme. It thus seems possible that the five stones of Monolith 4 may comprise fragments of two different but more or less identical monoliths.

Like Monoliths 1, 2, and 3, Monolith 4's Face I or front side appears to have depicted a single anthropomorphic being—or possibly, two nearly identical anthropomorphic beings. The arms are crossed over the torso in the opposite configuration of Monolith 1; that is, right above left. Just above the fragmentary right hand is a curled motif that may represent part of a small, ornamental head such as that on the chest of the central figure of the Wila Kala. Monolith 4's Face II or back side presents a long serpentine figure with feline ears and a tightly curled tail. Nearly all previous discussion of Monolith 4 has focused on this side of the monolith.

Monolith 4 differs stylistically from the others in a number of ways. First, while the monolith is more or less quadrangular, the corners are noticeably rounded, so that it would appear more ovoid in cross-section than either Monolith 1 or Monolith 2. Moreover, there is no indication among the remnant fragments that Monolith 4 was divided into distinct, compartmentalized panels as are the other preserved monoliths. Furthermore, Monolith 4 comes the closest of any of the Khonkho monoliths to representing a *two-faced* (Pajano-style) monolith, in that it has a frontal, humanoid figure on its reconstructed Face III. Taken together these features suggest that Monolith 4 may be slightly earlier chronologically than either Wila Kala or Jinch'un Kala.

Below the being's crossed arms is a figure that, due to its placement in the region of the navel, bears some resemblance to the "rayed head" motif (S. Chávez and K. M. Chávez 1975) seen on such Pajano/Yayamama sculptures as the Taraco and Mocachi stelae. However, on stone 4-2, this figure also represents the head and part of the wing of a raptor. Flanking this figure and descending from the left arm of the central personage are two of the familiar Late Formative serpent-like beings. One of these, however, is unique among the Khonkho monoliths in that the end of its tail is visible. While the tails of serpent-like beings are commonly represented in other Formative monuments of the Titicaca Basin, no other monoliths at Khonkho depict serpents with tails.

Below the serpents on stone 4-2 is a figure with a number of large, hydralike feline heads, similar to those on the winged camelid at the base of Monolith 2. On stone 4-1, the only decipherable carving depicts a raptorlike head facing upward, apparently on a thin, serpentine neck; the sharply pointed hooked beak on this representation is broadly similar to that of the winged attendants flanking the central figure on the Gate of the Sun at Tiwanaku (Browman 1972; Portugal Zamora 1941). The two images of predatory birds on Monolith 4 are unique among the Khonkho monoliths, and indeed among Yayamama/Pajano monoliths generally.

Portugal noted the small, subsidiary anthropomorphic figure on Face III (stone 4-2) and identified the finely incised depiction of its costume as a long tunic cinched at the waist. He considered it similar to the ceremonial garment known as *tipoy* in the Bolivian eastern lowlands, a type of long dress that "the Uru call *ira*" and that he also identified with the central figure on the Gate of the Sun, arguing that this Khonkho figure was a primitive version of the so-called Staff God (Portugal Zamora 1941:297). Beyond this garment, however, there is little iconographic evidence to connect this image to that of the personage from the Gate of the Sun, as Portugal himself admitted. The staves are absent here, for example, and rather than the solar headdress of the Staff God, the Khonkho figure appears to wear some kind of turban, perhaps similar to that depicted on the seated Pokotía sculptures (Portugal Ortiz 1998:Figs. 122, 123). Alternatively, the incised vertical lines on the head of the Khonkho figure may depict hair.

In any case, this figure stands atop a disembodied head, below which are a number of carved rings surrounding an anthropomorphic feline with human limbs. Each of these elements makes an appearance in other Formative monuments of the Titicaca Basin. Similar rings, for example, are common on other Yayamama/Pajano monuments, though they are nearly always depicted as single, isolated elements (Browman 1972, 1997). Similarly, disembodied heads characterize a number of stone carvings, and small, frontal figures can be found on others (the stela from Kala Kala may depict a garment similar to that seen on Monolith 4, see Portugal Ortiz 1998:Fig. 88). Nevertheless, while there are examples of these motifs on other monuments, their iconographic configuration on Monolith 4 is wholly unique. The number and dense composition of the rings, the attitude of the feline-human being, the careful depiction of clothing details and the disembodied head, together with the raptor imagery from the other face of the monument, all argue eloquently for a vigorous and distinctive symbolic system within the wider Yayamama/Pajano style of monumental carving.

Conclusions

Khonkho Wankane stone sculpture comprised two basic types. The first consisted of blocks carved to depict zoomorphic and human-like imagery. The two that were found constituted architectural elements of the east entrance to the north court of the Dual-Court Complex (Chapter 9). The second type consisted of four carved anthropomorphic monoliths, each of which may present an apical mythical ancestor who embodies critical elements and prominent features of surrounding landscapes. Drawing on Browman's criteria of increasing rectilinearity and empanelment—that is, the degree to which the surface of a sculpture is divided into discrete panels—we propose the following seriation (also Janusek and Ohnstad 2018); Monolith 4 (the Portugal Monolith, Ohnstad 2013) is earliest, dating to Late Formative 1, followed Monoliths 1 and 2 (Wila Kala and Jinch'un Kala), dating to Late Formative 1–2, followed, ultimately, by Monolith 3 (Tata Kala), dating to Late Formative 2–Early Tiwanaku. Furthermore, based on the chronology of Khonkho's four primary ritual-political spaces, we propose the following spatial contexts for these monoliths (Janusek and Ohnstad 2018; Ohnstad 2013). Monolith 4 likely originally inhabited the Sunken Temple, but was ultimately *ritually killed*, Monoliths 1 and 2 inhabited the two courts of the Dual-Court Complex, and Monolith 3 inhabited the space where it still lies slumped over on its back, the center of Khonkho's Main Plaza.

Part III

Excavations on the
Wankane
Platform

ᴄ◡ᴐ

The Wankane Main Plaza and its Subterranean Canal

John Wayne Janusek

In 2001–2002 we sought to expose features and cultural stratigraphy in the area Rydén (1947:87) designated as the "Northeast Courtyard." This is the largest of the three bounded monumental spaces that Rydén identified. He noted that it is the least clearly defined, demarcated largely by a slight depression with distinctive vegetation. The most prominent feature in the courtyard at the time of Rydén's visit was his Monolith 3, the Tatakala (see chapter 5). By all accounts, this massive carved stone was found lying in the same position that it still lies in today: near the center of the courtyard, face up and sculpted head to the east, with its lower portion slightly sunken into the present surface (Rydén 1947:Fig. 37). Nearby is a smaller rectangular carved orthostat with an inset upper edge that may have had some architectural function (e.g., a lintel socket). The subterranean drainage canal that Portugal identified and Rydén photographed was exposed some eight meters south of Tatakala.

Based on our geophysical spatial analysis and excavations we designated this area the Main Plaza of the Wankane platform. It measures approximately 55 meters on a side, and is slightly trapezoidal but roughly square. It is bounded to the south by the northeast portion of the Sunken Temple (Sector 2) and Compound 1 (Sector 6), to the west by the east platform wall of the Dual-Court Complex, and to the east by the west wall of Compound K (Sector 12), first identified and excavated in 2004. The objectives of our excavations in 2001–2002 were twofold (Figure 6.1). We sought to 1) define the cultural stratigraphy of the space that we identified as a plaza and 2) expose more of the drainage canal that Portugal Zamora first identified (1941:296–297).

A Stratigraphic Test Unit

Project members excavated a single unit (7.1) to determine the cultural stratigraphy of the Main Plaza (Figure 6 2). We opened the unit in the southwestern quadrant of the Main Plaza, just north of the Sunken Temple. This locale was chosen as opposed to the lowest area and presumed center of the plaza, located in the vicinity of the Tatakala to the northeast, for two specific reasons. First, the center of the plaza near the Tatakala and the original surface drain for the Wankane drainage canal clearly had been heavily

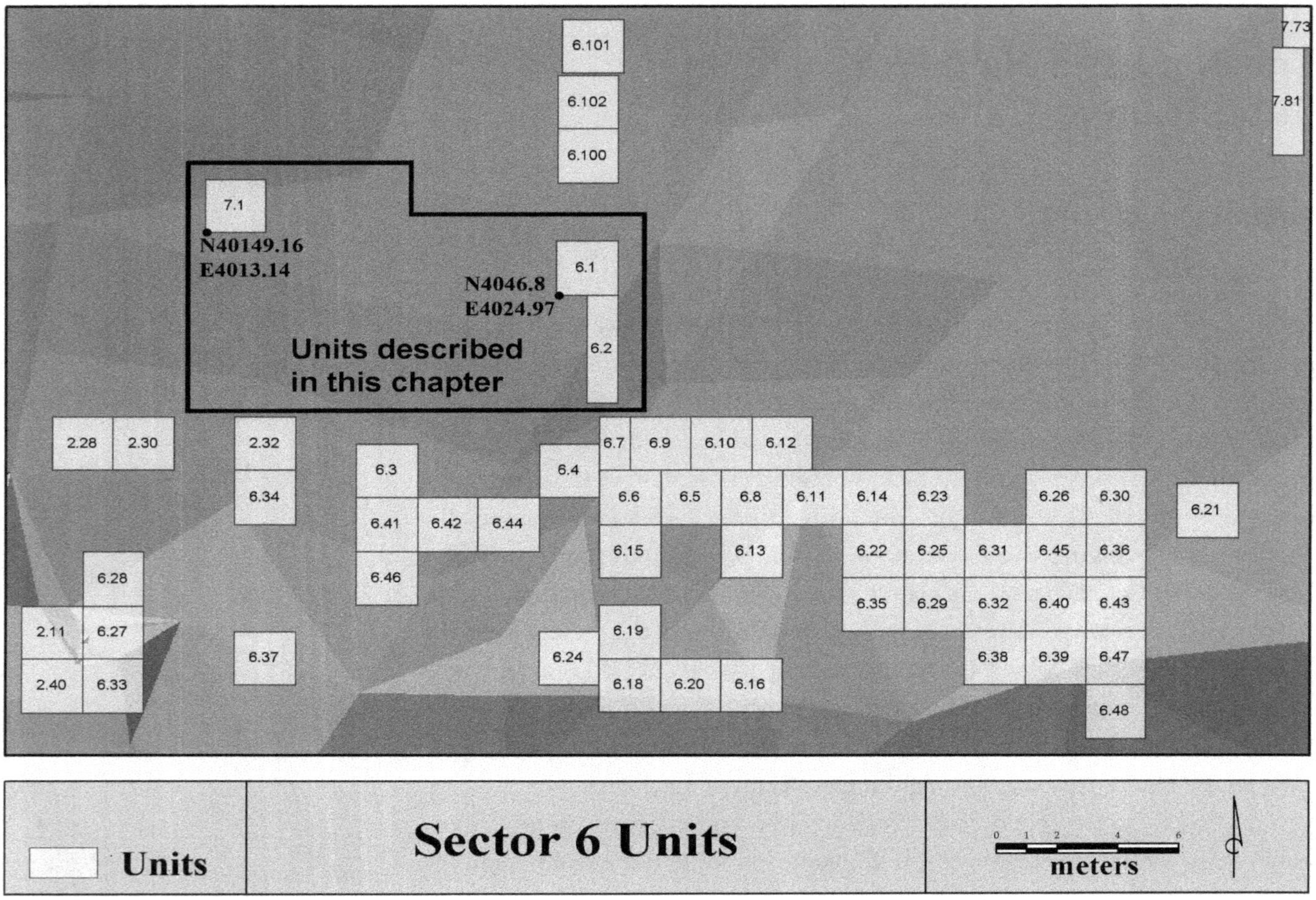

Figure 6.1 Plan of excavations in the Main Plaza (sectors 6 and 7). Base map by Scott Smith.

disturbed. Second, we hypothesize that this higher area would be covered by soil and debris from the eroded north wall of the Sunken Temple, and thus less disturbed by post-depositional activities. We opened this unit after conducting an east-west GPR transect across the site. Geophysical survey had revealed a feature, and possibly an occupation surface, that we considered worthy of excavation.

We excavated the unit to elucidate occupation surfaces and any related features. However, we found no clear occupation surface or features in the course of excavation (**Figure 6.3, Table 6.1**). We reached a clear soil change with moderately high artifact density in stratum 2, but it did not appear to be a surface. Rather, it appears to be an occupation zone with low density midden (visible as the interface between strata 1 and 2 in the south profile of the unit). At approximately 80 cm below the surface, in stratum 4, we reached a layer of sandy loam that became darker, moister, and purer with depth (strata 5 and 6). This sand was culturally sterile—that is, it contained no artifacts or cultural samples—and was very similar to the sterile sand that surrounded the primary canal (described below). At the time, we hypothesized that the

Figure 6.2   View of the south profile of the test unit in the Main Plaza Unit 7.1.

sand constituted a natural substrate on which the expanded platform and all of its architectural features were constructed. We later realized that the sand had been transported from the banks of Jach'a Jawira, located a few hundred meters to the south, in order to create an ideal permeable matrix for the canal.

Chronology

The chronology of the Main Plaza remains enigmatic due to the absence of a clear surface in the test unit. In light of the Plaza's structural associations, I hypothesize that it was used continuously throughout the Late Formative and Tiwanaku periods. What is certain is that the subterranean canal that we exposed just under the plaza was built no later than Late Formative 1, AD 1–300. It passed directly under the north wall of Compound 1, which was built in Late Formative 1 (chapter 8), and demonstrated no sign of having been reconstructed or substantially modified after it was first built.

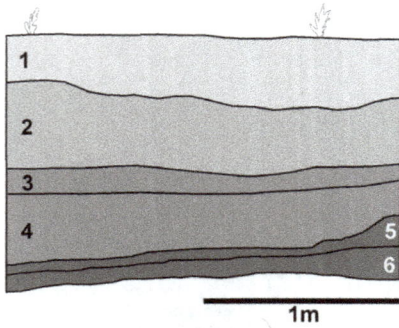

Figure 6.3   South Profile of Unit 7.1 in the Main Plaza.

Table 6.1   South profile of Unit 7.1 in the Main Plaza

Stratum	Color	Soil Consistency/Interpretation
1	7.5YR 5/3	sandy clay loam/topsoil–plow zone
2	5YR 5/3	silty clay loam
3	5YR 4/3	clay loam
4	5YR 4/4	silty clay loam
5	5YR 4/3	sand mixed with clay loam
6	5YR 3/3	sand

Subterranean Drainage Canal

We exposed a large subterranean drainage canal in the south-central portion of the Wankane Main Plaza, near the north wall of Compound 1. The northernmost portion of the canal, which would have had its intake basin in the Main Plaza, apparently had been removed prior to Portugal's and Rydén's early excavations. This left intact only a portion that extended southeastward under the Main Plaza toward Compound 1. The canal descends on a slight gradient to the southeast. It was in this direction that Rydén (1947:Fig. 29) located a similar canal eroding out of the southeast edge of the platform. We determined that this was the endpoint of the same canal.

We excavated two trench-like units (6.1, 6.2) just south of the previously-described section of the canal to expose an undisturbed section. Unit 6.1, excavated in 2001, included the disturbed north portion of the canal (**Figure 6.4**). The canal is almost a meter wide and stands 80 cm high. It consists of large, relatively flat stones, and includes both non-modified and roughly worked slabs. The crevices between slabs, including the exposed areas between upper slabs and side slabs, were caulked with pure black clay. A seal of lighter brown clay was then laid over the top of the canal. The soil surrounding the clay-sealed canal consisted of a pure sand similar to the sand recovered under the Main Plaza in Unit 7.1 (**Figure 6.5, Table 6.2**).

Figure 6.4   View of the remnant north portion of the canal under the Main Plaza.

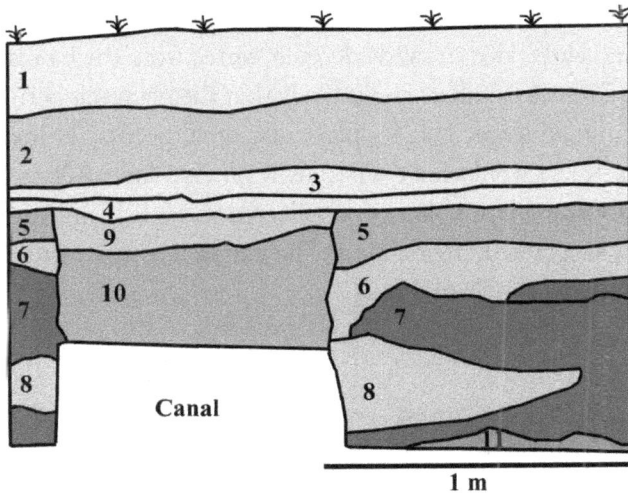

Figure 6.5   South profile of Unit 6.1, highlighting stratigraphy over and around the canal.

Table 6.2   South profile of Unit 6.1 around the canal

Stratum	Color	Soil Consistency/Interpretation
1	7.5YR 5/3	sandy clay loam/topsoil–plow zone
2	7.5YR 5/2	silty clay loam
3	7.5YR 5/3	silty clay loam
4	7.5YR 5/3	clayey silt
5	2.5YR 5/3	silty clay loam
6	5YR 5/4	silty clay loam
7	7.5YR 4/4	silty clay loam
8	2.5YR 6/3	silty sand mixture/canal sealant
9	2.5YR 6/4	silty clay loam
10	5YR 5/4	silty sand mixture/canal sealant
11	2.5YR 5/4	silty sand mixture/canal sealant

We extended excavations in 2002 to further expose the depositional stratigraphy of the sand and clarify its relation to the canal. Unit 6.2 was a long 4 m × 1 m unit that we opened to expose a relatively long section of the canal just south of Unit 6.1 and in the direction of Compound 1 (**Figure 6.6**). We left a baulk between Units 6.1 and 6.2 to preserve the stratigraphic context of the canal. This unit confirmed that the canal was oriented roughly to the cardinal directions, at least under the Main Plaza. We confirmed that the canal drained the Main plaza, passed under Compound 1, and drew water toward the sloping southeast edge of the Wankane platform. Further, comparative analysis of the sand surrounding the canal indicated that it derived from the banks of the Jach'a Jawira River south of the site. This was our first indication that the sandy substrate located under the southwest section of the Main Plaza in 2001, in unit 7.1, was not natural to the Wankane mound. It, too, derived from the banks of the Jach'a Jawira as part of the process of transforming the mound into a massive, monumental platform.

Conclusions

Rydén's Northeast Courtyard was Khonkho's Main Plaza and its most extensive space of social gathering. It was Khonkho's center of social and ritual gravity. The center's Sunken Temple, Dual-Court Complex, as well as its massive Compounds 1 and 3, all opened onto this plaza (see Janusek 2015; Smith 2009). The stylistically late Tata Kala monolith, stood in this space. An elaborate, over-engineered, stone-lined subterranean canal drained the plaza and

Figure 6.6   View of the top of the canal in Unit 6.23, stones and dark clay sealant intact.

its surrounding structures, carrying runoff toward the south. The canal was caulked with pure clay and embedded in sandy deposits carted from the banks of the Jach'a Jawira river. Project members find it likely that the plaza was periodically flooded to form a small iconic lake for particular ritual events, during which Monolith 3 (Tata Kala) would have stood as if on an island (Ohnstad 2013; Smith 2009). Draining vast volumes of collected water explains the canal's massive size and exaggerated engineering. The canal, in other words, simultaneously served pragmatic and ritual ends.

Chapter 7

ᔕ

The Sunken Temple and the Wankane South Platform

John Wayne Janusek and Adolfo Pérez Arias

A primary objective of Project Jach'a Machaca Phase One was to excavate and understand as fully as possible the sunken court first documented by Stig Rydén in 1947. Rydén (1947:88) referred to this as the "South Courtyard," and considered it the smallest of three monumental structures visible on Khonkho's surface. Alan Kolata was the first to conduct excavations in the courtyard itself. In October–November of 1937, members of Proyecto Wila Jawira excavated three blocks in the structure: one in the threshold of the south stairway (**Figure 1.14**), the structure's primary entrance; a second in the threshold of the structure's west stairway and entrance; and a third in its southwest corner. In the last two units, excavations continued to the base of several strategically-positioned orthostats that had been embedded 20–40 cm below the structure's internal floor. In 2001 we began work on the structure by removing the backfill of these units and continuing to expose substantial areas of the structure's walls and inner courtyard. This work continued through the 2002 field season (**Figure 7.1**).

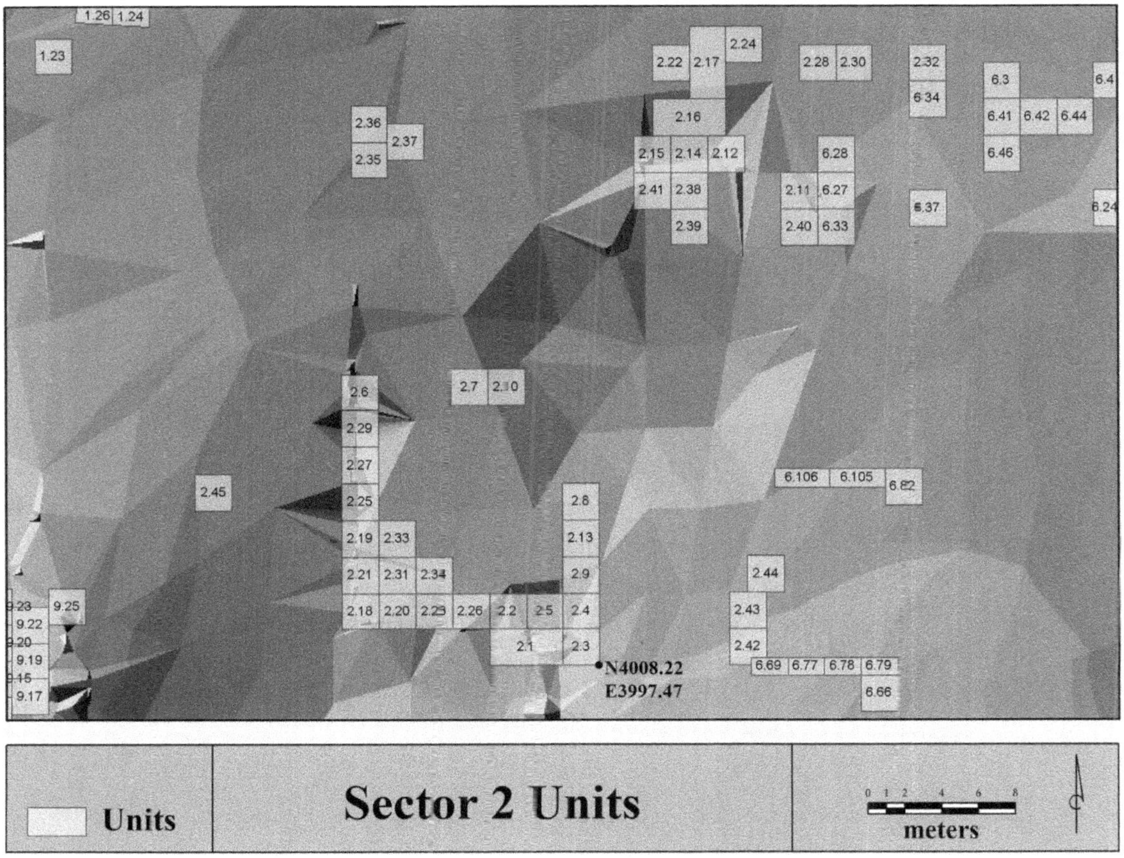

Figure 7.1 Plan of Sector 2 excavations. Base map by Scott Smith.

Sector 2 Units

Units

meters

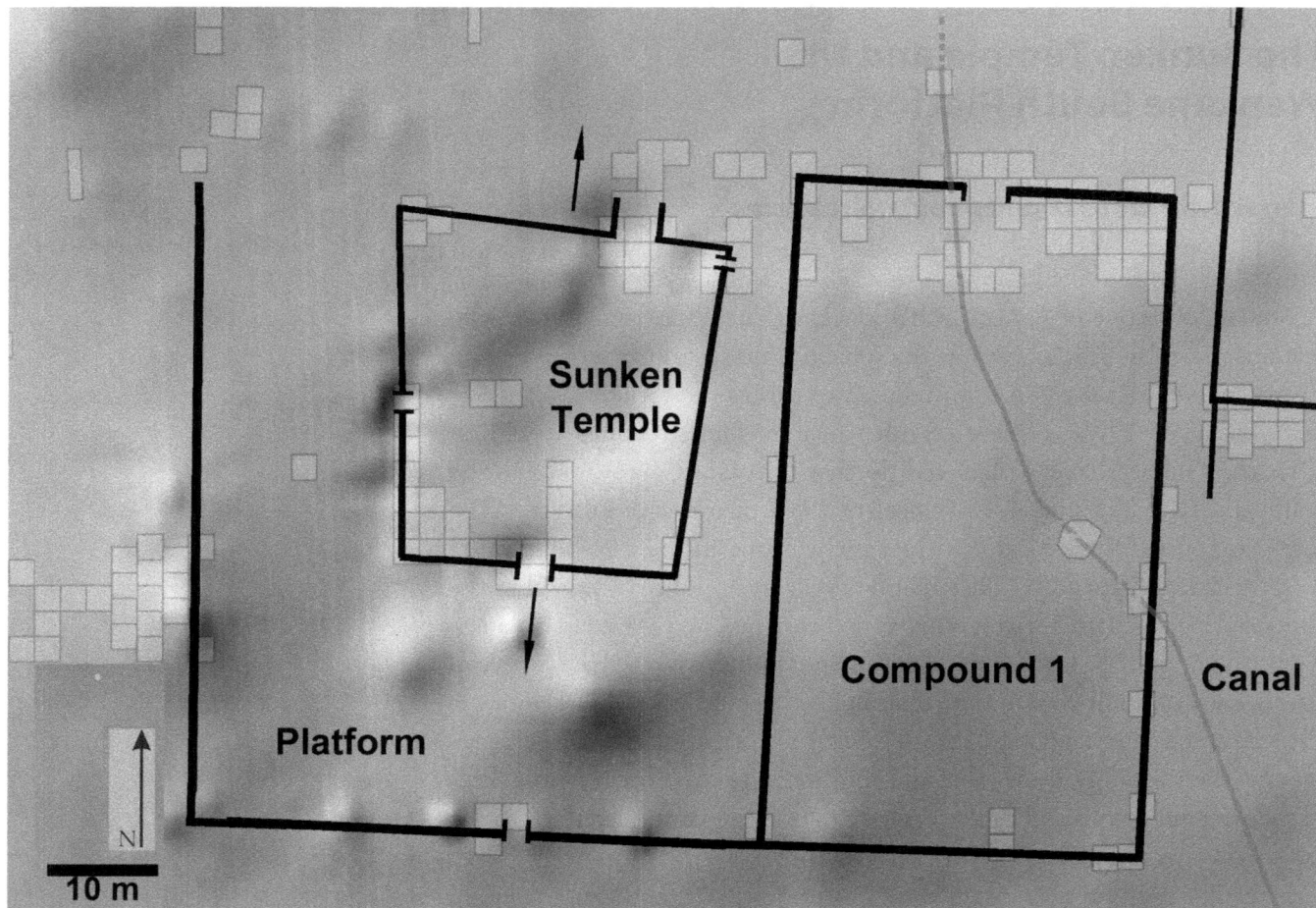

Figure 7.2   General plan of the Sunken Temple and its surrounds.

Spatial Layout

Our excavations in 2001–2002 determined that Rydén's South Courtyard was an early Sunken Temple different in construction and role from the other two "Courtyards" that he described **(Figure 7.2)**. The Sunken Temple was trapezoidal in plan. Its east and west walls were not parallel but rather diverged obliquely to form a north wall that is longer than its south wall. The south wall measures 21.6 meters and the north wall 26 meters in length. The west wall, at 27.6 meters, is more than a meter longer than the east wall, which is 26.2 meters long. The structure is more trapezoidal in plan than Tiwanaku's Sunken Temple, which appears to have been contemporaneous (Janusek 2008:94-95). The form appears to have been intentional, but to what end? Why was the north side of the structure broader, where it opened into a corridor that led into the Main Plaza?

Figure 7.3 View of the excavated south and west walls of the Sunken Temple, facing south.

Walls

The walls of the Sunken Temple were elaborately built. They consisted primarily of roughly hewn, rectangular sandstone slab masonry (**Figures 7.3–7.8**). Walls comprised segments of horizontally lain slabs braced by regularly place vertical pilasters. Wedged between many horizontally lain stones were smaller, relatively flat fieldstones that served to support the wall construction. Key orthostats, such as those at the corners of the temple and those framing its entrances, served as caissons that were sunk deep (20–40 cm) into the clay platform on which the structure was raised. Some of the pilasters extended above the stone wall foundation. These likely framed superimposed, earthen adobe or *tapia* walls that rested on the stone foundations and have long since eroded.

The Sunken Temple was built into a shallow natural slope that descended gently to the south. To level the structure, the south wall and south portions of the east and west walls consisted of substantial multi-course

Figure 7.4   (above) View of the south wall and entrance of the Sunken Temple, facing southwest.

Figure 7.5   (below) View of the excavated southwest corner of the Sunken Temple, facing south.

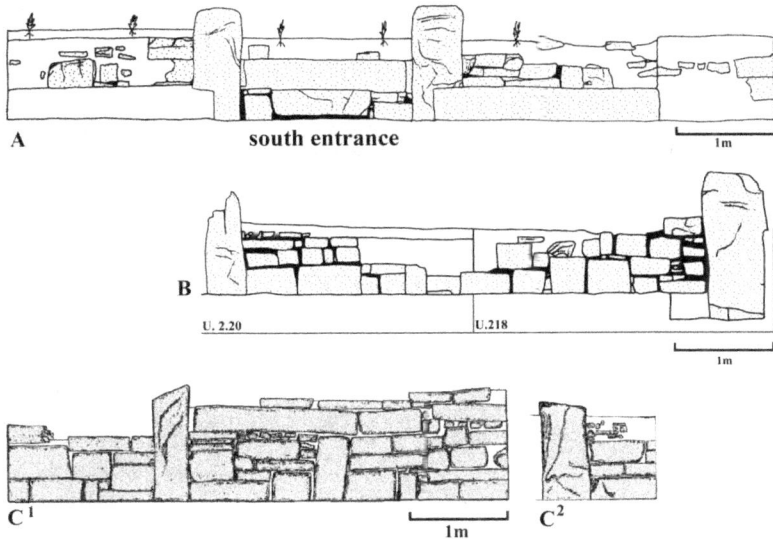

Figure 7.6   Profile views of the south (A, B, C2) and east (C1) walls of the Sunken Temple (wall profiles rendered by Adolfo Pérez).

Figure 7.7   View of the excavated west wall of the Sunken Temple, facing northwest.

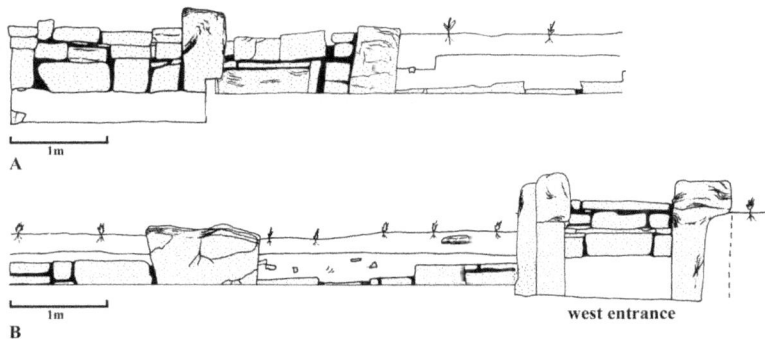

Figure 7.8   Profile views of the west wall of the Sunken Temple, including A) the south portion of the wall, B) the south portion of the wall including the west entrance (wall profiles rendered by Adolfo Pérez).

Figure 7.9 View of the excavated northwest corner of the Sunken Temple, facing west.

masonry foundations buttressed by tall pilasters sunk well below the Court's floor. This construction served to support the walls against the pressures of the soil in the thick clay platforms behind them. Stone masonry of the north wall and the north portions of the east and west walls was far less substantial (and most likely, being closer to the surface, has been more heavily disturbed by later activity). Wall foundations in these wall sections consist of, at most, one to three courses of sandstone masonry. No remnant masonry existed in the structure's northwest corner. Here, a strip of light orange clay identified the structure's wall foundations **(Figure 7.9)**.

The Sunken Temple appears to have been elaborately decorated. Its internal walls were plastered with a white lime precipitate. Flecks of white mineral covered the superimposed surfaces of its south, east, and west walls **(Figure 7.10)**. Furthermore, parts of the south wall may have incorporated colored designs. Superimposed surfaces in front of it revealed chunks of red, green, and yellow clay. Furthermore, the south entrance appears to have been fitted with an elaborate fired-brick portal or frieze. Excavations in front of it revealed numerous fired bricks fragments **(Figure 7.11)**. The bricks come in various shapes and sizes, but all are roughly rectangular and had been fired to a green, yellow, or orange finish. Their sides are gently concave. Yet for none of the bricks are all four long sides completely intact; in every case one or two sides appear to have been fixed to an original surface during firing. It thus appears that the bricks had been fired in place. A few bricks present fugitive red, orange, or white pigment, suggesting they depicted iconography.

Figure 7.10   View of the floor near the west wall showing plaster flakes.

10 cm

Figure 7.11   Fired brick fragments found near the south entrance of the Sunken Temple.

Stairways and Corridors

Unlike most other sunken courts published to date in the Lake Titicaca basin, Khonkho's has one stepped entrance in each of its four walls. Each entrance differs from the others in size, construction details, wall placement, and presumably, role. The north entrance linked the Sunken Temple to the Main Plaza, the west entrance linked it to a thick clay platform, the east entrance

Figure 7.12   View of the south entrance of the Sunken Temple. The raised stone toward the back of the image originally formed the top step of the staircase.

to Compound 1, and the south entranced linked it to a thick platform and, just beyond it, a possible early opening in the Wankane outer platform wall directly to the south.

The four openings formed points of movement into and out of the Sunken Temple. Most elaborate was the south entrance (**Figures 1.14, 7.4, 7.12, and 7.13**). It consisted of three stone steps that descended into the temple, framed by two sandstone pilasters. Its opening measured 1.6 meters wide. The top step consisted of a wide gray sandstone block, which rested on a carved red sandstone slab, which in turn rested on a carved slab of cream limestone. The top stone has since been removed and raised behind the entrance. Smaller roughly worked flat stones served to fit the blocks into the framework of the entrance and its supporting pilasters. The play of stone genre, texture, and color that facilitated one's descent into the structure—gray sandstone, red sandstone, white limestone—clearly had aesthetic value and likely other symbolic significance. Directly behind it, or south of the entrance, on the thick platform of red clay that bounded the structure, two lines of stones defined a passage that led persons toward the entrance and into the court (**Figure 1.14, Figure 7.13**).

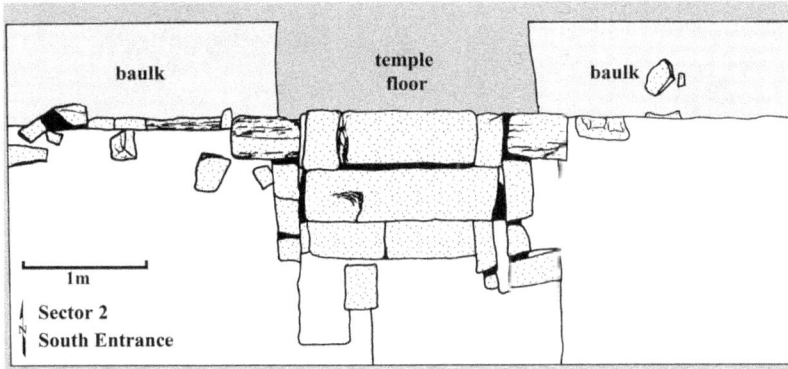

Figure 7.13   Plan of the excavated south entrance of the Sunken Temple (plan rendered by Adolfo Peréz Arias).

Figure 7.14   View of the west entrance into the Sunken Temple, facing west. Note the depth of the pilasters, excavated by Kolata's team in 1987.

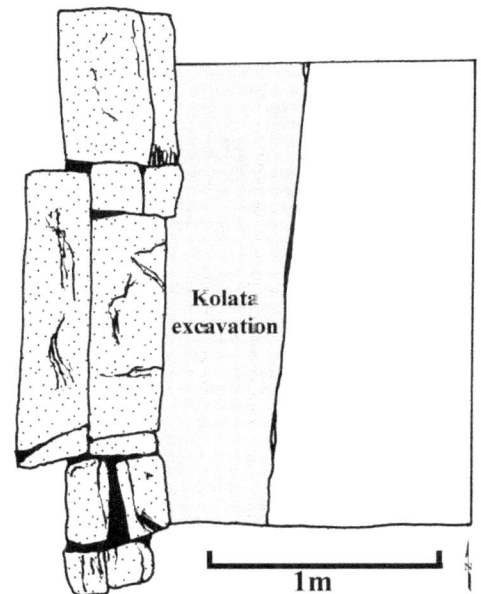

Figure 7.15   Plan of the west entrance into the Sunken Temple, indicating the extent of Kolata's excavations (plan rendered by Adolfo Peréz Arias).

The east and west entrances were positioned neither in the center of their walls nor in spatial opposition to one another. The west entrance consisted of a narrower opening (1.2 meters wide) located 1.1 m south of the center of the west wall (**Figures 7.14 and 7.15.**) It provided entrance into the Court from the thick, high clay platform that bounded it, and it consisted of two sandstone steps flanked by smaller sandstone blocks bound by the upright pilasters that framed the entrance. Somewhat reminiscent of the south entrance, a gray sandstone block formed the top step and a red sandstone block formed the bottom step.

The east entrance was set into the north part of the Sunken Temple's east wall. Its two small pilasters framed a narrow entrance 50 cm wide (**Figure 7.16**). Its threshold consisted of a single step consisting of two small sandstone

Figure 7.16 View of the small east entrance into the Sunken Temple, facing west.

blocks placed side by side. A more erratic and expeditiously made sandstone foundation ran parallel to the east wall of the Sunken Temple and on its east side. The Sunken Temple's east entrance provided access to the space that this expediently-constructed wall bounded. Excavations here determined that this space formed a sort of alley between the Sunken Temple and Compound 1. Originally, the Sunken Temple and Compound 1 had been spatially divided. At some point toward the end of Late Formative 1, the north wall of Compound 1 was extended westward to enclose this corridor and architecturally link the temple to the compound (see chapter 8). From this point forward, the east entrance provided direct access from Compound 1 to the Sunken Temple.

A wide corridor built into the north wall of the Sunken Temple connected it to the Wankane Main Plaza (**Figures 7.17 and 7.18**). The corridor was 3.25 m wide and its walls rested on a remnant foundation of roughly worked stones. Two large blocks formed the south corners of the corridor, though the east block recently has been removed due to plowing. The floor of the corridor consisted of a hard-packed sandy clay reinforced by a pebble aggregate surface. The northernmost portion of the corridor has been heavily disturbed by agricultural activity and thus its architectural components are difficult to discern. Some 1.3 meters north of the corridor's northernmost remnant foundations, the late extension of the wall linking Compound 1 to the Sunken Temple intruded into the northern portion of the corridor. The west part of this foundation, what we term its "west wing." may have formed a narrow doorway that restricted access from the Main Plaza into the Sunken Temple (**Figure 7.18**).

Figure 7.17   View of the north corridor of the Sunken Temple, facing north.

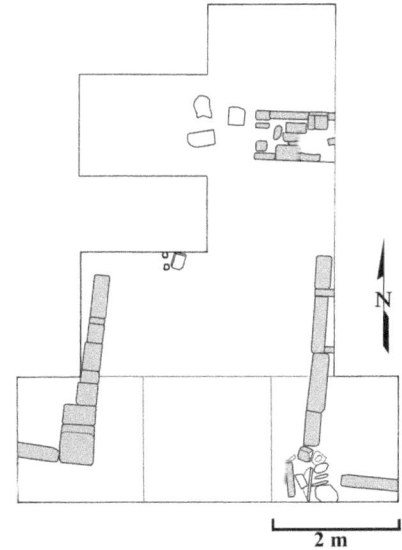

Figure 7.18   Plan of the north corridor of the Sunken Temple, showing the west end of the extension wall or 'wing' at its north end.

Surrounding Platforms and the South and West Entrances

Thick, durable clay platforms framed several portions of the Sunken Temple. Platforms framed the south and west temple walls, as well as the west side of the north wall and the south side of the east wall. The platforms consisted of light reddish-brown, finely selected silty clay loam. The south platform provided access to the temple's south entrance. Wall alignments behind the entrance define a hallway that linked this entrance to the Wankane outer Platform Wall, which is visible on the surface as an east-west alignment of massive pilasters several meters south of the temple **(Figure 1.16)**. The west platform provided access to the temple via its west stairway Platform Wall. A remnant north-south alignment of massive pilasters several meters west of the temple defines the western segment of this feature and the west edge of the Wankane platform. We excavated a single unit (U.2.45) between the Sunken Temple and the outer Wankane Platform Wall. It revealed a small ash lens in an otherwise homogenous and highly compact matrix of red sandy clay.

Floors, Artifacts, and Activities

Excavations in the temple revealed two superimposed prepared surfaces, similar to what was recorded in the Sunken Temple at Tiwanaku (Ponce 1990). The surfaces consisted of prepared floors made of a hard-packed, well-sorted clay loam. A lower surface was encountered in some units along the south wall

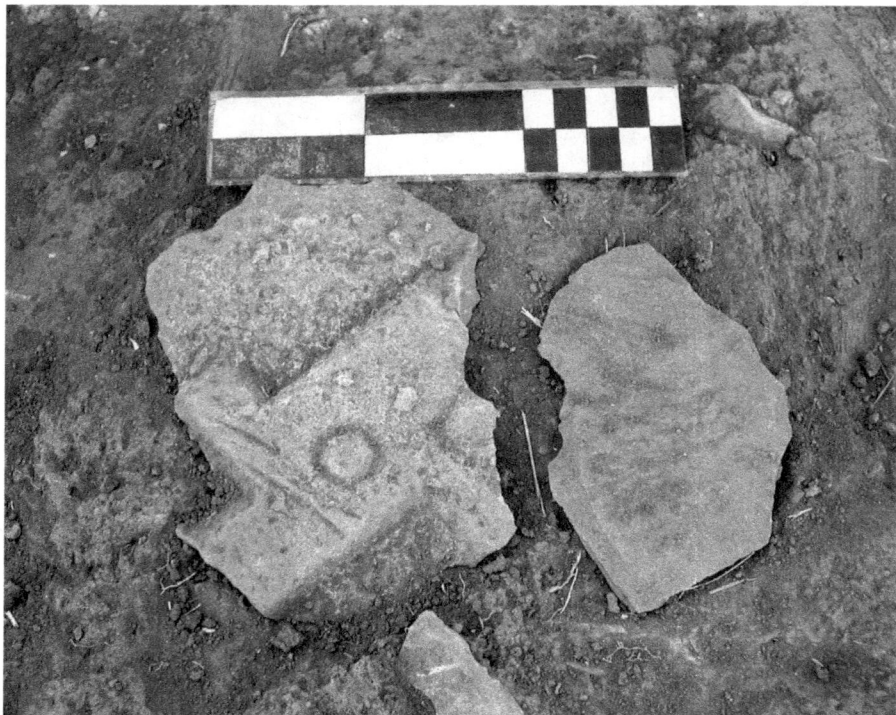

Figure 7.19   Fragments of sculpted stone found in the northwest corner of the Sunken Temple.

of the temple, in particular near its well-preserved southeast corner. Very little of this early surface was excavated, because we chose to keep most of the upper surface intact. The surface had been cleaned before it was covered by the final surface. Nevertheless, small artifacts, carbon flecks, yellow pigment, and ashy deposits covered the early floor's surface.

The final surface was encrusted with small, trampled artifacts and covered with thin ashy and silty deposits. The density of midden associated with the late surface was highest along the south wall, in particular near the south entrance to the temple. The surface revealed trampled fragments of ceramic vessels, splintered camelid bones, lithic debitage, and carbonized materials (including wood charcoal and camelid dung). Small flecks of white plaster speckled the floor along the south and west walls of the temple. Presumably, white plaster covered at least potions of the temple's interior walls. Large chunks of fired brick and small lumps of yellow pigment covered the surface near the south entrance. I suspect that these artifacts present the collapsed remains of a decorated fired-brick portal that covered the temple's south entrance.

Excavations just above the late floor near the northwest corner of the Sunken Temple revealed the flaked fragment of a stone sculpture that may be part of a monolith **(Figure 7.19)**. In that we interpret (chapter 5, Ohnstad 2013) the early Portugal monolith as having stood within this structure, could this be a part of that monolith?

Floor surfaces were best preserved near the temple walls. Long after the temple was abandoned, an extensive pit was dug into the center of the structure. Associated artifacts date this feature to the Early Pacajes phase. It likely was excavated during Early Pacajes to serve as a reservoir or sunken basin (*qocha*) to serve pastoral and horticultural productive practices. On the surface the pit appears to be ~18 m in diameter, but excavations demonstrated that it was larger and originally extended to within five meters of the south wall. Thus, much of the original floor of the Sunken Temple has long since been removed. Those who dug the basin took advantage of the existing sunken depression, appropriating ancient remains to contemporary purposes.

Stratigraphy

The interior of the Sunken Temple, in particular the overburden near the structure's south wall, produced excellent stratigraphic profiles. During its use and after its abandonment, the courtyard accumulated a distinctive sequence of deposits, leaving a slight surface depression that was expanded into a sunken basin in Early Pacajes. Directly over the upper floor in many areas was a thin lens (3–6 cm) of clean silty loam with charcoal flecks, yellow clay pigment, and fragmented artifacts that presumably represent the primary detritus of activities conducted within the temple. Covering this was a thicker (20–40 cm) stratum of light brown clay loam, most likely consisting of palimpsest use surfaces and accumulated deposits of eroding adobe from the temple's walls. This stratum included abundant chunks of fired brick and other artifacts. The upper portion of this stratum may have constituted a final use surface.

The stratum directly covering the last (Stratum 4), visible largely along the south side of the structure, was most distinctive. It consisted of a ~20 cm thick layer of soil with high organic content that sloped down to the north, approaching the floor some four meters north of the south wall (**Figures 7.20–7.22, Table 7.1**). This stratum included field stones, large fragments of fired bricks from the temple walls, chunks of white plaster, clay nodules in a variety of colors, and abundant ceramic sherds, camelid bone fragments, and lithic flakes. This stratum clearly marked the final abandonment of the temple, the collapse of its elaborate walls, and its subsequent conversion into an extensive midden.

A thick homogeneous layer of silt (10–30 cm thick) covering this stratum of collapse and abandonment included Tiwanaku and even denser Early Pacajes artifacts over the now-buried courtyard. The presence of a relatively well-defined interface between this and the abandonment stratum below may mark the intentional construction of a use surface, but as yet we have located no clearly defined structures. Tiwanaku activity was by all accounts ephemeral in this area of Wankane. Early Pacajes activity was more substantial and

Table 7.1   East Profile of Units 2.4 and 2.9

Stratum	Color	Soil Consistency /Interpretation
1	7.5YR 5/6	sandy clay loam /topsoil–plow zone
2	5YR 5/4	silty clay loam
3	5YR 4/4	silty clay loam /accumulated overburden
4	5YR 3/2	dark silty loam /accumulated midden with stones
5	5YR 3/3	silty clay loam /eroded adobe overburden

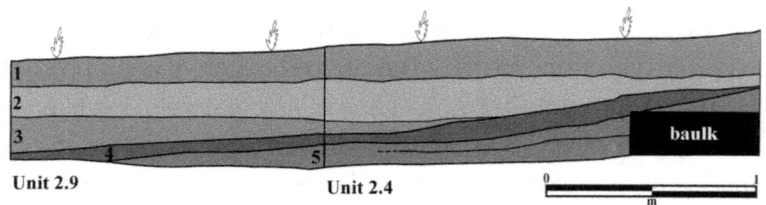

Figure 7.20   East profile of Units 2.4 and 2.9.

Figure 7.21   View of east profile of Units 2.4 and 2.9, highlighting the accumulation of stones in Stratum 4.

Figure 7.22   View of the north profiles of Units 2.2, 2.4, 2.5, 2.23, and 2.26, highlighting the same stratigraphic accumulation of midden and stones indicated in Figure 7.21.

likely centered on the basin excavated into the Sunken Temple. We located a shallow offering or refuse pit with camelid bones and Early Pacajes sherds near the east edge of the old south entrance.

Long Term History

The Sunken Temple endured a long history of construction, use, rehabilitation, abandonment, and repurpose spanning Late Formative through Early Pacajes periods. It constituted a sunken courtyard framed by a thick clay platform on its south and west sides, the south portion of its east side, and the west potion of its north side. The north potion of the courtyard's east side, and the east potion of its north side (east of its north corridor), were spaces that joined the Sunken Temple with Compound 1 and the relatively late west extension of its north compound wall. The courtyard's east entrance provided direct access into a corridor between the two complexes. As discussed in the next chapter, extending Compound 1's north compound wall westward coincided with the removal of an older north-south wall that had divided the west side of Compound 1 from the east side of the Sunken Temple. These architectural adjustments joined the northeast portion of the Sunken Temple to the northeast sector of Compound 1.

The earliest occupation activities in the Sunken Temple date to Late Formative 1 (Janusek 2011, 2013). Artifacts diagnostic of Late Formative 1 are found on the two early floors and in their superimposed occupation surfaces and debris. The Sunken Temple was first constructed and intensively used during this phase. The Sunken Temple appears to have been actively employed as a ritual space into Late Formative 2. Palimpsest surfaces over the second floor yielded ceramic sherds dating to this phase. Small fragments of fired bricks and angular stones in soils over the later floor may suggest that temple walls witnessed some rehabilitation during the LF 1–LF 2 transition. Later, sloping strata of dense midden with fallen wall material dated to Late Formative 2. Thus, it appears that the temple fell into obsolescence and began to collapse sometime during this phase. The Sunken Temple finally collapsed perhaps just as or after the Dual-Court Complex was constructed on the west side of Wankane.

Sector 2 continued to serve Khonkho Wankane long after the collapse of the Sunken Temple. Strata of midden and eroded silt in the old courtyard included artifactual material dating to Late Formative 2, Tiwanaku, and Early Pacajes occupations. The significance of this space in the later generations of Late Formative 2 is intriguing. Perhaps it intentionally constituted a visibly obsolete and eroding temple within an otherwise vibrant landscape of monumental structures and social gatherings. Perhaps its deteriorating presence served to remind later ritual participants of the obsolescence of older ritual practices and spaces in striking contrast to the potency of novel practices focused on newer monumental spaces such as the Dual-Court Complex. Or, perhaps, it reminded them of the long history of potent ritual practices at the site.

This sector of Khonkho Wankane was not intensively used again until the Early Pacajes phase. Tiwanaku style ceramics were present only in overburden at the northwest corner of the structure close to the Dual-Court Complex. It appears that Sector 2 was used only minimally during this phase, and perhaps only as an ancillary space along paths linking primary activity areas. Early Pacajes ceramic sherds were far better represented. It was during this time that the depression left by the collapsed Late Formative temple was expeditiously employed to fashion a small sunken basin (*qocha*) to support horticultural and/ or pastoral practices for a local community. We located two other such basins on the Wankane mound, and both dated to Early Pacajes: one due north of the Main Plaza and one on the north side of Compound 3 just to the east.

Conclusions

Excavations at the southwest edge of the Main Plaza revealed Khonkho's Sunken Temple. The Sunken Temple is trapezoidal in plan, which we later determined was due in part to its role in providing visual alignments with key landscape features and the rise and set of key celestial bodies and constellations (Benitez 2009, Janusek 2015). It incorporated four entrances, one in each wall. Each entrance likely addressed a particular group of persons. The north corridor leading from the Main Plaza, for example, countered the small, elaborate, three-stepped entrance to the south. Yet each entrance provided specific views of landscape and skyscape through other entrances. The Sunken Temple and its adjacent platforms occupied the west side of Compound 1. Constructing an outer north wall that linked the two structures toward the end of Late Formative 1 enveloped them as a single complex. We suggest that it manifests the shifting roles for Compound 1 and the Sunken Temple as Khonkho's incipient urban position changed during the Late Formative. Compound 1 appears to have become a 'backstage' for ritual productions in the Sunken Temple. Such productions were conducted in view of Monolith 4, which we argue stood here.

Drawing on Ohnstad and Janusek's monolith seriation, we propose that monolith 4, our Portugal Monolith (see Chapter 5), originally inhabited the Sunken Temple. Monolith 4 is stylistically earliest in our seriation, and the Sunken Temple incorporates the earliest sunken court at the site. Both date to Late Formative 1. More tellingly, both were decommissioned after (or toward the end of) the phase. The Sunken Temple was rendered obsolete and allowed to collapse. Monolith 4 was fragmented and buried just off of the platform to the west, in such a manner that we might consider it a *monolith interment*. If we are correct, structures and monoliths correlated intimately in Khonkho Wankane. We might consider that a monolith *inhabited* its enclosed ritual space on the Wankane platform, and that such a space was its *house*.

Chapter 8

Compound 1 and its Relation to the Sunken Temple

John Wayne Janusek, Andrew P. Roddick, and Maribel Pérez Arias

Compound 1 was the first major structure we identified that was not visible on the surface and had not been recorded prior to our research (**Figure 1.16**). It consisted of an enclosed compound on the Wankane mound that encompassed residual residential and ritual activities. Project members first located the compound—specifically, the foundation of its west wing—during the final days of the 2001 field season. We excavated several strategic units (**Figure 8.1**) to understand the length and function of this wall until we located a well-built, cobble-paved entrance approximately 23 meters to the east (**Figure 8.2**).

Continued operations in 2002 established that the east-west foundation in question was the west extension of a long masonry foundation that bounded

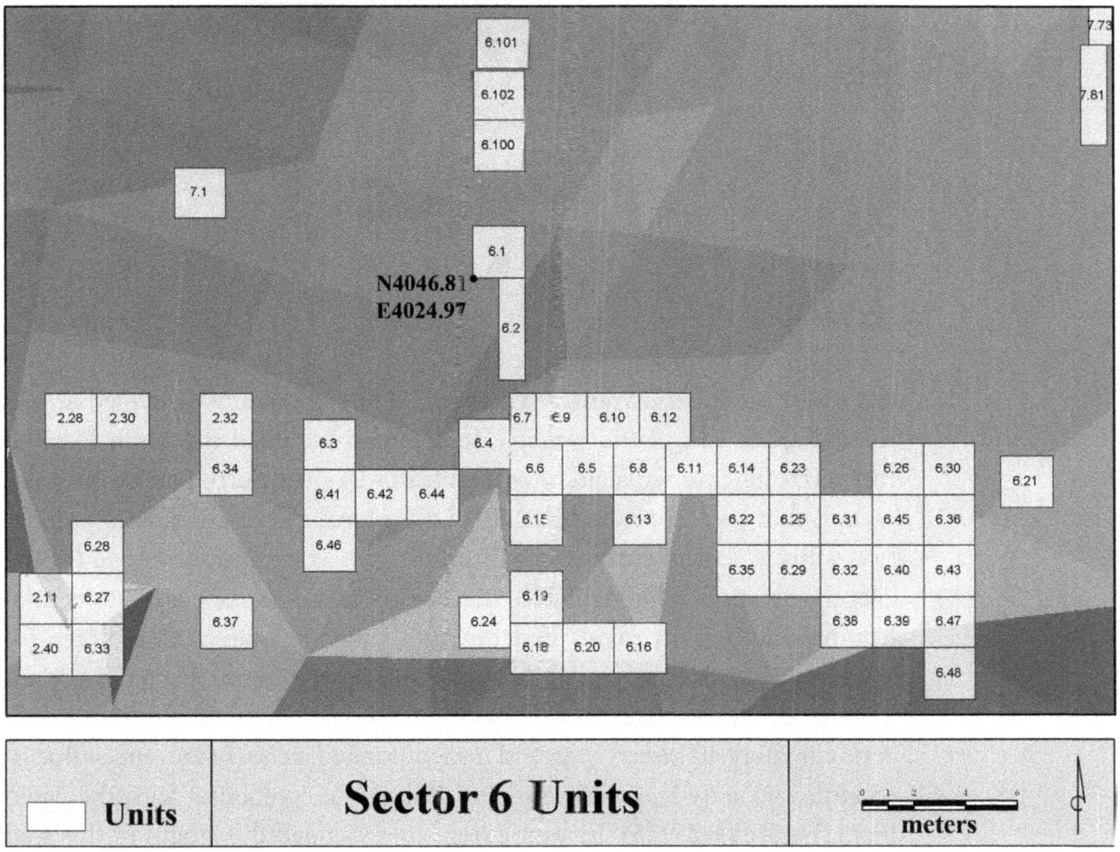

Figure 8.1 Plan of Sector 6 excavations. Base map by Scott Smith..

Figure 8.2 View of Compound 1 north compound wall and west wing, facing west.

the north side of an extensive compound. The compound occupied an extensive space east of the Sunken Temple and adjoined the Main Plaza to the north. The principal architectural features of the north part of the compound, that part excavated in 2001–2002, consisted of compound foundation walls, a central entryway or threshold, a west extension wall and corridor, and an enclosed, roughly-circular structure and its associated residential features and activity areas. Beneath the compound ran a long, north-to-south trending drainage canal that collected waste and runoff from the Main Plaza (see **Figures 1.6 and 6.4**). The original north compound wall measured approximately 30 meters long and it incorporated a cobble entrance—located almost exactly in its center—that linked the compound with the Main Plaza **(Figures 8.3–8.5)**. Its west extension extended the length of this wall

Figure 8.3   Aerial view of the northwest section of Compound 1, highlighting the north entrance and circular Structure 6.C1. North is up.

Figure 8.4   View of the excavated north portion of Compound 1, facing west. Circular Structure 6.C1 is in the foreground.

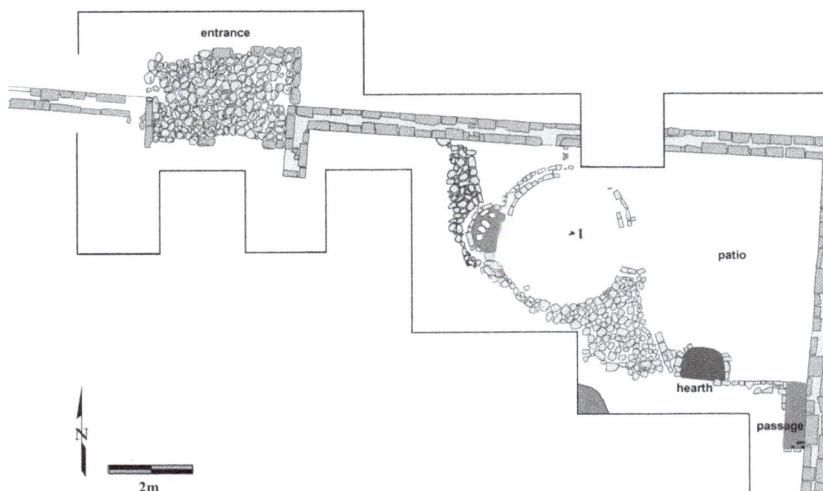

Figure 8.5   Plan of the excavated northeast section of Compound 1, highlighting the elaborate entrance Structure 6.C1, and its associated features. Image rendered by John W. Janusek.

20.5 m west, and linked the north compound wall with the Sunken Temple's north corridor.

Compound Walls

Substantial walls set on stone foundations (~60 cm wide) bounded the perimeter of Compound 1. Wall foundations in most instances consisted of two rows of large angular field stones, many roughly worked, filled with clayey soil and in some areas stone rubble. In several areas the foundation consisted of multiple stone courses; this was most clear in the east wall foundation, which consisted of 5–6 remnant stone courses. The top sides of the foundation stones of the north compound wall, those facing the Central Plaza, had been prepared. Their plaza-facing upper edges had been painstakingly beveled and rounded such that the foundation stones extended slightly beyond the base of the adobe or *tapia* walls they supported (**Figure 8.6**). Analysis of soil over the wall foundations indicates that the earthen portion of the walls consisted of finely selected adobe bricks of reddish-brown sandy clay. Artifact densities north of the north compound wall, in the Main Plaza, tended to be slightly higher than those south of the wall, or inside of the compound.

The west wing of the north compound wall appears to have been added relatively late in the history of Compound 1. It articulates with the main part of the north compound wall some 13 m west of the main north entrance. The construction technique of the west wing is substantially different from that of the original north compound wall and the other compound walls exposed to date. The later foundation did not consist of double-coarse stone construction and the north edges of the northernmost stones were not beveled as they had been in the original north compound wall. The stones comprising the west wing foundation are more often randomly placed in relation to those of the original compound walls.

The west wing foundation was attached to the west edge of the original north compound wall (in Unit 2.32) at a point where it formed the

Figure 8.6 Detail of the north compound wall, facing west, emphasizing the beveled foundation stones facing the main Plaza, to the right.

northwest corner of the compound. The original west wall of the compound articulated with the original north wall at this point. The original west wall foundation demonstrated the same construction techniques (e.g., double-row construction) as those of the original north compound wall. Further, stones of the west and north compound walls interlocked at the points of articulation in this corner. The stones of the west wing foundation simply abutted those of the original corner. Importantly, most of the foundation of the original west compound wall had been removed, leaving only the interlocked stones of the original articulation plus a withering trail of stone rubble to the south of the corner (**Figure 8.7**). Did the removal of this wall correspond with the construction of the west extension wall? We return to this question below.

An Elaborate Primary Entrance

An elaborate entryway approximately 3.8 meters wide occupied the center of the original north compound wall (**Figures 8.3 and 8.5**). It constituted what appears to have been an unobstructed threshold that joined the north part of the compound to the Main Plaza. Two short, south-trending foundations framed the south part of the entrance that led into the compound. The floor of the entrance was elaborately prepared and it extended some 0.8 meters into the space of the plaza. It was rectangular and consisted of tightly-packed, medium-sized cobbles (**Figure 8.8**). The cobbles are heavily worn, attesting years of treading. Most fascinating, the interstices between the stones revealed

Figure 8.8 View of the elaborate north entrance, facing west. Note the trample-wear of the cobbles.

Figure 8.8 View of the elaborate north entrance, facing west. Note the trample-wear of the cobbles.

small fragments of valued minerals and objects. They included flecks of red pigment, a piece of light blue sodalite, a broken arrow point, and a trapezoidal piece of gold lamina.

The Circular Structure and its Associated Features

The most striking architectural feature in the excavated portion of Compound 1 was a circular structure (Str. 6.C1, Smith 2009) situated between the main entrance and the northeast corner of the compound (**Figures 8.3–8.5**). The outline of the structure was ovoid; inside dimensions are ~2.6 m east-west (outside dimensions: ~3.2 m) and ~3.1 m north-south. Architectural characteristics of its foundations are unique. The north half of the structure foundation consisted of remnant aligned, roughly worked rectangular stones. Most of the south half consisted of rounded, flatter, and less precisely aligned cobbles. It is difficult to distinguish the south foundation from the stones that formed an outdoor pavement. The significance of the opposing foundation is unclear, though it was likely in part historical. That is, it is possible that the south portion of the building was rebuilt and embellished sometime after it was originally constructed.

Key features built into the structure included an entrance, which opened to the east, and opposite this, to the west, a semi-circular subterranean annex (U.6.22, F. 1). The doorway is fairly wide, measuring approximately 90 cm between its innermost jambs. Excavations in the threshold revealed a rem-

Figure 8.9 Artifacts left on the floor of Structure 6.C1, including an antler tine and ceramic disk.

nant pebble aggregate surface. The annex is formed by a collar of angular field stones and incorporates a yellow-green plaster surface 15 cm below the living surfaces of the structure. The fill over the surface consisted of a dark ashy loam with charcoal and burnt and splintered bones, and it contained a cluster of rounded cobbles. Our interpretation is that the annex originally served as an interior storage bin and was later converted into a smaller interior hearth.

The structure revealed no clearly prepared interior floor. Rather, its interior consisted of a palimpsest of thin, superimposed surfaces of fine loam (5 YR 4/3), some of which appear to have covered only sections of earlier surfaces. The surfaces were encrusted with low frequencies of artifacts including ceramic sherds, broken camelid bones, stone objects, and lithic debitage. Most remarkable was a double-tined deer antler that rested on top of the final surface at the center of the structure (**Figure 8.9**). Archaeologists have recovered antlers from the tops of Tiwanaku period tombs in Lukurmata (Janusek and Earnest 1990), and one is depicted as the headdress centerpiece of a high status personage on a Tiwanaku style *kero* from Tiwanaku. The antler placed on our floor appears to have been part of a closing ritual for the structure. Thus, it appears antlers had ritual significance in the region pre-dating Tiwanaku regional hegemony. Was there some indexical parallel between the placement of the antler on the floor of the circular structure and the placement of antlers on top of interments and human heads? Did antlers form an element of long-term rituals of interment for both structures and humans?

The circular structure and its associated activity areas formed a residential unit in the northeast corner of Compound 1. A swath of cobble pavement linked the structure and its annex to the north compound wall. A halo of soil around the perimeter of the annex defined an area where adobe brick walls once surrounded its stone core, indicating that the cobble pavement was laid after the circular structure and its annex had been constructed. The stones bounding the pavement's east edge are nicely aligned, indicating that the adjacent enclosure was of some importance. A small alignment of rectangular stones joins the north side of the circular structure to the north compound wall, and appears to bound the east side of this enclosure. Was this enclosure, perhaps, added after the initial construction and occupation of the circular structure as ancillary *internal* space? Whatever the case, the outdoor surfaces behind the structure and its north pavement descended to the southwest.

A more extensive cobble pavement extended southeast of the structure, bounded by an oblique, if highly disturbed, alignment of quadrangular stones on its east edge. Just south of the pavement was a sand-filled, clay-lined basin that may have served as a drainage feature. The alignment connected the structure to a hemispherical outdoor hearth to the southeast (**Figure 8.5**). The soil above the cobble pavement differed from that of surrounding areas in that it consisted of dark ashy silt with high organic content that contained large ceramic and camelid bone fragments, and fire-split, soot-covered angular stones. The hearth abutted an east-west wall foundation and was fitted with a semi-circular stone collar. Hearth fill consisted of a soft bluish-gray ash with chunks of baked orange clay and clay chunks, and its hard-packed cream clay base was covered with thin lenses of dark gray ash. The area behind the hearth, south of the east-west foundation, consisted of a dark ashy midden. Soils above the cobble pavement and south of the east-west foundation appear to contain residues of periodic hearth cleanings.

The east-west foundation stops short of the east compound wall to form a corridor that opens to the south. It seems likely that this corridor served as a narrow entrance into the space of this residential unit. A remnant east-west alignment of stones less than two meters to the south marks the southern edge of the corridor. The corridor was filled with refuse that included fire-split rocks, splintered camelid bone (including a partial vertebral column), and large ceramic sherds. The refuse rested on a substrate of orange clay, which may have constituted a prepared floor.

The circular structure and its associated features, foundations, pavements, and activity areas comprise a discrete residential space in the northeast corner of Compound 1. It forms a relatively well-bounded space with a likely entrance in its southeast corner, adjacent to the east compound wall. The space enclosed an open patio that consisted of superimposed palimpsest trampled surfaces encrusted with moderate densities of cultural artifacts, including sherds, splintered bone, and lithic debitage. This was an open outdoor space that served a variety of residential practices, including food preparation and cooking near its south edge.

Other Activity Areas in Compound 1

Excavations outside of the northwest corner of the compound exposed nothing as visually dramatic as the residential unit focused on Structure 6.C1. Excavations south of the primary entrance exposed a reddish-brown silty clay floor supported in some areas with an aggregate pebble substrate. Covering the floor was a moderately dense midden consisting of dark silt with faunal remains, ceramic sherds, and lithic fragments. Units 6.19 and 6.24 revealed remnant portions of wall foundations that require further study.

The northwest sector of the compound revealed several enigmatic but intriguing features. Sparse small cobbles encrusted the floor of the compound near the north compound wall. One unit (U.6.46) revealed an oblique double-row alignment of stones surrounded by ash lenses (**Figure 8.10**). Nearby were extensive deposits of yellow clay and dark gray ash (in Us. 6.42 and 6.44). Interspersed among such features were two small circular pits that may have been postholes. We recovered the most unique objects near the original west compound wall close to the Sunken Temple. Resting on the compound's clay floor, near the remnant north-south wall, was a boulder of bright green andesite.

Figure 8.10   Remnant foundation of a circular structure located in northwest quadrant of Compound 1.

This boulder had been partially carved. We had already identified four other stones of this striking material *ex situ*, on the surface of the southeast quadrant of the Wankane mound. Our *in situ* find determined that the green andesite boulders constituted an important element of Late Formative ritual at Khonkho Wankane.

The Compound 1–Sunken Temple Connection

The small east entrance for the Sunken Temple opened into the northwest sector of Compound 1. It established a clear passage toward the compound. The relationship between Compound 1 and the Sunken Temple shifted over time. The original west compound wall and the east temple wall ran parallel to one another and some 10 meters apart. However, much of the original west compound wall was ultimately dismantled, most likely upon the construction of the west extension of the north compound wall. The west extension wall joined the north compound wall to the Sunken Temple's north corridor and completely enclosed the spaces east and northeast of the temple within the confines of the larger compound. Whatever relation had held between the adjacent structures before this event, after it they formed an interlinked architectural ensemble.

Architectural changes created an intimate relationship between Compound 1 and the Sunken Temple. The Sunken Temple's original east entrance, located near the northeast corner of the structure, now opened directly into the west side of a refashioned Compound 1. If Compound 1's west extension wall constricted access to the Sunken Temple from the Main Plaza, it created a second east-west entrance (~1.2 m wide) that joined Compound 1 with the old corridor to the Sunken Temple. It appears that the Sunken Temple's early, highly constricted east entrance provided exclusive entry during Late Formative 1 while the new north corridor entrance provided entry for larger numbers of persons during later Late Formative 1 and early Late Formative 2.

The East Side of Compound 1

Project members excavated a single unit (U.6.21) outside of the northeast corner of Compound 1. It was excavated in order to locate the northeast corner of the compound, which was later located in Unit 6.30, just to the west. The soil was very different from that in units inside of the compound, in that it consisted of a clean, dense, reddish (5YR–7.5YR 3/3) clay loam with very low artifact density. Further excavation after finding the true northeast corner of the compound revealed no other features.

In 2007, excavations directly adjacent to the east side of Compound 1 revealed additional patterns. A trench (U.7.14) excavated 14 m south of the northeast corner of the compound revealed a pavement of sparse, small cobbles outside of the wall foundation **(Figure 8.1´)**. The pavement formed an exterior alley that provided movement between Compound 1 and Compound 3, which we first identified in 2004.

Stratigraphy and Chronology

Stratigraphic profiles in the north part of Compound 1 were straightforward due to the shallow depth of the occupations below the present surface (**Figure 8.12, Table 8.1**). Near the north compound wall, soil consisted of a ~20 cm stratum of dark reddish-brown, silty loam topsoil (7.5YR 4.5/6) covering a rich, 10–30 cm stratum of reddish-brown clay loam (5YR 5/4). A thin stratum of fine light clay, in some places mixed with dark silty lenses or yellowish sandy pockets, formed remnants of construction fill or slumped walls that covered the palimpsest surfaces of the Compound 1 occupation.

Figure 8.11 Remnant pavement in the alley between Compounds 1 and 3, viewed facing east (photo by Maribel Pérez).

Figure 8.12 South profile of Units 6.16, 6.18, and 6.20.

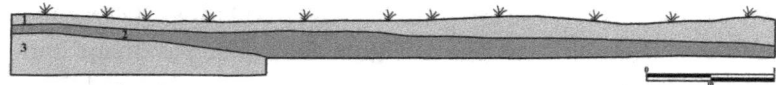

Table 8.1 South profile of units 6.16, 6.18, and 6.20

Stratum	Color	Soil Consistency/Interpretation
1	7.5YR 4.5/6	sandy clay loam/topsoil–plow zone
2	5YR 4/4	silty clay loam
3	5YR 4/3	silty clay loam with compact sandy pockets

The depth of the soil overburden increased several meters to the south, inside Compound 1. The base of the excavated occupation descends gradually as the soil overburden rises to form a low platform. The northeast side of the platform incorporated a later occupation consisting of a single foundation alignment associated with fallen wall rubble and ashy midden containing Tiwanaku and Pacajes style ceramic sherds (U.6.38). This later midden rested on a thick layer of fill that incorporated small pockets of cream-colored, hard clay loam **(Figure 8.13, Table 8.2)**. The cobble foundation was oriented slightly west of

Figure 8.13 South Profile of Unit 6.38.

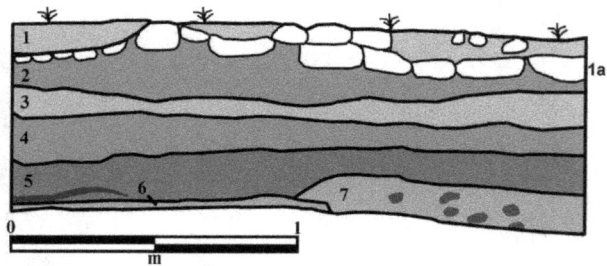

Table 8.2 South profile of Unit 6.38

Stratum	Color	Soil Consistency/Interpretation
1	7.5YR 5/6	sandy clay loam/topsoil–plow zone
1a	N/A	Tiwanaku period stone foundation
2	7.5YR 4/4	ashy silt loam
3	5YR 5/4	silty clay loam
4	5YR 4/4	silty clay loam
5	5YR 3.5/4	silty clay loam
6	7.5YR 5/4	silty loam/occupation surface
7	5YR 4/4	silty clay loam with sandy inclusions

north, differing from earlier alignments. In units to the west (Units 6.34, 6.37) excavations revealed a Late Formative surface with abundant gravel and small angular stones, likely rubble fill from the dismantled west Compound 1 wall.

Ceramic assemblages and radiocarbon results collectively indicate that the earliest and most intensive occupations in Compound 1 date to Late Formative 1. Ceramic assemblages included Kalasasaya style wares, and specifically burnished bowls with red-painted rims and non-burnished bowls with opposing, horizontal strap handles (see Janusek 2003a). Primary Late Formative 2 occupations covered some of the early occupations in the compound. They included cooking and other vessels containing fine, dense mica inclusions and burnished orange-ware forms such as *vasijas*. Tiwanaku and Pacajes period occupations covered parts of Compound 1. These occupations were more expedient and less substantial than those during the preceding Late Formative.

Conclusions

Compound 1 was a massive compound that project members later determined measured 29.6 m east-west by 51.5 m north-south (Smith 2009:106). An early, small doorway in the northeast corner of the Sunken Temple led into a corridor aligned along the west side of the compound. It is thus intriguing that a residential complex centered on a Late Formative 1 circular structure occupied the northeast corner of the compound. This was the first direct archaeological evidence for a residential complex at Khonkho since Portugal's (1955) excavation of two circular structures in the 1940's. Excavations in 2004–2007 revealed more than thirty other circular structures at the site, most concentrated in two patio groups within Compound 3, just to the northeast (Janusek 2015; Marsh 2012; Smith 2009). Compared to most of these other structures, Compound 1's was relatively elaborately constructed and the extent of its residential features relatively expansive. We suggest that the person or family that occupied this structure enjoyed relatively high status. In light of the antler tine placed over its floor, the valued minerals and objects embedded in the compound's primary entrance, the partially-carved green andesite boulder further west, and the exclusive entrance with the Sunken Temple, we suspect that the inhabitants were some of Khonkho's key ritual specialists and perhaps those who orchestrated the ceremonies conducted in the Sunken Temple.

Toward the end of Late Formative 1 or in early Late Formative 2, the southern two-thirds of Compound 1 was converted into a massive platform consisting of elaborately selected and placed fill deposits (Janusek 2015; Plaza Martinez 2007). At least one other similarly-sized circular structure located in the compound's southeast corner, and by all accounts contemporary with

Str. 6.C1, was obliterated in the process. So was the entire original south wall of the compound. Compound 1 during this event was repurposed to support one of three platforms that constituted a new proxemic character for the site focused on an east, a west, and a south platform—the one built over the south portion of Compound 1. Structure 6.C1 appears to have been abandoned at approximately the same time.

᷍

Chapter 9

A Dual-Court Complex on Wankane's West Platform

John Wayne Janusek and Maribel Pérez Arias

One of the primary objectives of excavations in 2001–2002 was to clarify the area of Khonkho Wankane that Rydén (1947:88) referred to as the "North Courtyard," our Sector 1 **(Figures 1.10, and 9.1)**. It is located on the west side of the Wankane platform. Visible above the surface in this area are large stone blocks and long pilasters that at first sight appear to define a large open court-yard somewhat more extensive than the Sunken Temple. The area was the subject of test excavations over the years. Most notable was a 2 m × 2 m unit that Kolata and colleagues excavated in the north portion of the presumed courtyard late in 1987. Our excavations in one of the courtyard's entranc-es indicated that another unit had been excavated prior to Kolata's project. We surmised that this undocumented excavation was the work of either Maks Portugal Zamora or his son, Max Portugal Ortiz.

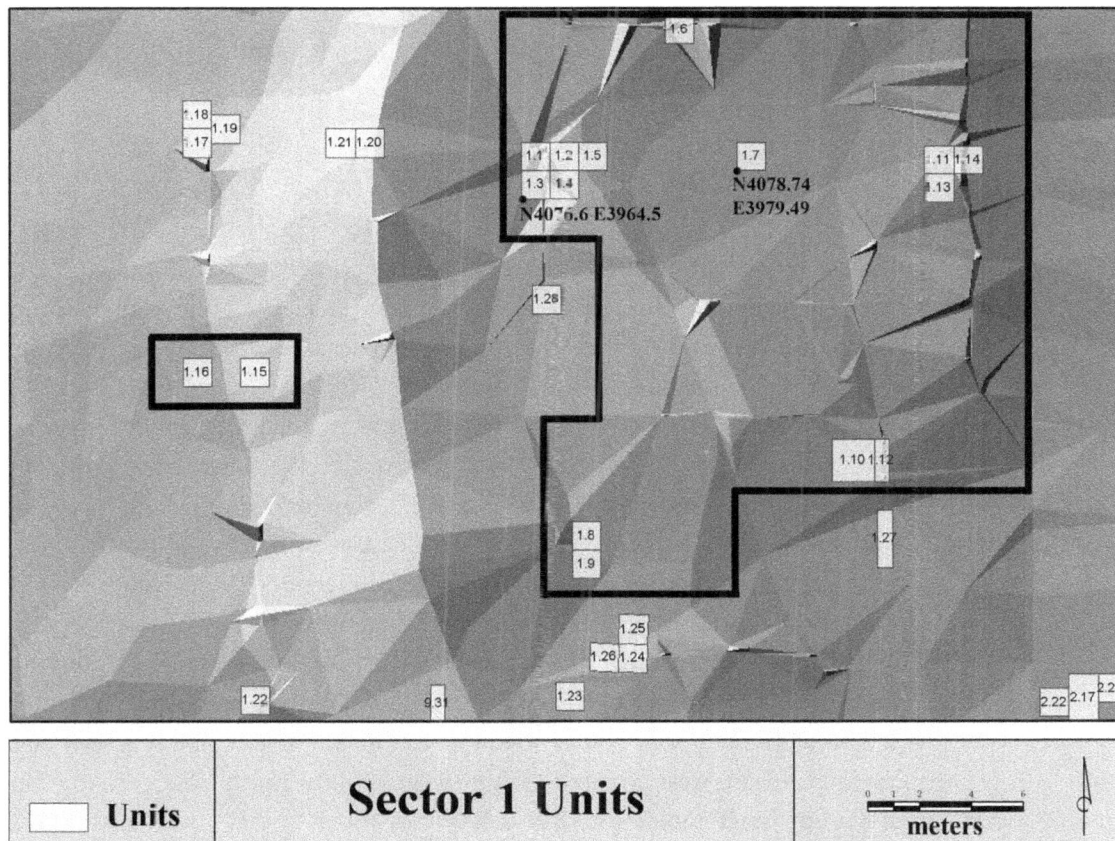

Figure 9.1 Plan of Sector 1 excavations, Base map by Scott Smith.

Figure 9.2 View of surface architecture associated with the North Court of the Dual-Court Complex.

Spatial Layout

Our excavations indicated that the Sector 1 portion of the Wankane platform housed not one large courtyard but two adjacent courtyard–platform structures. We refer to this structural ensemble as the Khonkho Wankane Dual-Court Complex. Its east wall constituted the west wall of the Main Plaza **(Figure 9.2)**. Each structure consisted of a sunken patio and a raised earthen platform, and their platforms consist of compact reddish–brown silty clay loam fortified by stone revetments. The North Platform structure measures 52.6 m east–west and its inner courtyard 23.8 m east–west by 20.7 m north south. The slightly smaller south platform structure measures 51 m east–west and its inner courtyard 21.1 m east–west by 17.7 m north–south. The rectangular spaces formed by the outer revetments and the inner courtyards are all slightly trapezoidal, though not nearly to the degree of the Sunken Temple in Sector 2. This architectural complex called for rectilinear architectural spaces. It also required an east–west orientation that broke from the north–south orientation of the Sunken Temple.

Although the two courts ultimately formed a single complex, they may have been constructed separately, beginning with the South Court. Their sequential construction is most evident in the west platform of the conjoined Dual-Court complex (**Figure 9.3**). The North Court extends 1.5 meters west of the South Court, and its west platform and revetment extends 1.5 meters further west to encompass its greater size. Ceramic sherds recovered from the

Figure 9.3 Two views of the west extension of the outer platform wall of the North Court: A) facing east toward the west outer platform wall of the South Court, gray bands representing unexcavated wall section; B) view of the corner of the west outer platform of the South Court and the west extension wall of the North Court, facing northeast.

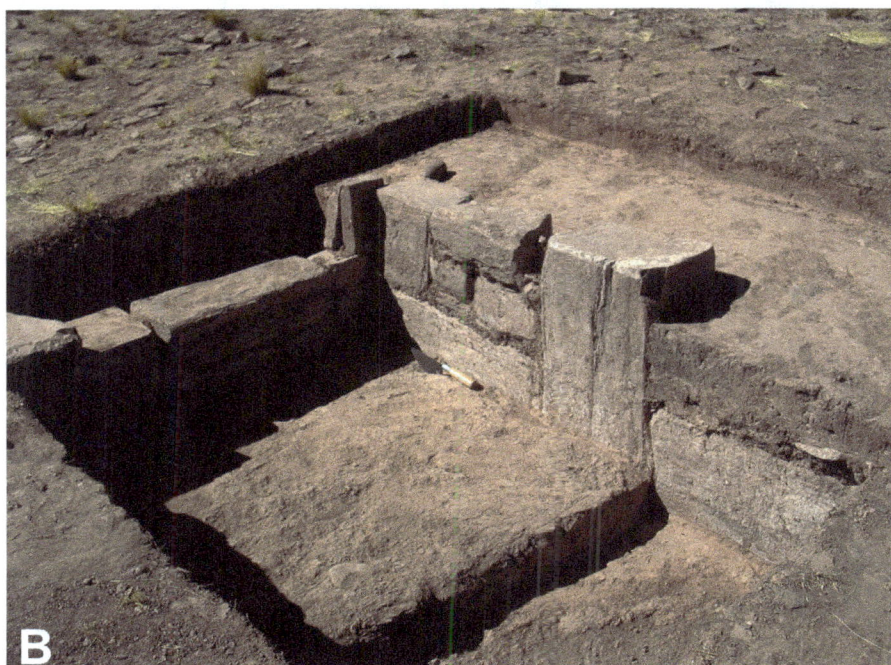

two courts indicate that the South Court had an earlier history dating to Late Formative 1, and that the North Court was likely constructed in Late Formative 2 and may have even continued to be used, if only informally, into the Tiwanaku period. Nevertheless, during much of Late Formative 2 the two courts formed a unified Dual-Court complex. Its construction history was built into its west platform revetment.

We located three clear entrances, two of which had been visible on the surface of the Wankane platform. The two surficial entrances were stairways that descended into the courtyards of the two structures (**Figure 9.4**). Each was

Figure 9.4 East-facing views of the a) west entrance to the North Court and the b) west entrance to the South Court of the Dual-Court Complex. Note the placement of a large rectangular sandstone block as the upper step for each (original side pilasters for the south entrance have since been removed).

built into the west wall of its respective courtyard. The west stairway of the North Courtyard had two stone steps— though the lowest step may be missing—and the west stairway of the South Courtyard had three. Excavations in 2002 revealed a narrow corridor in the east platform of the North Courtyard complex. This corridor opened between two large pilasters that occupied the west wall of the Main Plaza (one of which has since fallen over and blocked the passage) and was precisely aligned with the west stairway on the other side of the courtyard. It is possible that a similar corridor was built into the east wall of the South Courtyard structure, but excavations revealed that this area of the Wankane platform has been heavily disturbed by later agropastoral and other activities.

The South Courtyard

Two areas of the South Courtyard were targeted for excavation in 2002: one to expose its monumental west stairway (Units 1.8–1.9), and one in the northeast corner of the court where a possible passage to the Main Plaza had been identified on the surface (Units 1.10, 1.12). The stairway consisted of three superimposed and elegantly carved sandstone blocks **(Figures 9.5–9.6)**. The top stone consisted of gray hued and the bottom two red hued sandstone. Three flat stones supported the middle step. The steps clearly demonstrate use wear, and the second two have shallow loaf-shaped surface depressions indicating that their sides supported stone or earthen foundations. It is likely that the sandstone steps formed parts of an elaborate entrance that incorporated

Figure 9.5   Remnant west entrance to the South Court, facing southwest. Note the fine rectangular form of the bottom two sandstone steps, as well as the beveled areas for use.

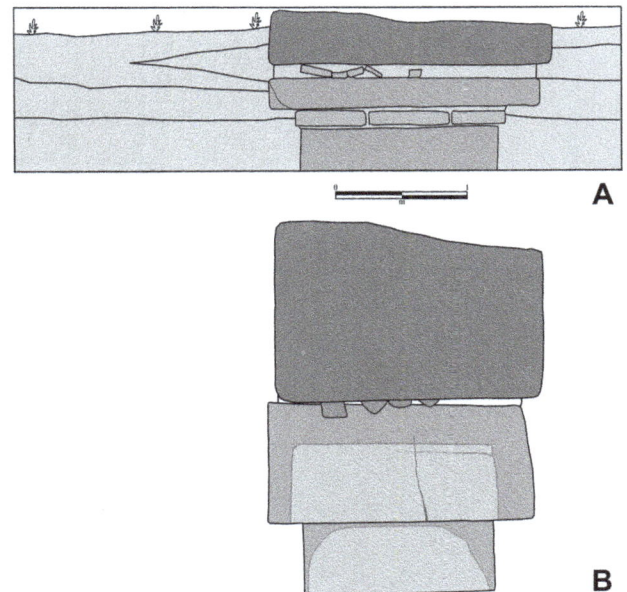

Figure 9.6   West profile (A) and plan (B) of the west entrance to the South Court. Note the beveled areas for use.

Figure 9.7 View of surface architecture and excavations in the northeast portion of the South Courtyard, facing northwest (Units 1.8 and 1.9). Excavations of the west entrance to the North Courtyard are in the distance.

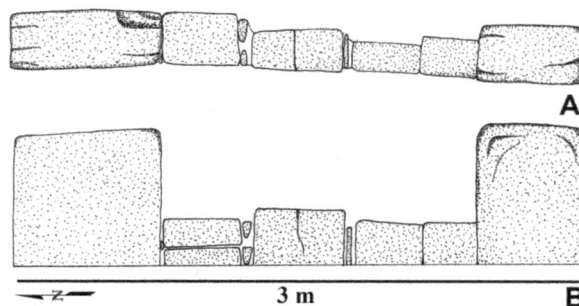

Figure 9.8 Rendering of the (A) plan and (B) profile of the excavated north portion of the east inner platform wall of the South Court (Units 1.8 and 1.9).

door-jamb pilasters and smaller, easily removed blocks. The bottom of the lowest step rested a few centimeters over the surface of the sunken courtyard.

The presence of two sandstone blocks on the surface near the northeast corner of the courtyard prompted excavations in this area **(Figures 9.7 and 9.8)**. Two excavation units were opened to determine whether or not this area of the courtyard incorporated a passage to the Main Plaza. The stones in question were relatively large rectangular blocks that appeared to have served as pilasters framing an opening. Yet excavations revealed several smaller stones that formed a remnant wall foundation between them. Thus, this area did not constitute a passage between the South Courtyard and the Main Plaza. We then hypothesized that the passage was located further south, at or near the center of the east wall of the South Courtyard. Excavations in 2004 and 2005 indicated that this portion of the courtyard's foundation has been heavily disturbed, but that the passage likely was originally located near the center of the east wall.

Excavations in the courtyard itself revealed several superimposed ephemeral surfaces rather than an elaborately crafted or plastered floor. These surfaces were very similar to those located inside of the Sunken Temple, and like them, were difficult to distinguish during excavations. We located an initial subsurface of prepared clay loam just under the lowest step of the west stairway and underneath the east wall foundation near the structure's northeast corner. A superimposed *occupation zone* included remnant palimpsest trampled surfaces and occupation overburden associated with the long-term use of the structure. Some excavated areas, and most clearly the northeast corner of the courtyard, revealed trampled surfaces reinforced by sparse pebble aggregates. Overall, identifying clear surfaces was challenging across the courtyard.

Figure 9.9   View of the west entrance to the North Court, facing west.

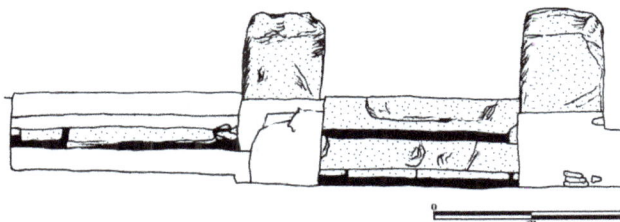

Figure 9.10   Rendered profile of the west entrance to the North Court, facing west.

The North Courtyard

The west stairway of the north courtyard and its north revetment were targeted for excavation in 2001 (Units 1.1–1.5). As in the South Courtyard, a large, gray sandstone slab constitutes the top step, but here surrounded by two intact pilasters (**Figure 9.9–9.11**). The pilasters have slumped down into the entrance. Our excavations confirmed that this was due in part to prior excavations in this area. They revealed the clear outlines of a previous excavation unit in this sector (**Figure 9.11**). It appears to be a 2 m × 2 m unit oriented slightly askew of the cardinal directions. Although some community members suggested that this was one of Kolata's units from 1987, its fill was durable and its edges less systematically formed and oriented than his other units. We suggest that the unit was most likely excavated prior to 1987.

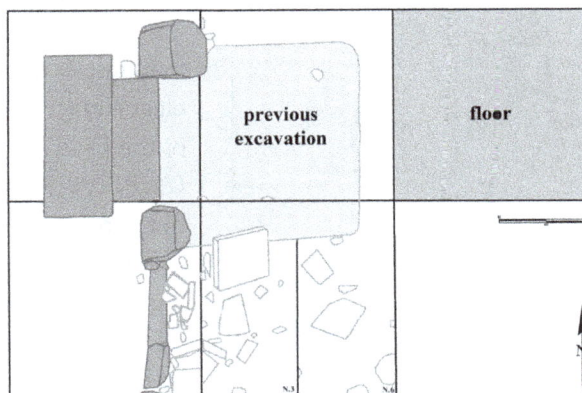

Figure 9.11   Plan of the west entrance to the North Court, showing outline of an early excavation.

The stairway leading into the courtyard consisted of two carved, superimposed sandstone blocks. The bottom of the lower block rests on a prepared bed of flat carved slabs. The wall foundation on the south side of the stairway has partially collapsed, but is still better preserved than the foundation in the same area of the South Courtyard. The base of the foundation and at least part of its upper courses consisted of carved rectangular ashlars and expediently worked fieldstones. Sections of the upper courses consisted of small fieldstones and cobbles. Overall, the blocks comprising the lower wall foundation were much better carved and more rectangular in shape than those in the Sunken Temple. Prior excavation had removed the original floor surface near the steps, and possibly even the stone that formed the basal step of the original stairway.

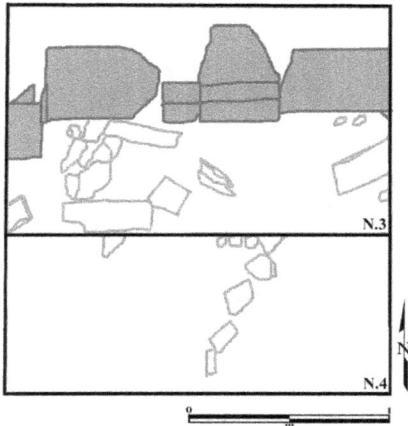

Figure 9.12 Plan of excavation (Unit 1.6) in the north platform wall of the North Court.

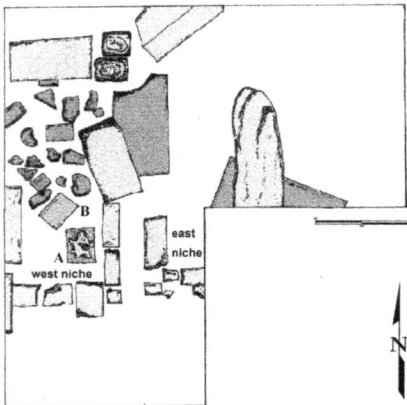

Figure 9.13 Plan of the excavations in the corridor that linked the Main Plaza with the North Court (Units 1.11, 1.13 and 1.14). It highlights the two niches and carved blocks (A and B) found in the west niche (plan rendered by Maribel Peréz Arias).

Nevertheless, we located an intact portion of the surface of the North Court-yard a couple of meters east of the stairway, in Unit 1.5.

An excavation unit in the north wall foundation of the courtyard—Unit 1.6—confirmed the architectural characteristics found at the entrance (**Figure 9.12**). The wall here rested on a foundation of large ashlars and partial-ly carved fieldstones, and in some places an upper course of smaller fieldstones and cobbles. Although we located no prepared surface, we did locate a durable stratum of red sandy clay at the base of the foundation, similar to the likely surface exposed at the base of the west staircase.

Broadly considered, the floor inside of the courtyard consisted of a durable stratum of sandy clay that was slightly laminated, suggesting exposure to wind and rain. It was located approximately 60 cm below the current surface. Every-where it was exposed, the floor was clean and contained a very low density of artifacts. To further expose the floor, we re-opened Kolata's 1987 excavation pit near the center of the courtyard by removing the backfill and cleaning the profile walls. The walls of the unit (Unit 1.7) consisted of a dark silty loam very much unlike the compact red clay soil that formed the court's platforms, and manifests sediment that has accumulated over centuries. We failed to locate a clear surface in this unit, suggesting the possibility that the North Courtyard of the Dual-Court complex was later—and perhaps during the Pacajes Period (AD 1100–1450)—converted into a sunken basin (*qocha*) and reservoir. The Sunken Temple suffered a similar transformation.

Excavations in the platform east of the courtyard revealed a corridor lead-ing from the sunken court to the Main Plaza (Units 1.11, 1.13, 1.14). The platform here is approximately six meters wide and is bounded on either side by large stones and tall pilasters. It has been used most recently as a road for truck traffic, and thus its soil is highly compacted. The possibility of a corridor was noted on the surface as east-west aligned stones within the east platform. Excavations revealed a corridor paved with expediently carved fieldstones and more finely carved ashlars, bounded on either side by large, rectangular cut stone blocks (**Figure 9.13**). The corridor opening, where it meets the Main Plaza, was originally flanked by two massive sandstone pilasters. The south pilaster has since fallen over and today blocks the entrance.

Two niches framed by carved stone foundations occupied the south side of the corridor near its opening into the plaza. The west niche incorporated two blocks with sculpted decoration (**Figures 5.4, 9.13 and 9.14**). One, found lying flat on the floor of the niche (A), depicts what appears to be a winged camelid, and in light of its gracile features, perhaps a vicuña. The second, found ly-ing on its side, depicts a human head in profile (B) (**Figure 9.15**). The face has the convex nose reminiscent of monolithic iconography at the site and is more broadly representative of Late Formative lithic and ceramic iconography (Janusek and Ohnstad 2019).

Figure 9.14   Detail of the location of the carved block depicting the winged camelid in the west niche of the corridor that linked the North Court to the Main Plaza.

Stratigraphy and Chronology

Stratigraphic profiles in the Dual-Court Complex were fairly straightforward. Near the west stairway of South Courtyard, the original use surface rested on a prepared floor of dark brown clay loam (Stratum 5, **Figure 9.16, Table 9.1**). Covering the surface was an *occupation zone* of palimpsest occupation surfaces (Stratum 4b, 10–12 cm thick), capped by a stratum of lighter silty loam that manifests the accumulated sediment of eroded adobe walls (Stratum 4a, 4). Two thick, vaguely distinguishable strata of accumulated sediment covered these early layers: the lower of brown clayey silt (Stratum 3) and the higher of slightly darker brown clayey silt (Stratum 2). A shallow plow zone (Stratum 1, 20 cm thick) capped these strata. Between the uppermost stratum of sediment and the plow zone were scattered ash lenses that date to the Tiwanaku period (e.g., Stratum 1a). Stratigraphy in the court's northeast corner consisted of the same floor substrate and surfaces capped by a thick layer of accumulated sediment (brown silty loam, 7.5 YR 3/2), all under the same plow zone.

Stratigraphy in the North Courtyard was similar, though secondary upper strata incorporated redder soils due to the bright red clay of its eroding west platform (**Figure 9.17, Table 9.2**). The soil under the floor consisted of dark brown pre-cultural clay (Stratum 4). The prepared thin floor above it consisted of reddish-brown clay loam (Stratum 3) covered by a thin stratum of palimpsest surfaces and, above it, a thick layer of finely sorted sediment that most likely represented eroded adobe from earthen wall superstructures (Stratum 2).

Figure 9.15   The two carved sandstone blocks of the North Court's east corridor: (A) winged camelid and (B) profile head (see Figure 5.4).

125

Figure 9.16 Representative stratigraphy of South Courtyard. Unit 1.9, south profile.

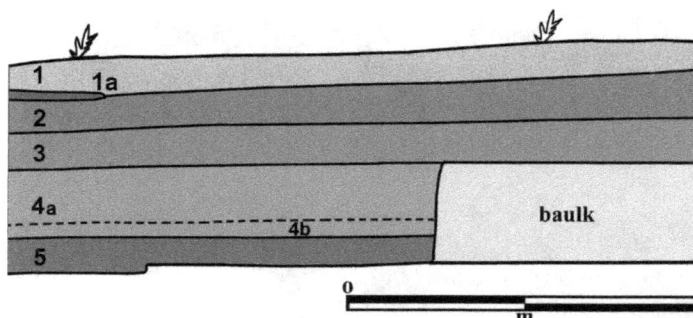

Table 9.1   South Profile of Unit 1.9 in the south courtyard

Stratum	Color	Soil Consistency/Interpretation
1	7.5YR 4/3	sandy clay loam/topsoil–plow zone
1a	5YR 3/3	ashy silt
2	7.5YR 3/4	silty clay loam
3	7.5YR 4/3	silty clay loam
4a	7.5yr 5/3	silty clay loam (eroded adobe)
4b	7.5yr 5/3	occupation zone above surface
5	5YR 4/4	silty clay loam

Figure 9.17 Representative profile of north courtyard, Units 1.3–1.4, south profile.

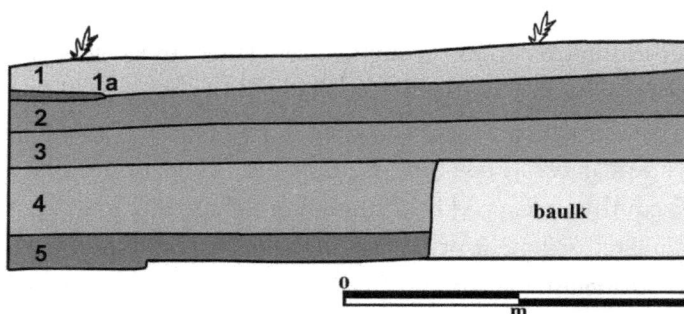

Table 9.2   South profile of Units 1.3–1.4 in the North Courtyard

Stratum	Color	Soil Consistency/Interpretation
1	7.5YR 4/3	sandy clay loam /topsoil-plow zone
2	5YR 5/4	silty clay loam
3	5 YR 4/3	silty clay loam
4	7.5YR 5/4	silty clay loam

Above this layer was a thin stratum of secondary midden that dates to the Tiwanaku and Early Pacajes periods, capped by a thin (15 cm) plow zone that slopes down towards the middle of the courtyard area (Stratum1).

The chronology of the Dual-Courtyard Complex is relatively complex. The courtyards appear to have been used at slightly different times in the history of the site. Ceramic sherds dating primarily to Late Formative 2 are directly associated with surfaces and immediate overburden in the south courtyard, whereas ceramics dating to Late Formative 2 and Tiwanaku IV are associated with surfaces in the north platform structure. The two structures appear to have been constructed at different times during Late Formative 2—the south courtyard followed by the north courtyard—but were joined as a single monumental complex upon or shortly after the north courtyard's construction. Both were initiated in Late Formative 2 and for some time operated together as monumental loci for ritual-political activities. It is undoubtedly important that early in Late Formative 2, and possibly shortly after the construction of the south courtyard of the Dual-Court Complex, the Sunken Temple just to the southwest fell into obsolescence and began to deteriorate. It is also significant that the floor and superimposed surfaces of the north courtyard revealed evidence for early Tiwanaku (IV) period use.

We located no evidence for later activity directly associated with the complex. Ceramic sherds diagnostic of Tiwanaku V and Early Pacajes were recovered, but associated nearly exclusively with accumulated sediment, secondary midden, and thin ash lenses stratigraphically above the original surfaces of the courtyards. By all accounts, the Dual-Court Complex fell into disuse early in the Tiwanaku period.

Conclusions

Excavations in Rydén's North Courtyard revealed an architecturally intricate ensemble that we term the Dual-Court Complex (Janusek 2011, 2015; Janusek et al. 2003; Smith 2009). The complex was constructed early in Late Formative 2, relatively late in Khonkho's formative history. Although the South Courtyard may have antedated the North Courtyard, both were incorporated into a unified, east-west oriented complex during Late Formative 2. The east-west alignment of the courtyards centered on the east-west axes of their primary entrances, a stark shift from the primary axis of the early Main Plaza Sunken Temple articulation. A similar shift was occurring at approximately the same time in Tiwanaku, as manifested in the construction of Kalasasaya and Pumapunku. Among other relations, this new axis manifested a novel proxemic and visual orientation to solar horizon events, in particular facilitating visual connections with solstice and equinox rise and set places in relation to architectural features of the new constructions (Benitez 2009, Vranich 2009). Many critical alignment stones are no longer in place on the platform of the Dual-Court Complex, but we suggest that it, like Kalasasaya, facilitated alignments for a solar-centered calendar in Late Formative 2.

The Dual-Court Complex incorporated stone sculptures. Two carved blocks were incorporated into a pair of niches built into the east entrance of the North Court. We suggest that these niches comprised places for rendering offerings or paying homage as celebrants entered the relatively intimate, enclosed space. Drawing on the monolith seriation developed by Ohnstad and Janusek, and as noted in Chapter 5, we suggest that paired monoliths 2 and 3 occupied each of the two courts of the Complex. Entering into either court from the east or west facilitated an encounter with one of those monoliths.

Part IV

〜

Excavations in Residential and Mortuary Sectors of Khonkho Wankane

Chapter 10

༄

Residential and Mortuary Activity on the Northwest Slope of Wankane

John Wayne Janusek and Deborah E. Blom

Project members initiated excavations on the northwest slope of the Wankane platform in 2001 to expose residential and mortuary contexts (**Figure 10.1**). According to community members, the Bolivian archaeologist Gregorio Cordero conducted excavations here in the mid-1900s. They indicated that he found burials. Recalling research in the Katari Valley (Janusek and Kolata 2003), we suspected that the edges of the Wankane mound might have served as prime locations for Tiwanaku burials. We excavated twelve units in an area where the Wankane mound slopes down to the northwest. Units 3.1–3.8 and 3.10 were excavated in the sloping portion of Sector 3, and Units 3.9, 3.11, and 3.12 on the flat edge of the platform. We hypothesized that the flat portion of Sector 3 housed the west edge of primary occupations, while the sloping

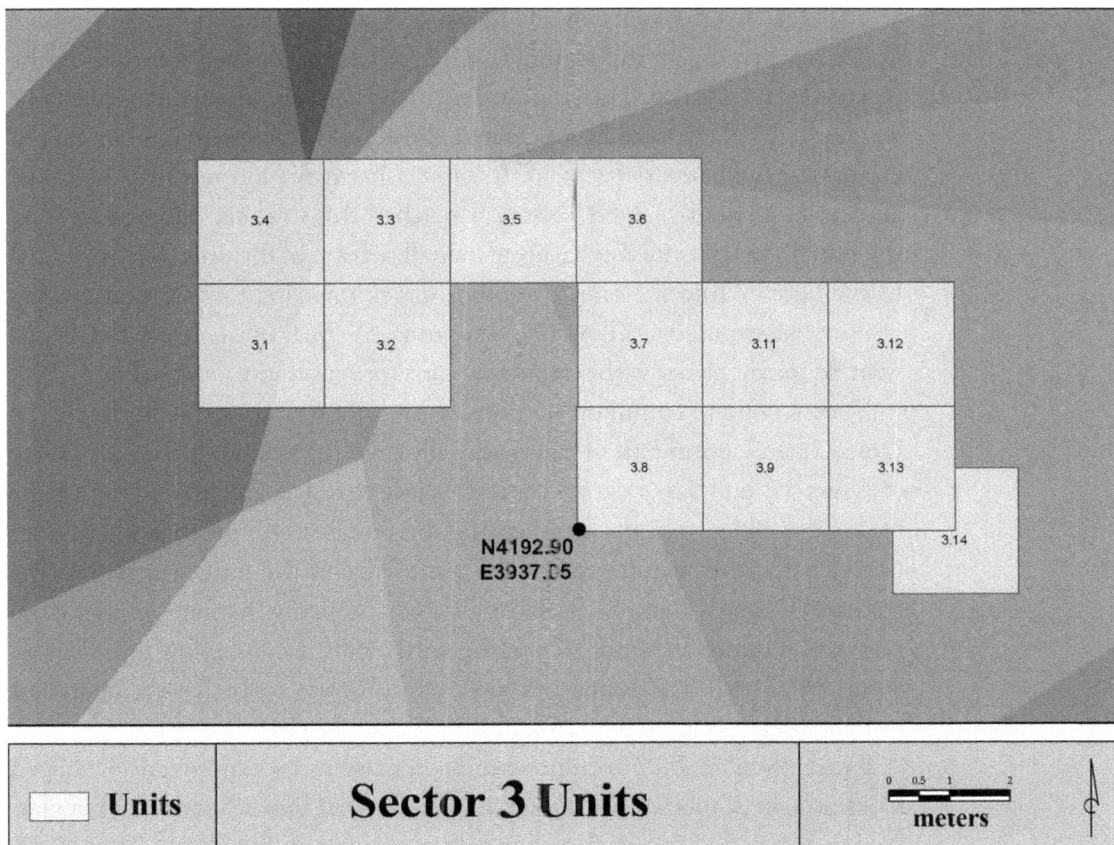

Figure 10.1 Plan of Sector 3 excavations. Base map by Scott Smith.

portion to the northwest may have been dedicated to past mortuary activities.

Excavations corroborated these hypotheses. They indicated that the edge of the platform was home to a residential occupation during the Late Formative. The occupation extended several meters further west, continuing under the sloping, heavily eroded portion of the mound. During the Tiwanaku Period, the sloping edge of the mound, much like the edges of smaller mounds in the Katari valley, were prime areas for burying deceased persons. Excavations revealed six human interments in this area.

Late Formative Occupation

We initiated excavation in 2001 by exposing a 4 m × 4 m excavation block (Units 3.1–3.4) in a gently sloping area of Sector 3 to remove the plow zone, which averaged 10 cm thick. We did this to expose the upper origin points of subterranean mortuary contexts. While we exposed the upper origins of two burials, depositional contexts were more complex than expected. We next excavated several 2 m × 2 m excavations to the east, to 1) expose what we considered to be an occupation context and 2) reveal any other interments in the immediate area.

The 4 m × 4 m block exposed the west edge of a compact orange stratum. To further investigate this feature (Unit 3.5, F. 1), we opened two units to the east, units 3.5 and 3.6. The stratum continued through these units. Its surface was pocked and encrusted with ceramic, lithic, and faunal remains but did not continue evenly across Sector 3. In Unit 3.7, excavation reached the upper portion of a burial (3.7, F.1) before it reached this stratum. After excavating the burial, we continued excavating a small portion of the unit (0.8 m × 2 m) to the floor. While the orange stratum was not apparent, at its stratigraphic position we exposed a yellow clay stratum (2.5Y 7/6). Both appear to be remnant floors associated with a relatively early, pre-mortuary occupation.

We encountered remnant portions of the yellow floor in the north part of Unit 3.8, and a thin lens of green ashy silt (like that found in the east profile of Units 3.2 and 3.3) near its center. Adjacent to the green lens was a layer of dense cobbles, possibly representing the remains of a fallen wall (Feature 6). Abutting this feature, and at the south edge of the unit, were two other features (Features 7 and 8). They originated at roughly the same stratigraphic position as Burial 5 (Feature 9), to the north. Both were shallow pits. Feature 7 was filled with fieldstones and loose silt, on top of which were abundant camelid bones. Feature 8 was filled with dark silt (5YR 4/3).

Excavations in 2002 continued these operations by exposing an L-shaped block of units (Units 3.9, 3.11, and 3.12) adjacent to Units 3.6 and 3.7. They clarified that the area housed a Late Formative occupation (**Figures 10.2 and 10.3**). Excavations in Units 3.9 and 3.12 revealed two sections of a highly fragment-

Figure 10.2   View of a remnant, north–south trending Late Formative structure wall.

Figure 10.3   View of the remnant south portion of the Late Formative structure wall.

ed fieldstone wall foundation oriented roughly north-south and slightly east of the cardinal directions. The foundation straddled the east wall of Unit 3.9 and the west wall of Unit 3.12. Wall segments were associated with an occupation surface consisting of a thin lens of reddish-brown (5 YR 4/4) sandy clay loam. This surface extended through Units 3.11 and 3.9, and appears to have been associated with an adobe block in Unit 3.8 and, to the west, the remnant orange and yellow floors located in 2001. Associated ceramic sherds dated to Late Formative 1 **(Figure 10.4)**. Floor surfaces were laid over a red, pre-cultural clay or platform fill.

Figure 10.4   Kalasasaya bowl recovered from the surface of the Late Formative structure.

The remnant structure, floors, and occupation surfaces were the first in a long sequence of habitation activities in Sector 3. Superimposed surfaces, including patches of a dark brown stratum (7.5 YR 4/2) of sandy clay along the west edge of the remnant fieldstone foundation, indicate that the first floor was resurfaced at least once. This patchy upper stratum was associated with ceramics diagnostic of both Late Formative 1 and 2, and included burnished ollas with dense mica temper. Several later refuse pits and ashy deposits intruded into these superimposed surfaces. Their ceramic assemblages tended to date to Late Formative 2 but also included early Tiwanaku period vessels.

Tiwanaku Period Mortuary Contexts

We encountered six subterranean interments in 2001, all of them in the sloping western portion of Sector 3. All were subterranean cist burials. These included four simple cist burials and two slab-cist burials. Two of them had been seriously disturbed by later cultivation (3.1 R.1, 3.4 R.1). All dated to the Tiwanaku Period, and thus postdated the Late Formative occupation features just described. I organize their description according to their subterranean morphology as simple or slab-cist burials.

Simple cist burials

3.1, F.1 (Burial 1)   This was a small, simple, unlined cist burial. Covered the cist were two capstones that had sunk onto and partially crushed the human remains. The interred individual was a female 49–80 years in age who had been buried in a flexed position, presumably lying on her side and facing south. The thoracic vertebrae were twisted almost 180 degrees in relation to the lower body, suggesting that the body had been disturbed before, upon, or after interment. There were no preserved burial offerings.

3.4, F.1 (Burial 2)   This was the base of a small, simple cist burial that had been heavily disturbed by later cultivation. We exposed this burial in the north profile of Unit 3.4, and excavated the feature as a micro-salvage operation. The interred individual was only partially represented and was associated with no offerings.

3.6, F.3 (Burial 3)   This was also a small simple cist burial. Although it originated further under the surface than the first two, it appears as though the burial had been disturbed sometime in the past. It contained remains of a poorly preserved child aged 3.5 to 6 years. No preserved burial offerings were recovered.

3.9, F.10 (Burial 6)   This was a simple cist tomb located in the southwest corner of Unit 3.9. The top of it became apparent very close to the present surface, as it was covered by several large stone slabs (**Figure 10.5**). The interment consisted of the remains of an 8–12 year old juvenile. As in other cist burials, the interred individual was very poorly preserved. Accompanying the interment were two Tiwanaku vessels: a red-slipped *tazon* and inside of it a small domestic *vasija* (**Figure 10.6**).

Figure 10.5 Stone slabs covering human burial, 3.9, F. 10.

Figure 10.6   Tazon and domestic *vasija* that accompanied the human remains of 3.9, F.10.

Figure 10.7   View of the excavated human burial, 3.7, F. 1.

Slab-cist burials

3.7, F.1 (Burial 4)   This was the first of three slab-cist burials we encountered while attempting to reach the orange floor feature. It was outlined in a roughly square manner by five stone slabs **(Figure 10.7)**. The remains of the interred individual, a female adult approximately 40 years old, were better preserved than those in the other burials. The remains were apparently seated in a flexed position on a large flat slab that served as a tomb base. On the south side of the burial was a small ovoid feature consisting of baked dark red clay. It contained ceramic and bone fragments and a chunk of white kaolin clay. Preserved offerings included camelid bones that appear to have been placed over the seated body, and a Tiwanaku style black-on-red *cuenco* **(Figure 10.8)**.

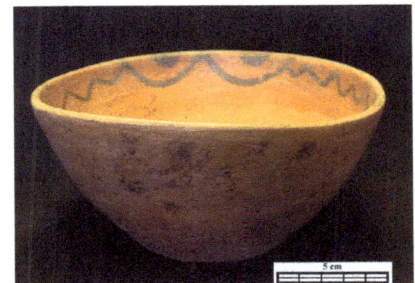

Figure 10.8   The black-on-red cuenco that accompanied the human remains of 3.7, F.1.

Figure 10.9 View of the excavated human burial, 3.8, F. 9. Note poor bone preservation.

Figure 10.10 Polychrome *tazon* and *vasija* that accompanied the human remains of 3.8, F. 9. The *vaijsa* manifests the popular Cochabamba Tiwanaku style (Janusek 2003a).

3.8, F. 9 (Burial 5)   This slab-cist burial straddled Units 3.8 and 3.9 (**Figure 10.9**). The collar was ovoid in plan and supported by fieldstones placed on end. The interment consisted of a late middle-aged to elderly adult, whose sex was unclear. Like the individual in Burial 4, this one was poorly preserved. He/she appears to have been seated in a flexed position, facing north. Accompanying the interment were two red-slipped, polychrome Tiwanaku vessels, a *tazon* and a *vasija* (**Figure 10.10**).

Offering Features in Unit 3.10

At the beginning of the 2002 field season, we opened one unit just southwest of the main excavation block. We did this to determine the context of two small features apparent on the surface. The features had not been noticed in 2001. They either had been placed in the previous year or had eroded out of the mound during the 2001–2002 rains. Each feature consisted of a narrow cist lined with field stones. Each intruded through a thin stratum of occupation midden and into the pre-cultural, red clay subsoil of the mound slope. Diagnostic ceramics from the midden dated to late Formative 1. They appear to have been slab-lined offering deposits, yet their temporality remains unclear. It is possible that they were created in 2001–2002, in association with community ritual practices following the first season of excavation at the site.

Stratigraphy

Because this sector encompasses the edge of the Wankane platform, the westernmost units (Units 3.1–3.8, 3.10) were much shallower than the easternmost. Excavations in Units 3.1–3.4 and 3.10 simply removed the upper plow zone. Units 3.9, 3.11, and 3.12 revealed a deeper and more complex stratigraphy. The south profiles of Units 3.8 and 3.9 (Figure 10.11, Table 10.1) revealed abundant evidence for cultural activity. The densest evidence for primary cultural activity was apparent in stratum 5, a stratum of dense occupation debris. In the east profiles of Units 3.8 and 3.9, this stratum revealed the habitation features and surfaces described above.

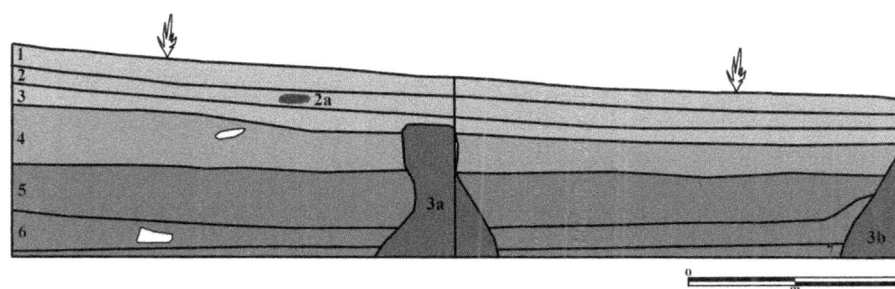

Figure 10.11   South stratigraphic profile of Units 3.8 and 3.9.

Table 10.1   South Profile of Units 3.8 and 3.9

Stratum	Color	Soil Consistency/Interpretation
1	7.5YR 5/3	sandy clay loam/topsoil–plow zone
2	5YR 5/3	silty clay loam/upper midden
3	5YR 4/3	silty clay loam/upper midden
4	5YR 4/4	clay loam/midden
5	7.5YR 4/3	silty clay loam/midden
6	7.5YR 3/3	silty clay loam
7	7.5YR 3/3	clay loam/precultural soil or cultural fill

Another revealing stratigraphic profile was obtained from the north walls of Units 3.11 and 3.12 (Figure 10.12, Table 10.2). It revealed some clear chronological relationships. Importantly, Late Formative occupations are deep and are associated with a structure as well as abundant cultural strata and features. Tiwanaku occupations, which consist largely of secondary midden, are limited to the upper strata of the stratigraphic profile. No later occupations, such as Early Pacajes or Pacajes Inca, were located in Sector 3.

Figure 10.12 North stratigraphic profile of Units 3.11 and 3.12.

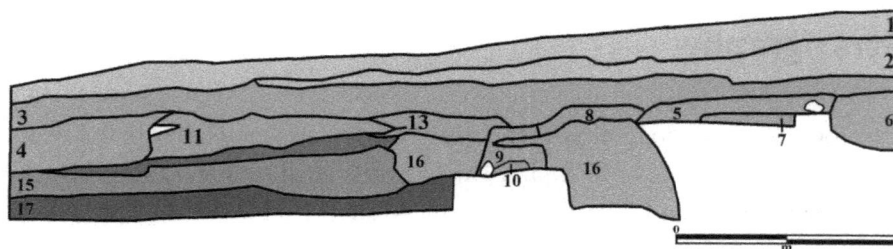

Table 10.2 North Profile of Units 3.11 and 3.12

Stratum	Color	Soil Consistency/Interpretation
1	7.5YR 5/2	sandy clay loam/topsoil-plow zone
2	7.5YR 5/1	silty clay loam/upper midden
3	7.5YR 4/3	silty clay loam/Tiwanaku occupation zone
(lower Tiwanaku occupation zones include strata 4–11, 13, 16, and their associated features)		
12	7.5YR 4/3	silty clay loam/Late Formative 1 occupation zone
15	7.5YR 5/4	silty clay loam/Late Formative 1 occupation zone
17	7.5YR 4/4	red clayey silt/pre-cultural substratum

Chronology and Conclusions

Excavations in Sector 3 exposed an area with a long history of occupation and mortuary activity located off of the central platform of Khonkho Wankane. Excavations revealed several superimposed strata and numerous cultural features dating to the Late Formative period. These included the badly damaged remains of a structure with rectilinear wall foundations oriented roughly north-south and slightly east of the cardinal directions. The structure rested on the remains of a well-prepared floor with orange and yellow colored components, and was associated with superimposed surfaces, occupation zones, and pits. The early floor dated to Late Formative 1 and its superimposed surfaces, manifested in remnant patches, revealed ceramic assemblages diagnostic of Late Formative 1 and 2. Above this was a less distinct occupation zone associated with several pits that yielded Late Formative 2 ceramic assemblages, some of which included early Tiwanaku period sherds.

Covering this Late Formative 2 stratum, in turn, was a thin midden that petered out toward the west. The last yielded ceramics squarely diagnostic of the Tiwanaku period. Six human burials, including four cist and two slab-cist burials, descended from this Tiwanaku Period occupation zone. Three of the six burials contained preserved offerings. No post-Tiwanaku occupations were encountered in this area of Wankane.

〰

Chapter 11

Tiwanaku Period Residence and Specialized Production at the North Edge of the Wankane Platform

John Wayne Janusek, Arik Ohnstad, and Dennise Rodas

Excavations at the north edge of the Wankane platform yielded evidence for primary occupation and specialized activity. Sector Four consists of a low platform bounded to the west by a shallow depression north of the Main Plaza and to the north by a thick cobble wall that defines the north edge of the Wankane platform. Surface collections revealed dense artifact scatters, and subsurface cores indicated deep occupations with dense ash and carbon (chapter 12). We excavated nineteen contiguous units in this sector (**Figure 11.1**). Due to their proximity to the surface, pre-Hispanic occupation had been heavily disturbed by post-depositional cultural practices.

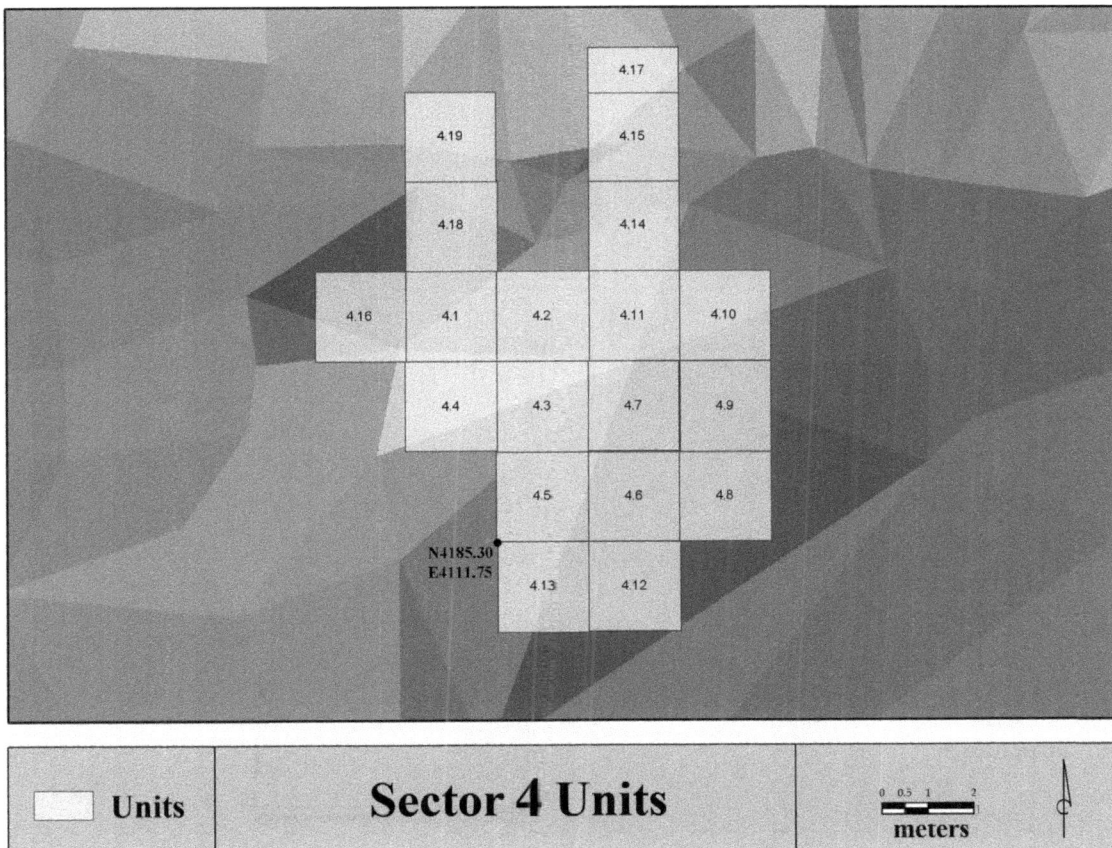

Figure 11.1 Plan of Sector 4 excavations. Base map by Scott Smith.

Units | **Sector 4 Units** | meters

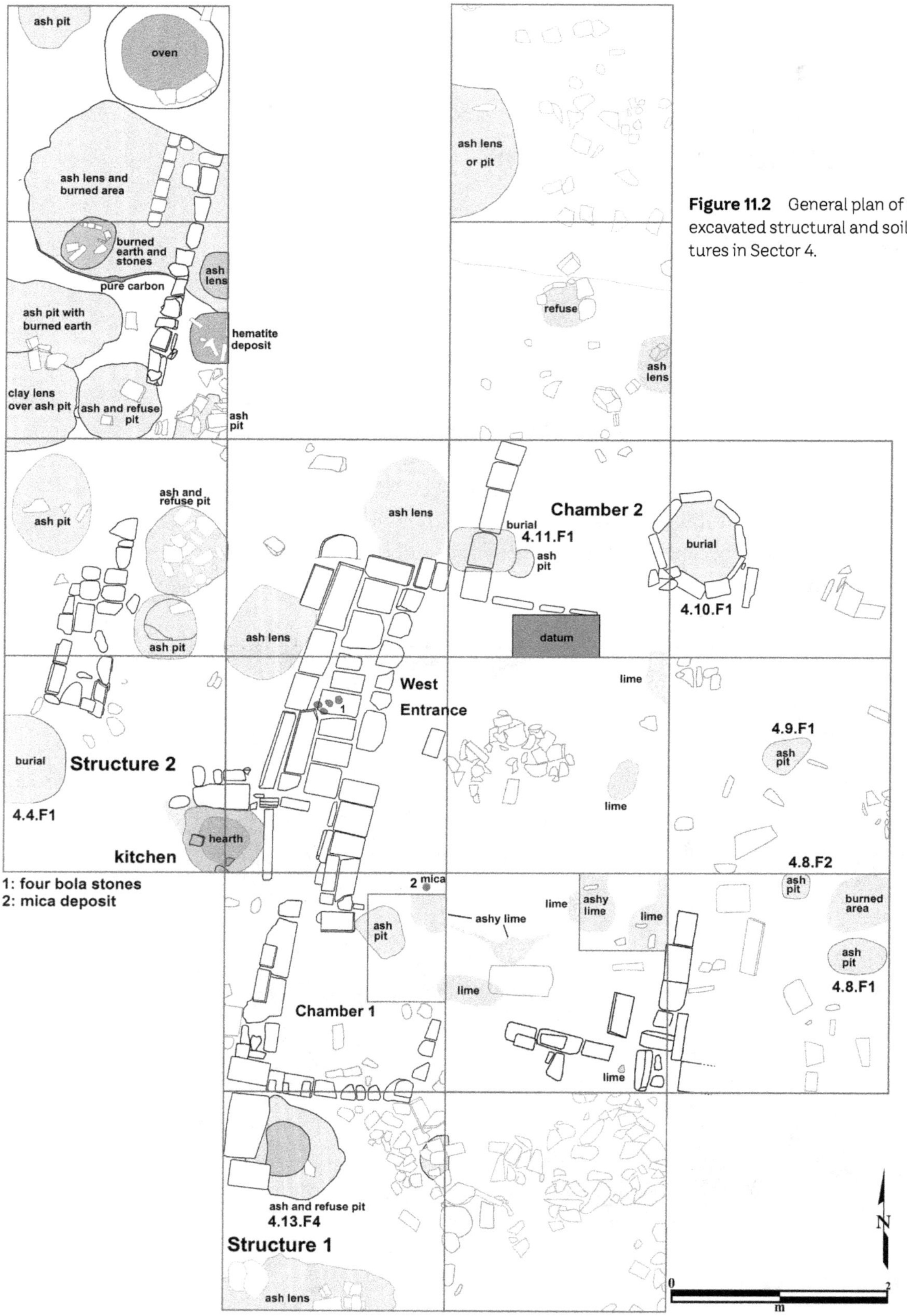

Figure 11.2 General plan of major excavated structural and soil features in Sector 4.

Excavations exposed a large Tiwanaku period multi-room structure and an adjacent parallel wall **(Figure 11.2)**. Associated with the structure were remnant surfaces and occupation zones associated with dense artifactual refuse, ash lenses, and subterranean features. Features included refuse pits, at least one hearth, and human burials. Several features and artifact deposits indicate evidence for a specialized activity that remains unclear. They include extensive burned ashy areas, a deep oven at the north edge of the occupation, extensive deposits of pulverized lime, and caches of cinnabar and mica.

Research in 2006 continued excavations in Unit 4.19, at the north edge of the excavations block. Deep excavations in this unit revealed Late Formative occupations directly under Tiwanaku period middens and occupation surfaces.

Structures 4.1 and 4.2

Project excavations exposed the foundations of a relatively large multi-room structure that we designate Structure 4.1 **(Figures 11.2–11.4)**. It consisted of stone foundations supporting adobe walls that have long since eroded over the associated occupations. Foundations varied slightly in spatial orientation but ranged between seven and ten degrees east of north, comparable to structures excavated at Tiwanaku and Lukurmata (Janusek 2004). The foundations were relatively well built in the scheme of Tiwanaku residential construction. In several places foundations consisted of multiple superimposed courses. They consisted of angular, expediently worked sedimentary stones quarried from the

Figure 11.3 View of 2001 excavations in Sector 4, facing south, showing the foundations of Structure 4.1, Structure 4.2, and surrounding features.

Figure 11.4 View of Structures 4.1 and 4.2, facing north, after completing 2002 excavations.

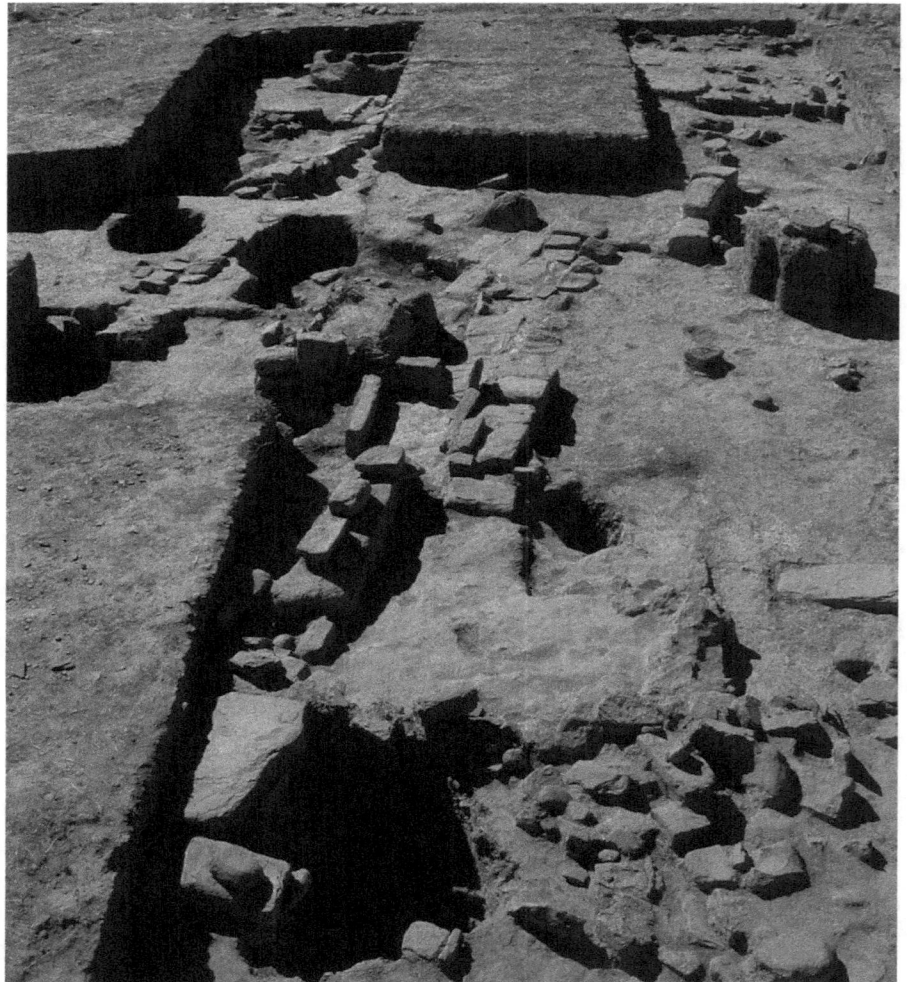

foothills of the Corocoro range located a few kilometers to the north. Portions of the foundations incorporated large and well-carved sandstone blocks.

Structure 4.1 incorporated a principal room surrounded by at least two smaller chambers. The main room measured approximately 3 m east-west by 4 m north-south. It incorporated several ashy deposits and shallow pits in addition to lenses of pulverized ashy lime and a small deposit of raw mica. The northeast corner of the structure, that closest to the contemporary surface, has been demolished in the course of post-depositional activity at the site. A small chamber (1) flanked the southwest corner and another (2) the northwest corner of the room. While the southwest chamber is fairly well preserved, the northwest chamber, the foundations of which are just a few centimeters below the current surface, is only partially extant. It is unclear what purposes these side chambers served.

The structure incorporated an elaborate west entrance. The entrance is approximately two meters wide and incorporates an apron paved with relatively

Figure 11.5 View of structure foundations and surrounding features, facing
southeast, showing abundant lime deposits and residues.

large, well-worked stones. The apron served as a short set of steps that drew
people up from the west and into the main room of the structure. A cluster of
four spherical *bola* stones was found lying just over the steps. They may constitute the remnant stone ballasts of a *bola* sling for hunting deer and smaller
animals. Excavations in the main room exposed several small areas of intact
trampled surface (or *apisonado*), yet in most areas occupation consisted of a
thicker palimpsest of surfaces, detritus, and artifactual debris that we define
as a 4–8 cm thick occupation zone. Complex lenses of gray ash mixed with
carbonized camelid dung and other organic matter constituted significant portions of the occupation zone. The occupation zone yielded relatively high densities of artifacts, in particular camelid remains and ceramic sherds. A cache
of raw mica occupied the southwest corner of the main room **(Figure 11.2)**,
and mica flakes were prominent in some of the ash lenses located within and
around the structure.

A distinctive characteristic of the structure and its associated occupation
zones was the presence of deposits and residues of lime—whether calcium
oxides or hydroxides **(Figure 11.5)**. No other occupations at Khonkho Wankane demonstrated such a density of lime deposits, so we suggest that they manifest the mineralized residues of specialized activities that occurred in Sector
4. Lime residues formed around the edges of the stones that comprised the
entrance to Structure 4.1. Close inspection indicates that it crystallized as a
thin layer just above the stones. Lime also concentrated as lenses in several
portions of the occupation zone within the main room of Structure 4.1. Excavation in the northeast quadrant of Unit 4.6 revealed a thick deposit of lime

just below the occupation zone, associated with extensive lenses of gray ash. These lime deposits may well manifest an erosional precipitate that crystallized after the abandonment of the Sector 4 occupations. Yet we suggest that post-abandonment crystallization of these deposits manifested a reaction to elements infused in the soils in the course of Tiwanaku occupations. If we are correct, they indicate some form of specialized production that involved the employment or production of substantial densities of calcium-based minerals.

A stone-lined nook built into the south edge of the stairway, abutting the southwest wall of the structure, formed the northeast corner of a kitchen (Figure 11.2). The nook contained a deep and well-defined hearth (4.4, F.1). Lining the hearth was a thick, oval-shaped ring of reddish-orange backed earth, supported in places by medium-sized field stones. An opening lined with small stones faced south. The hearth was filled with greenish-gray ash that contained moderately dense, carbonized camelid dung pellets and charcoal fragments. It also contained large cooking vessel sherds. Little of the kitchen was discernable beyond the hearth. It occupied a space between the south portion of Structure 4.1 and the double-row wall to the west that we designate Structure 4.2.

Structure 4.2 denotes the north-south trending wall just west of Structure 4.1. It correlates with the west edge of a shallow platform that is visible on the current surface and demarcates Sector 4. This was a substantial wall that consisted of up to three stone courses and averaged 50 cm wide. Its foundation rests approximately 40 cm below that of Structure 4.1, but also dates to the Tiwanaku period. It appears to be contemporaneous with Structure 4.1, even though it is slightly lower in elevation and its trajectory is a few degrees shallower east of north than that of the west walls and stairways of Structure 4.1. In fact, the elaborate entrance to Structure 4.1 consists of steps that rise from approximately the level of the Structure 4.2 wall up into the main room of Structure 4.1. The wall we designate as Structure 4.2 may form the west wall of an adjacent structure. Yet we favor the hypothesis that it constituted the foundation of a compound wall that enclosed Structure 4.1. Residential sectors bounded by encompassing compounds constituted a fundamental pattern of spatial organization at Tiwanaku and Lukurmata (Janusek 2004).

Features, Activity Areas, and Human Interments

A defining characteristic of Sector 4 was the density of ash lenses and ash-refuse pits recovered in the course of excavation. This was particularly the case outside of Structure 4.1; in fact, an absence of large, deep pits helped to define its boundaries in addition to remnant wall fragments. The density of ash and refuse pits was particularly high north, west, and south of the structure. Large, deep, and in some cases amorphous pits containing enormous amounts of ash, carbonized dung, and artifact fragments characterized Tiwanaku occupations at Tiwanaku, Lukurmata, and other sites in the region (Janusek 2004). At Khonkho, Lukurmata, and sites across the southern basin, they mark the onset of Tiwanaku period occupations and manifest a novel social practice.

The area immediately surrounding Structure 4.1 yielded a number of shallow ash lenses and deeper pits (**Figure 11.2**). All contained relatively high frequencies of carbonized organic matter and substantial densities of artifacts. Three subterranean features located on the east side of Structure 4.1 stand out in light of their depth and globular—that is, roughly bottle-shaped—profiles. These were Features 4.8.1, 4.8.2, and 4.9.1. The form and volume of these pits suggest that they may have been originally excavated to serve as subterranean storage bins. They were subsequently, like many similar subterranean features in residences at Tiwanaku, rendered obsolete and filled with ash, carbonized dung, and artifactual refuse. Located at the south edge of Structure 4.1, Feature 4.13.4 stands out in regard to its depth (>70 cm) and stratigraphic complexity. Like deep ash pits associated with Tiwanaku occupations at other sites, its form was difficult to define. Its opening contained numerous angular fieldstones. Furthermore, its fill alternated strata of relatively pure, reddish brown silty clay with darker, carbon and artifact rich ash to ashy silt. One stratum of ash contained a lens of hematite, reminiscent of the large deposit found in Feature 4.18.4 (see below).

Specialized Activities in Units 4.18 and 4.19

The area immediately west and northwest of Structure 1 revealed an embarrassment of features and activity areas (**Figure 11.6**). This is particularly the case for the units that were most deeply excavated and thoroughly investigated, Units 4.18 and 4.19. It is important to first elucidate the stratigraphic relations that we were able to discern among architectural and other features. The earliest strata we excavated in 2001–2002 revealed a large, amorphous area of grayish-blue silty ash bordered by a ring of pure carbonized organic matter (4.18, F.3 and 4.19, F.7) (**Figure 11.7**). For the most part, this feature was left unexcavated. Yet the area clearly manifested residues of extensive burning *in situ*, and to an extent uncommonly located in Tiwanaku occupations. The closest parallels to such an area are the amorphous *pit kilns* of the Ch'iji Jawira sector of Tiwanaku that were dedicated to firing pottery vessels (Rivera Casanovas 2003).

Covering part of the feature at the north edge of Unit 4.18 was a concentrated deposit of burnt clay and soot-covered, fire-cracked stones. The wall foundation of Structure 4.2 appears to have been set directly on top of the amorphous grayish-blue silty ash feature. Its construction was roughly contemporaneous with the burnt clay deposit. It also appears to have been

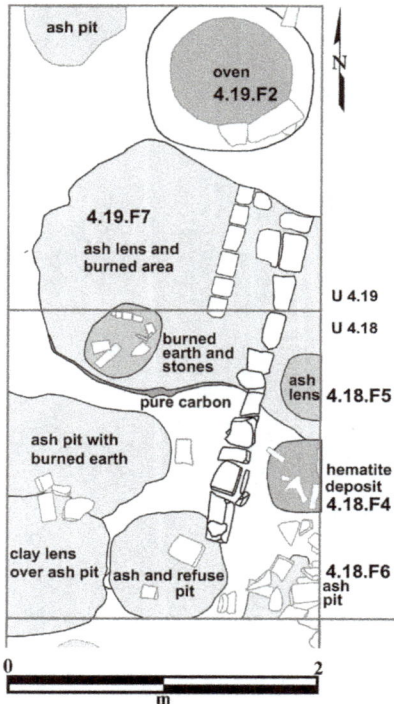

Figure 11.6   Plan of Units 4.18 and 4.19, the northwest portion of Sector 4, demonstrating abundant pits, burning, and activity areas.

Figure 11.7   Close-up view of the northeast quadrant of Unit 4.18, facing west, highlighting an extensive area of burning and carbonization to the right (4.18, F.3 and 4.19, F.7) and a thick deposit of hematite in the foreground (4.18, F.4) associated with the foundation of Structure 4.2.

more or less contemporaneous with an unusually large and thick deposit (> 3 liters) of red, powdered hematite on its east side (4.18, F.4), as well as a nearby ash lens (4.18, F.5) and pit (4.18, F.6) **(Figure 11.7)**. Hematite is commonly used to make red pigment in the region. The deposit further indicates that Sector 4 was dedicated to a specialized activity that continued over multiple occupations.

A deep pit (4.19, F.2) superimposed over the north section of the foundation of Structure 4.2 presents even further evidence for specialized production **(Figures 11.8 and 11.9)**. It formed a deep oven located precisely on the north edge of the Sector 4 sub-platform. The opening of the feature was relatively small and was alternatively lined with adobe bricks and angular field stones. The feature expanded in circumference with depth, ultimately forming a rounded-edge bell shape. The base of the oven contained a distinctive yellowish-green ash that contained dark pulverized organic matter, abundant chunks of burned earth, and soot covered, heat-split stones. It also yielded larger chunks of partially baked clay. Two superimposed lenses of grayish-green ash divided this low stratum from a superimposed stratum (Level 2) of ash mixed with carbonized dung pellets. This stratum also yielded heat-cracked stones and burned earth, in addition to smaller chunks of baked clay than those recovered in the lower stratum of the feature. At the interface of the two strata, excavators recovered a small unfired clay vessel 5–6 cm high and 4–5 cm in diameter.

Figure 11.8   Oblique view of the deep oven (4.19, F.2) encountered in Unit 4.19, facing southeast.

The oven was built into the north edge of the sub-platform, at the best position to take advantage of the predominant northwesterly winds that regularly pass through the region. It was well positioned to create an especially oxidized place for firing ceramic vessels or producing some other heat-crafted things. A stone feature was built into the south wall of the feature approximately 25–30 cm above its base **(Figure 11.10)**. It was a rectangular flue that consisted of two horizontally laid cap stones that covered one remnant, perpendicularly set wall stone. The flue provided ventilation from the south, on the platform just northwest of Structure 4.1. It may have served as a built-in *blow tube* to afford additional ventilation and even human-induced heat from on top of the platform.

The oven clearly produced things that required high firing temperatures and left substantial burnt debris. Furthermore, the fill of the feature included baked clay and at least one small, unbaked ceramic vessel. Earlier features in Sector 4 are uncannily similar to the *pit-kiln* features that Claudia Rivera Casanova (2003) excavated in the Ch'iji Jawira sector of Tiwanaku, and that were, by all

Figure 11.9   Aerial view of the deep oven in Unit 4.19.

accounts, dedicated to the production of specific forms of ceramic vessels. Furthermore, the hematite cache located in nearby 4.18, F.4 and in other features of the sector (4.13, F.4) likely provided the red pigment so distinctive of Tiwanaku red-slipped wares. The mica deposit located in the northeast corner of Unit 4.5 may have been used to produce the inclusions that helped afford Tiwanaku vessels their inimitable durability and surface brilliance. It is unclear what the lime deposits found inside of Structure 4.1 would have added to the production chain. Perhaps it was unrelated to ceramic production. If it was related, it may have been employed in the production of Tiwanaku ceramic pigments or pastes.

Human Interments

Project excavations uncovered four human interments in Sector 4. Three of them appear to be late, dating either to the late Tiwanaku or Early Pacajes periods. None of them contained preserved burial offerings, which is uncommon for Tiwanaku period burials. All of them were located outside of or on top of the wall foundations of Structure 4.1.

The human interment of Feature 4.11.1 was found on top of the north portion of the west wall of Structure 4.1 (**Figure 11.11**). It was located very close to the present surface, and thus had been disturbed by recent plowing. The interment presented no clear burial context, perhaps due to its post-depositional disturbance. Nevertheless many of the bones were relatively well

Figure 11.11   Feature 4.11.1, a surficial human interment that likely dated to Early Pacajes.

preserved. While the mandible was present, the interred person's cranium was missing. Deborah Blom's (2005) osteological analysis indicated that the person was an adult aged 25 to 58 years old and probably male. Upper limbs presented slight arthritis and lower limbs moderate to severe arthritis. Post-dating the Structure 4.1 foundation, this burial likely dated to Early Pacajes.

The human interment of Feature 4.10.1 consisted of a stone-lined cist burial located in or just outside of the northeast chamber of Structure 4.1 (Figure 11.12). The burial appears to have intruded into the structure. Although the interment itself had been placed further below the surface than Feature 4.11.1, it contained no preserved offerings. A conjunction of stratigraphic evidence, burial type, and lack of offerings point to a very late Tiwanaku or Early Pacajes affiliation for this burial. The human interment itself was very poorly preserved. Remnant bones manifest a young adult, likely male, aged 15 to 24 years based on pubic symphysis characteristics (Blom 2005).

Excavation in Unit 4.4 revealed yet another intrusive human interment, Feature 4.4.1. Like the two interments previously described, this one appears to have intruded into the primary Tiwanaku occupation of Sector 4. It contained no preserved offerings. Only the lower portion of the body of the interred person was preserved enough for detailed bioarchaeological analysis. Blom's analysis indicated that the knees, feet, and left ankle of the individual demonstrated slight lipping characteristic of arthritis.

Figure 11.12 Feature 4.10.1, a cist-lined human burial dating to Late Tiwanaku or Early Pacajes.

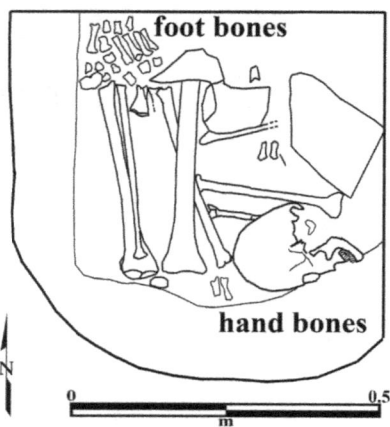

PAJAMA
Unit 4.10
Level 3
Feature 1
Human burial

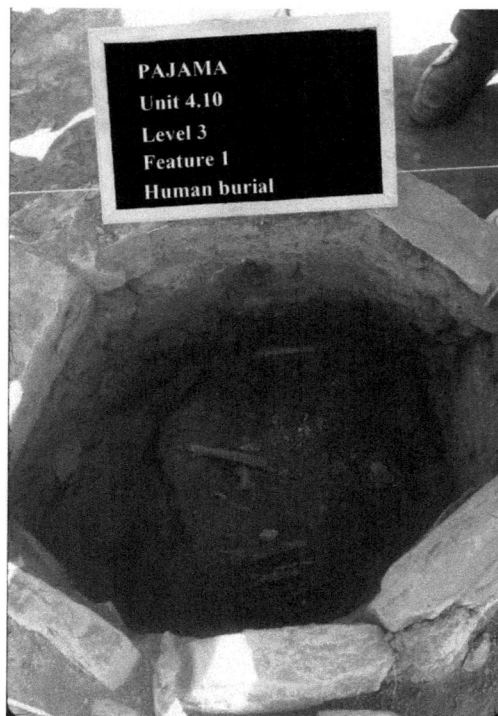

foot bones

hand bones

N

0   0.5
m

Figure 11.13 Rendering of the human interment of Feature 4.19.13.

Unlike the others, the interment of Feature 4.19.13 likely dated to the Late Formative **(Figure 11.13)**. It was located while conducting deep excavations in Unit 4.19 in 2006. The purpose of the 2006 excavation was to determine if there was any continuity between Late Formative and Tiwanaku period occupation in Sector 4. The burial was located in the southwest corner of Unit 4.19, stratigraphically below the foundation wall of Structure 4.2 and the oven. The interment consisted of a very well preserved adult person with no apparent burial offerings. The remains have yet to be analyzed by a bioarchaeologist. Assuming this was a Late Formative interment, it is one of only four known from Khonkho Wankane (see chapter 1).

Excavations in 2006

Follow-up excavations in 2006 focused on Unit 4.19. They were conducted specifically to determine whether the Tiwanaku occupations of Sector 4 were founded over Late Formative occupations; and if they were, to determine the character of the gradient between Late Formative and Tiwanaku occupations. It had been unclear whether there was or was not a hiatus between Late Formative and Tiwanaku occupations at Khonkho Wankane. Excavations in 2006 in Sector 4 and Sector 14 (Ohnstad 2007) indicated no stratigraphic hiatus. Excavations in two key long-term sectors indicate that Khonkho Wankane was continuously occupied from the Late Formative through the Tiwanaku periods. There is no evidence for a hiatus between Late Formative and Tiwanaku period occupations. The transformation from one 'period' to the next is one of predominant practices, technologies, and material assemblages.

Stratigraphic Profiles

Excavations in most units were shallow. Excavations in 2002 exposed deeper strata in certain units (4.13, 4.18–19) while excavations in 2006 sought to expose the cultural stratigraphy of the northernmost unit in Sector 4 (U.4.19). Local stratigraphy varied and in some instances was complex, so here I present them as numbered strata of increasing depth. A broad stratigraphic formula consisted of the following:

1. Plow zone/topsoil, 10–15 cm: brown sandy clay loam (7.5 YR 5/3)

2. Midden/Occupation Zone, 10–15 cm: dark reddish brown, hard sandy clay loam (5 YR 3/3)

3. Occupation Zone/Midden, 20–25 cm: dark reddish brown, soft sandy clay loam (5 YR 3/3)

4. Fill, 10–20 cm: dark reddish brown sandy clay with ash and burned soil (5 YR 3/3)

Most features associated with Structure 4.1 appear to have originated in Stratum 2. Features associated with Structure 4.2 appear to have originated in Strata 4.

Units 4.18 and 4.19 exposed deeper strata. The east profile of Unit 4.18 is somewhat representative of deeper strata and shows the relative position of three key features in the unit, U.4.18, F.4, U.4.18, F.5, and U.4.18, F.6 **(Figure 11.14, Table 11.1)**. The stratigraphy of this portion of Sector 4 consisted of the following major strata:

1. Plow zone/top soil, 10–25 cm, brown sandy clay loam (7.5 YR 5/3).

2. Midden/Occupation Zone, 10–15 cm, reddish brown sandy clay loam (5 YR 3/3)

3. Occupation Zone, 10–15 cm, reddish brown clay loam (5 YR 3/3)

4. Fill and Midden, 10–15 cm, dark reddish brown sandy clay (5 YR 4.5/3)

Three features located in the east portion of Unit 4.18 were deposited at the interface between strata 4 and 3. They demonstrated the following characteristics:

4.18, F.4 a lens-shaped deposit consisting of light reddish brown silt containing carbonized matter, burned earth, and light densities of ash, capped by a layer of pure, ground hematite.

Figure 11.14 East Profile of Unit 4.18, showing key features.

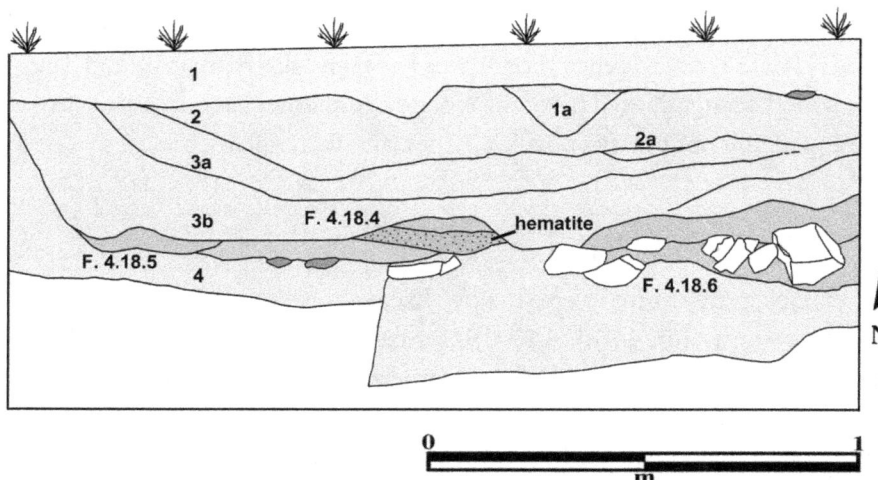

Table 11.1 East Profile of Unit 4.18

Stratum	Color	Soil Consistency/Interpretation
1	7.5YR 5/3	sandy clay loam/topsoil–plow zone
1a	7.5YR 4/4	sandy clay loam
2	5YR 3/3	compact silty clay loam
2a	5YR 4/3	silty clay loam
3a	5YR 4/3	loose silty clay loam
3b	5YR 4/3	loose silty clay loam with ash and carbon inclusions
4	5YR 3/3	compact sandy clay loam with baked soil inclusions
4.18, F. 4	5YR 3/2	soft ashy soil over hematite deposit
4.18, F. 5	10.5YR 3/2	greenish-gray ash with dense carbonized remains
4.18, F.6	10Y 7/1	greenish-gray ash with carbon, stone rubble

4.18, F.5 a shallow, localized, lens-shaped deposit consisting of dark and light-colored ash mixed with a sandy loam. Inclusions included carbonized matter and burned earth.

4.18, F.6 a more complex, lens-shaped pit of and angular field stones. It consisted of an upper matrix (4.18.6.1) of greenish-gray ash (10 Y 4/1) with fine inclusions of carbonized matter and burned earth. Its thinner, lower matrix (4.18.6.2) consisted of a compact, dark gray ash (7.5 YR 3/1) with coarser inclusions of carbonized matter and large field stones.

Unit 4.18 revealed a clear occupational stratum associated with residential and more specialized activities. The oven of Unit 4.19 post-dated this stratum. Specialized activity had a long term history in Sector 4 during the Tiwanaku period.

Conclusions

The north edge of the Wankane platform—our Sector 4—appears to have been inhabited continuously from the Late Formative through a substantial portion of the Tiwanaku period. Despite substantial post-depositional disturbance, this sector revealed some of the best evidence for Tiwanaku period residential activity at Khonkho Wankane. We hypothesize that it constituted part of a neighborhood of Tiwanaku period residential compounds. Like residential compounds at Tiwanaku and Lukurmata, this one included human interments. Deceased relatives were buried under vital living spaces.

Sector 4 was simultaneously dedicated to some specialized activity that transcended at least three superimposed occupations in this area. One strong hypothesis is that inhabitants of the complex produced ceramic vessels for several generations. We acknowledge that evidence for ceramic wasters and partially-baked vessels—relatively common in the ceramic production sector of Ch'iji Jawira in Tiwanaku—was relatively light. A secondary hypothesis is that Sector 4 was dedicated to producing metal objects. The nearby Corocoro range is rich with copper and silver ores. Yet we recovered no slag from nearby floors or middens.

It is also possible that inhabitants of Sector 4 continued a tradition of specialized production initiated at Khonkho Wankane during Late Formative 1 (Janusek 2009:40–42; Smith and Pérez Arias 2014). Early inhabitants of the southwest portion of Compound 3 dedicated themselves to the production of human interments and reliquaries. Key evidence for such production included vast quantities of lime and mineral pigment. While highly speculative, it is possible that Tiwanaku period inhabitants of Khonkho Wankane, already masters at transforming the dead, were conscripted into curating the deceased as part of their participation in Tiwanaku hegemony.

Chapter 12

⌇

Subsurface Cores and Test Excavations on the Wankane Mound

José Luís Paz Soria

Three complementary archaeological activities were conducted during the first season of the Jach'a Machaca Archaeological Project at Khonkho Wankane: 1) intra-site survey, 2) opening various test pits, and 3) extensive block excavations. The intra-site survey was aimed to identify the extent of the various cultural periods of occupation, and if possible, their respective activity areas (domestic, ceremonial, funerary, etc.). To fulfill this commitment, we proceeded to: 1) undertake a systematic collection of surface materials by stratified sampling, 2) conduct geophysical survey using ground-penetrating radar and electro-magnetic resistivity, and 3) conduct geological coring to gain an understanding of the relationship of variable surface (soil color changes, elevation differences, and changes in the density and type of vegetation) and sub-surface conditions.

Subsequently, in sectors where archaeologists identified Formative and Tiwanaku occupations, several small-scale excavations and test pits were placed in order to verify more robustly whether surface deposits corresponded with subsurface depositions and to ascertain the nature of their stratigraphic deposition. All of this work was supplemented by block area excavations to understand specific monumental, residential, and mortuary sectors of the site (see chapters 6–11 and 13). Within this framework, I carried out the following tasks: 1) geological coring during the intra-site survey, and 2) opening of three test pits and one small-scale block excavation on the north slope of the Wankane mound. Excavation areas were denominated Sectors 5 and 8 (Figures 1.4 and 12.1).

Subsurface Cores

The site of Khonkho Wankane is characterized by numerous architectural features (walls and stone alignments corresponding to an undetermined number of structures and buried platforms) and surface indicators (subtle changes in soil coloration, marking differences in elevation and fine differences in the density and type of vegetation) that are differentially interspersed on the surface. These characteristics necessitated the use of a geological hand auger with a 2-inch diameter in order to: 1) determine the number and nature of

Figure 12.1 Plan of Sector 8 excavations. Base map by Scott Smith.

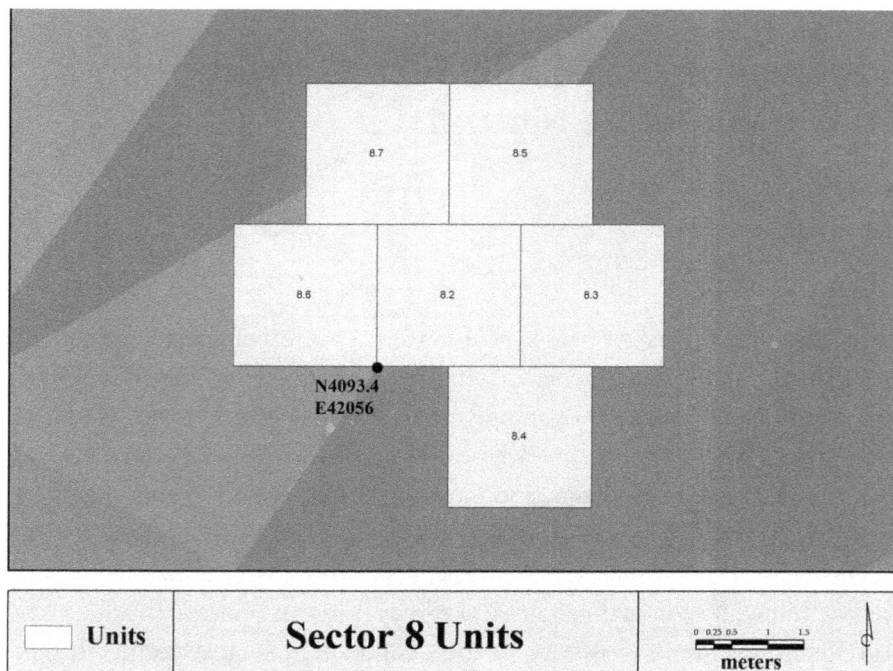

stratigraphic events within the architectural features and below the surface indicators, 2) identify evidence for cultural activity (organic deposits, archaeological features, and abrupt interfaces), and 3) to obtain diagnostic material (Barba 1990; Hester et al. 1997; Roskams 2001). The results presented below summarize the results of coring.

The core samples taken on the central part of the Wankane mound revealed a thick stratum of lamellar structure, consisting of sandy loam and loose soil, attributed perhaps due to the erosion of adobe walls. The entire sector is within the monumental core, and although the coring did not detect formally constructed floors, we were able to identify faint yellow clay lenses where few existing materials are concentrated. Possibly, the walls of these large enclosures were raised first, and then the structures were occupied without further considerations, perhaps because of the large investment of time and labor demanded in the placement of a formal floor. A more likely interpretation is that the absence of a floor is the result of its degradation due to the constant action of natural disturbance processes. Additionally, a lower stratum of orange, granular, silty clay loam, undoubtedly deposited due to water or wind action (Schiffer 1996; Waters 1992), is overly compact, despite its status as pre-cultural sub-soil, revealing an intense and sustained episode of trampling.

The south slope of the mound revealed a curious variety of stratigraphic deposits in the current vicinity of the Jinch'unkala and Wila Kala monoliths. Around the monoliths, we recorded a complex sequence of thin grayish, clay-rich sediments devoid of cultural materials. Excessive soil moisture due to the proximity of the water table resulted in the suspension of this work. The east and west sectors of the mound appear to be large residential platforms. Nevertheless, core samples identified only two small strata of orange granular silty clay loam lacking in cultural material similar to that recovered under the center of the mound.

The north portion and slope of the mound revealed the most interesting finds. We identified a large area with several superimposed strata of differing soil types, in addition to various abrupt interfaces of a grayish color containing a good deal of cultural material. These attributes warranted the placement of several excavation units in this area. The first three of these units (Sectors 5 and 8), located on the north slope of the mound, are described below. Excavations in Sector 4, located on the platform south of Sector 8, are described in chapter 11.

Finally, the team drilled core samples on the smaller Putuni mound some 200 meters north of Wankane. Atop this promontory cores identified several irregularly distributed grayish clay lenses, which seem to be a characteristic of Tiwanaku period occupation at the site. Paradoxically, the cores from the south slope of Putuni did not find any trace of sub-soil cultural activity, despite the considerable amount of artifacts and stains on its surface.

In conclusion, the use of a geological augur allowed us to locate several cultural features below the surface. Nevertheless, the survey was less successful in and near the monumental core, where many sub-surface soils appear to be relatively 'clean' and free of dense cultural lenses and artifacts.

Test Excavations

Each of the three pits was initiated based on the results of the core samples and according to specific objectives, which will be mentioned at the beginning of each stratigraphic description. Two-by-two meter test pits were excavated using stratigraphic criteria, although exceptionally, arbitrary levels were applied in problematic contexts or when it was necessary to better control deposits which were substantially thick. In addition, complex stratigraphic sequences and excessive moisture retention in the deeper layers hindered the separation of some events. Despite this drawback, most contexts, both cultural and natural, were adequately differentiated during excavation. Additionally, Unit 8.2 preceded the opening of several contiguous units, due to the discovery of a structure near the surface in one of its side-walls. These additional units were excavated in order to better define the characteristics and dimensions of the structure.

In order to register stratigraphic deposition, individual forms were used for strata, features, and burials. The Kroeninberg Method was used to identify soil texture, and the soil color was established using Munsell color charts. Cultural features and stratigraphic profiles were recorded in plan and profile drawings and conventional photo-graphic registries (Harris 1989; Hester et al. 1997; Roskams 2001).

Cultural materials (ceramics, lithics, bones, etc.) from each stratum were recovered in a quarter-inch screen, but the artifacts and carbon samples associated with cultural features (structures, burials, pits, etc.) and use surfaces were registered and collected individually using three-dimensional coordinates (Joukowsky 1980; Renfrew and Bahn 1991; Roskams 2001). Flotation samples were collected using three-dimensional registration for subsequent archaeobotanical analysis (Hastorf et al. 1996). Upon completion of an excavation, the corners of test pits were marked with materials to facilitate their future location, and then they were back-filled with sieved soil to prevent the collapse of the profiles and the accumulation of moisture.

Unit 5.1

Early excavations in Sector 3, on the northwest portion of the mound, revealed several Tiwanaku period tombs while augur tests identified complex stratigraphic sequences in their vicinity. Test Unit 5.1 was opened on the flat portion of the mound southeast of Sector 3. It revealed a complex stratigraphic profile (**Figure 12.2, Table 12.1**).

Highlights in the analysis of this stratigraphic sequence include the following:

1. Several ash lenses (Features 1 through 6) of variable thickness were interspersed with strata of natural origin. These ash lenses may represent pre-Hispanic use surfaces, since they have abrupt interfaces that originated due to a sudden accumulation of sediments over a stable deposit (Walters 1992). Moreover, the lenses are irregular and discontinuous across the length and width of the unit and slightly more compact than the natural strata, typical of occupation surfaces (Thierry et al. 1993; Matthews et al. 1997; Schiffer 1996). The lenses revealed relatively low densities of materials, which may indicate that the activities associated with them were occasional.

    Yet other explanations are possible. The lenses may be secondary sheet middens created by dumping the ashy residues of activities conducted in the monumental core to the south and east, or even, in part, the result of periodic water-based erosion of ashy deposits from those higher portions of the mound.

2. The sources contributing to the deposits appear to have changed over time, since the upper strata (I through V) consisted of *loamy* silty clay, while the lower strata (VI through VIII) consisted of *sandy* silty clay. Tentatively, we believe that that the upper deposits were altered

Figure 12.2   View of west profile of Unit 5.1.

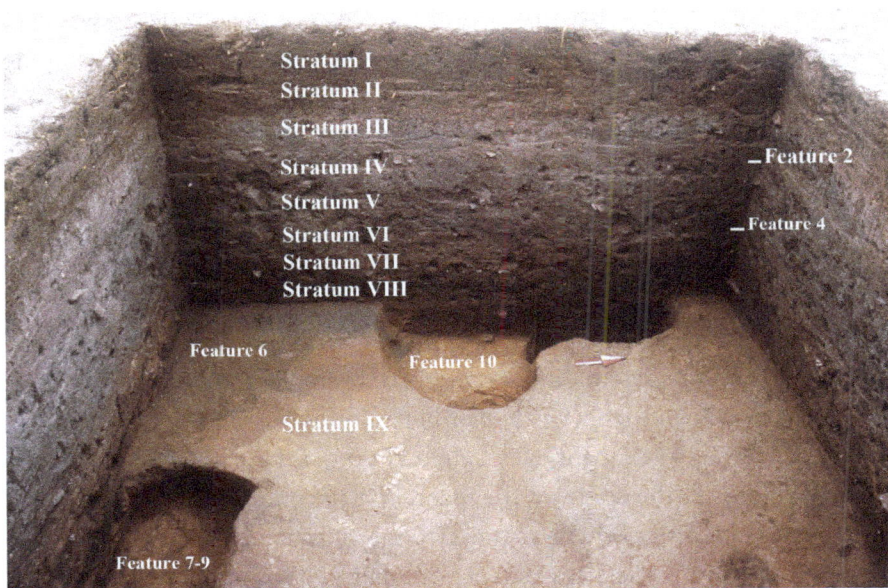

Table 12.1   West profile of Unit 5.1

Stratum	Color	Soil Consistency/Interpretation
I	7.5YR 3/4	sandy clay loam/topsoil-plow zone
II	7.5YR 3/3	silty clay loam/plow zone
III	7.5YR 3/3	silty clay loam
IV	7.5 YR 4/3	silty clay loam
V	7.5YR 4/3	silty clay loam
VI	7.5YR 3/4	sandy clay loam
VII	7.5YR 3/4	sandy clay loam
VIII	7.5YR 3/4	sandy clay loam
IX	7.5YR 3/4	sandy loam/cultural fill or precultural substrate
Feature 2	5Y 6/2	clay loam/greenish-gray ash lens
Feature 4	10YR 3/3	clay loam/ash lens
Feature 6	10YR 3/3	thin ash lens
Features 7–9	10YR 3/3–3/6	ashy-sandy loam/refuse pit
Feature 10	10YR 3/3	silty loam with clay lenses/refuse pit

through plow-zone activity, which affected the inclusion of silt in the soil matrix and generated slight changes in the color matrix. In contrast, the deeper strata may have been formed by the erosion of adobe walls, etc., in higher eroded areas, which would have contributed a greater amount of sand to the texture of the strata and influenced the orientation of the materials according the inclination of the slope.

3. The deposits are slightly thicker in the south profile, owing to the three-degree incline of the strata relative to the slope. This does not apply to the events registered below (Strata VIII and IX and Features 7–9 and 10), because their surfaces were virtually horizontal.

4. Intrusive pits excavated into pre-cultural soil (i.e., Features 7–9 and 10) tended to be similar in texture (loamy silt) and in soil color (dark brown), but there were also notable differences in the form, base, cut, and the size of these features, and even in their inclusions (e.g., the absence of guinea pig crania in Feature 10). Such differences suggest that the features represent different uses. For example, the first pit (Features 7–9) may have been a ritual offering, as it was *respected* by not being disturbed by subsequent events. In addition, its base and cut were more elaborate. To the contrary, the second pit (Feature 10) appears to be a refuse pit, since other pits intruded into it (characteristic of such features during the Tiwanaku period). Further, its walls and base were simpler.

5. There are marked differences in the clay lenses within these features. For example, in the first case (i.e., Features 7–9), the clay lens is undoubtedly intentional, and probably would have served to separate and/or preserve the contents of the feature as at other Tiwanaku sites. In the second case (i.e., Feature 10), the clay lenses were more randomly deposited and slightly inclined.

Unit 8.1

Geological cores in the north sector of the site detected an extensive area of human occupation bisected by the thick wall of a much-deteriorated platform. The upper part of this platform, Sector 4, was further exposed in a block excavation (chapter 11), while the lower sloping portion, Sector 8, was first excavated in Test Unit 8.1. This unit was excavated in order to observe the stratigraphic deposition on both sides of this architectural feature. Its stratigraphic sequence was highly complex (**Figure 12.3, Table 12.2**).

Analysis of this complex stratigraphic sequence established that:

1. The strata were irregularly distributed relative to the length and width of the unit and were variable in thickness, surface form, texture, and color. This great diversity was due to the action of differing contributing factors during the process of site formation. For example, the orange colored strata which had a higher inclusion of clay (e.g., Strata III, V) may have formed from the erosion of adobe walls. Conversely, deposits with inclusions of silt and of darker colors (Features 1, 2, and

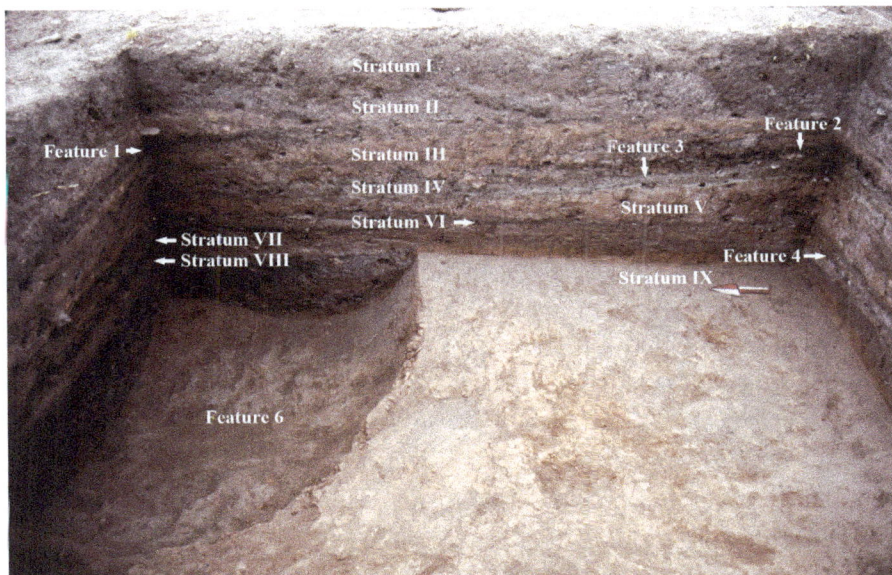

Figure 12.3   View of east profile of Unit 8.1.

Table 12.2   East profile of Unit 8.1

Stratum	Color	Soil Consistency/Interpretation
I	10YR 4/3	sandy clay loam/topsoil–plow zone
II	10YR 4/3	silty clay loam/plow zone
III	5YR 4/4	silty clay loam
IV	7.5YR 3/3	silty clay loam
V	7.5YR 3/3	clay loam
VI	7.5YR3/4	silty clay loam
VII	7.5YR 3/3	silty clay loam
VIII	5YR 3/4	silty clay loam
IX	5YR 3/4	clay loam/cultural fill or precultural substrate
Feature 1	7.5YR 4/3	sandy clay loam/ash lens
Feature 2	10YR 4/2	sandy clay loam/ash lens with carbon
Feature 3	2.5Y 4/3	sandy clay loam/continuous greenish–gray ash lens
Feature 4	7.5YR 4/4	sandy clay loam/ash lens
Feature 5	7.5YR 3/4	clay loam/ash lens
Feature 6	10YR 3/4	sandy loam/refuse pit

4) seem to have originated from the decomposition of organic matter (Schiffer 1996; Stein 1992; Waters 1992).

2. Lower events (Strata VI through IX) were horizontal, but from Stratum V up to Stratum II, including intermediate features, the slope ascended six degrees to the south. This marked change in slope can be

attributed to a rapid accumulation of sediments and/or changes in the direction of erosion. This undoubtedly had an impact on the distribution of cultural materials (Petraglia 1993; Rosen 1993; Schiffer 1996), although its impact is unknown at the site of Khonkho Wankane.

3. The occupational surfaces (Feature 3 and Strata VI and VIII) are better defined than those of the last test pit, despite their thinness, because they were very horizontal, had continuity for almost the entirety of the unit, contained a good deal of associated materials, and were more compact. Interestingly, the faint concentration of carbon flecks on the use surfaces indicates that after some activities were completed a small amount of ash was immediately deposited. These features lead us to think that these were the result of more formal/stable occupations rather than representing a brief or occasional use.

4. Feature 6 presents several attributes that make it comparable to Feature 10 of Unit 5.1, for example, the concave walls, the rear intrusion of a smaller pit, and its location above the sterile soil. However, there are radical differences in texture and content. Regarding the texture, this feature does not have an organic character, but tends to be sandy, and erosion of the slope likely filled the event. Regarding the content, the presence of several irregular sand lenses can be attributed to the disintegration of the adobe cores, or perhaps, to the gradual erosion of the outer part. These considerations lead us to think of a large feature that was open for a considerable period of time, and most likely pit lined with pre–Hispanic adobes or perhaps part of an enormous *midden*.

Units 8.2.–8.7

Unit 8.2 was also excavated in the lower portion of the north platform, some thirty meters west of Unit 8.1. The objective of this test pit was to obtain a second stratigraphic sample to compare with the complex stratigraphy of Unit 8.1. Upon locating the foundation walls for the southeast corner of a pre-Hispanic structure (Feature 1) in the east profile of the unit, five additional units were opened (Units 8.3–8.7) around Unit 8.2 **(Figure 12.4)**. These six units invariably demonstrated the same stratigraphy: an upper plow zone covering a second horizon (Stratum II). Units 8.2 and 8.3 revealed the heavily disturbed portions of a thin use surface associated with both sides of the foundation. Once the remnant walls were defined, it was decided to continue excavating deeper in places where an occupation surface was unclear (for example, Unit 8.6). However, a 40 cm space in the south profile was left intact in order to preserve the foundations of adobe that existed in that area.

The complex stratigraphy of Units 8.2–8.7 merits discussion: **(Figure 12.5 and Table 12.3)**:

Figure 12.4   View of remnant Tiwanaku structural foundation in Sector 8, facing east.

Figure 12.5   View of south profile of Unit 8.6, highlighting the profile of Feature 9 (human burial).

Table 12.3 South Profile of Unit 8.6

Stratum	Color	Soil Consistency/Interpretation
I	7.5YR 4/4	sandy clay loam/topsoil–plow zone
II	7.5YR 3/4	sandy clay loam
III	7.5YR 3/4	clay loam
IV	7.5YR 3/3	clay loam
V	7.5YR3/4	silty clay loam
VI	7.5YR 3/4	sandy clay loam
VII	7.5YR 3/4	silty clay loam with high density of stones
VIII	5 YR 4/4	clay loam/cultural fill or precultural soil
Feature 9	10YR 4/2	silty clay loam/human burial

1. Strata I and II constituted the plow-zone. Both had the same texture and color, but showed slight differences in hue. The division between these two deposits may be fictitious, as both would form a single event.

2. Regarding the pre-Hispanic structure, the discontinuity of the stones in the foundations and the dispersion of several worked stones in Strata II are likely due to the destructive action of plowing. The unprecedented conservation of its southeast corner seems to be due to either the greater durability of mortar here, or perhaps to the conjunction that offered additional strength to this part of the structure.

3. The use surface of the building was best preserved adjacent to the foundations, but it was apparent on both inside and outside of the corner. Both areas revealed a low density of cultural material. Yet no well-prepared floor was found associated with the structure. It may be that the structure had no formally constituted floor, but it may also be that centuries of plowing and erosion have degraded and destroyed it.

4. The small area of the excavation, the large number of intrusive pits, and the great heterogeneity of the deposits render stratigraphic interpretations difficult. The structure was undoubtedly used for an extended period of time, but its particular purpose—residence, storage, temporary housing, etc.—remains unclear.

5. A burial (Feature 9) was clearly associated with the structure, as the tomb's upper orifice descends from the level of the structure's surface (i.e., Stratum II) (Figure 12.5). Ceramic offerings in the burial included a Tiwanaku style *kero* and *tazon* (Figures 12.6 and 12.7). Other features and events originated well below the surface and did not have direct contact with the building, indicating that they likely pre-dated its construction. It is clear that this structure was built over pre-existing

Figure 12.6   Aerial view of human burial 8.6, Feature 9, highlighting vessel offerings.

Figure 12.7   The red-slipped *kero* and *tazon* interred with human burial 8.6, Feature 9 (photos by John Janusek).

deposition, but it is unclear whether it had a temporal (i.e., during the same phase of occupation) or functional (e.g., reoccupation of the domestic area) link with the underlying sequence.

6.   The tomb consisted of an intrusive cut 80 cm deep and 70 cm in diameter. It lacked clearly-defined cist walls and intruded into an extensive refuse pit below. Once the burial was excavated, its bottom was leveled to facilitate placement of a flat ceramic slab, perhaps to separate the lower earlier event, and the body of an adult was placed on top (**Figure 12.8**). Although the human remains were fragmentary, osteological analysis indicated that the individual was a probable male between 50 and 80 years old at the time of death. The individual was buried in a seated position, leaning slightly on his vertebral column. After the flesh decomposed, the cranium, torso, and upper

Figure 12.8 Poorly-preserved human remains resting on a stone slab at the base of tomb U. 8.6, Feature 9.

extremities fell on the rest of the body due to the weight of deposition above. Within the fill used to cover the burial was a pile of stones that included an exhausted ground stone tool. The upper tomb was filled with silt loam up to the level of the structure surface.

7. Two pits that intruded into sterile soil (i.e., Features 5–6 and 9–B) are somewhat amorphous and share three characteristics: a) they are enormous, b) they contain dense quantities of material, especially camelid bones, and c) they were not covered, verifying their status as open pits. Soil fill varied widely between and within them; textures ranged from clayey silt to loamy silty clay, colors ranged from dark brown to dark grayish brown, and artifacts other than camelid bones, ceramic sherds, and lithic debitage varied.

I believe the pits were excavated for different purposes. Feature 5–6 likely was a refuse and/or an adobe pit based on its similarities to other events (i.e., Feature 10 of Unit 5.1 and Feature 6 of Unit 8.1). By contrast, Feature 9–B included two partial camelids and thus may include the residues of offerings.

Conclusions

Three test units and a small block excavation allowed us to generate an overview of 1) the stratigraphic deposition and 2) the sequence of occupation in two sectors of the northern portion of the Wankane mound. Stratigraphic deposits resulted from a combination of natural and cultural processes. Erosion by wind and water contributed significantly to the overall form of the Wankane and Putuni mounds. This included early weathering of the pre-cultural stratum of clay-rich soils and later weathering of human occupations on the mounds. Other natural processes included the erosion of the adobe walls such as those that the partial foundation exposed in Sector 8 would have supported. Another possible result of erosion was the sloping, fine strata exposed in Unit 5.1, which may be a result of erosion from the central part of the mound.

Judging by their associated materials, all of the features appear to date to the Tiwanaku period. Analysis of these contexts suggests a sequence of occupation consisting of two pre-Hispanic stages. The first phase corresponds to the intrusive pits excavated into pre-cultural soil (i.e., Features 7–9 and 10 of Unit 5.1, Feature 6 of Unit 8.1 and Features 5–6 and 9B of Unit 8.6). Unit profiles did not show cuts descending from the upper events, and it is likely these features are contemporaneous. When compared to one another, it can be seen that each was unique in form and content.

Several of the pits (i.e., Features 7–9 and 10 of Unit 5.1, and Features 5–6 and 9B of Unit 8.6) were located only a few centimeters away from each other, and in some cases, smaller pits had intruded into the larger, earlier ones. The concentration of features in Sector 8, in particular, cannot be attributed to a lack of space at the site, since the Wankane mound alone is larger than 10 ha in total area. Rather, this sector likely was home to a permanent, intensive residential occupation much like those exposed at Tiwanaku and Lukurmata (Bermann 1994; Janusek 2004). Test Unit 5.1, on the other hand, revealed either—or both—superimposed sheet middens or refuse eroded from the higher, central portion of the Wankane platform. The remains of a pre-Hispanic structure and an intrusive burial (Feature 9) manifest a second phase of occupation. The function of this structure is unknown; it is difficult to infer its use based on the excavation of an isolated corner. Bermann (1994) and Janusek (2004) encountered similar structures at Tiwanaku and Lukurmata. After the structure was abandoned, erosion of the adobe walls produced several superimposed clay-rich lenses that covered the foundations and its remnant surface. The human burial associated with the structure is similar to Tiwanaku period burials at Tiwanaku and Lukurmata, in the form of the cist, the position of the interred individual, and the inclusion of distinctive Tiwanaku style ceramic vessels.

Test excavations identified a long sequence of occupation and secondary debris on two sectors of the north Wankane mound. Excavations in Sector 5 exposed stratified secondary midden deposits. Excavations in Sector 8 exposed part of a primary Tiwanaku period domestic occupation. Early occupations in this sector include large, deep pits excavated into pre-cultural strata. Later occupations consist of the southeast corner of a structure—likely a domestic structure—associated with a subterranean cist burial. Though occupations were heavily disturbed by centuries of natural erosion and human plowing, future excavations in both sectors may shed further light into the occupational history of two sectors that incorporate particularly dense residues of human occupation at the site.

Chapter 13

ᢗᢞ

Investigations on the Putuni Mound

Jake R. Fox

In 2002, project members initiated excavation on the east and south sides of the Putuni mound. We designated these areas Sectors 10 and 11, respectively. Investigations on the east side of the mound took the form of a wide trench that produced a stratigraphic cross-section of that portion of the mound (**Figure 13.1**). This portion of the mound is relatively steep and has been eroded by the flow of a stream descending from a spring in the Corocoro range to

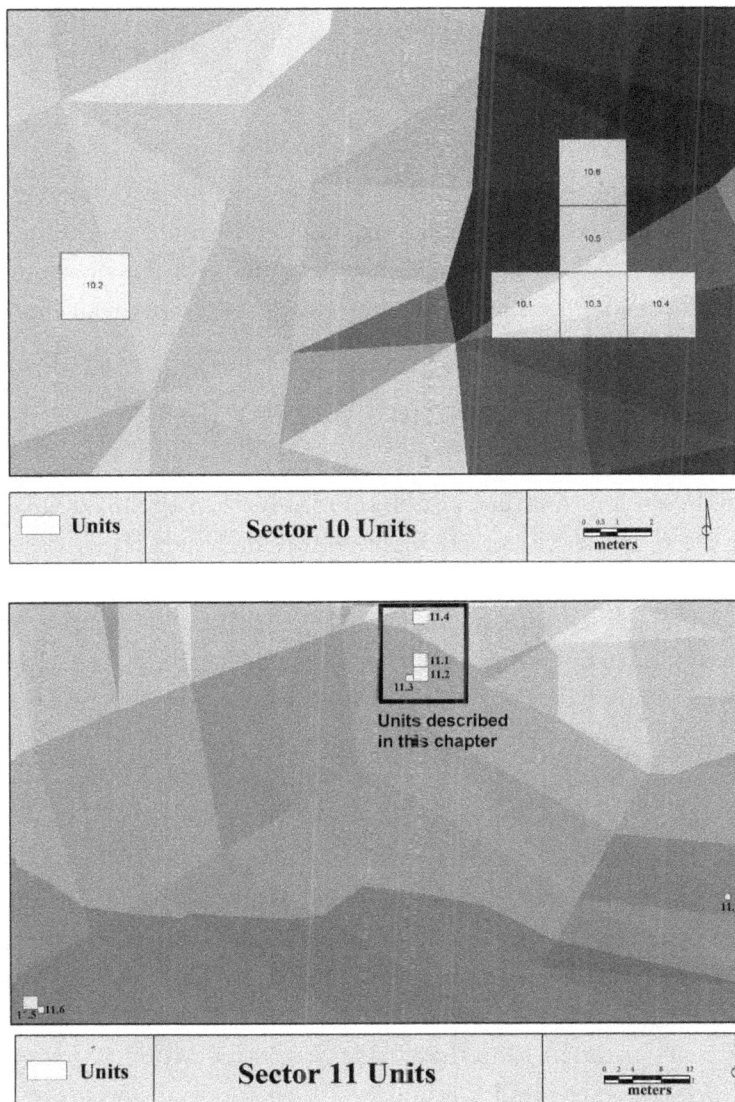

Figure 13.1 Plans of Sector 10 and 11 excavations. Base maps by Scott Smith.

the north **(Figure 13.2)**. Unit 10.2 was excavated directly west of the trench, on the high, level portion of the mound. On the south side of the mound, the portion that faces the larger Wankane mound, excavations exposed at least one surface and a number of features dating to the Tiwanaku period.

Putuni East Excavation: Sector 10

Two excavations took place on the eroded east face of the Putuni mound. The first was a trench comprising units—10.1, 10.3, and 10.4—that collectively measured 2 m × 6 m **(Figure 13.3)**. The location for the Putuni East trench was chosen based on the presence of dense Late Formative ceramic sherds beneath the steep mound face. The sherds appeared to be eroding out of a low, dark band of soil that was visible in stratigraphic exposures across the east side of Putuni.

The uppermost 10–15 cm of soil in the trench excavation contained low densities of ceramic sherds, most of which appear to date to the Tiwanaku period. No features or surfaces were observed in these deposits. Beneath this plow zone we encountered culturally sterile strata of sediments that extended to a depth of 140 cm below the surface in the west part of the unit. These sterile deposits were underlain by a very thin sandy stratum of midden-like sediment high in organic content and ash **(Figure 13.4)**. This sandy organic deposit—stratum 14 in the profile illustration—corresponds with the dark band visible on the eroded east side of the mound and appears to represent an

Figure 13.3   View of excavated Units 10.1, 10.3, and 10.4, facing southwest.

occupation surface, though we located no constructed floor or clear features associated with it. The inference of a surface is based on its horizontal orientation and organic content, patterns that contrast with the culturally sterile and discontinuous stratigraphy of overlying layers.

In addition, our team recovered a number of splintered camelid bone fragments and Late Formative ceramic cooking wares in Stratum 14. Although artifact densities were relatively low, they were exclusively associated with Stratum14 and no other superimposed stratum. Stratum 14 was underlain by an extremely compact stratum of homogeneous clay (Stratum 15). This deposit was sterile, and probably represents the top of the natural landform that preceded the Late Formative period occupation.

Putuni East stratigraphy was complex **(Figure 13.4 and Table 13.1)**. Most strata contained high volumes of discontinuous inclusions of clay chunks, sandy silts, and gravel. In general, sediments were extremely poorly sorted, with inclusions varying widely in size, texture, color, and composition. The deposits cannot be attributed strictly to geomorphic—that is, alluvial or aeolian—processes. Because they do not slope down from the edge of the mound and because their composition cannot be accounted for from uphill deposits, colluvial deposition is unlikely. Stratum 14 was the only flat-lying stratum that did not include high volumes of randomly-sorted inclusions. It contained much higher densities of artifacts and organic debris than any of its overlying layers. Later research determined that Stratum 14 comprised a palimpsest of

Figure 13.4 South stratigraphic profile of Units 10.1, 10.3, and 10.4.

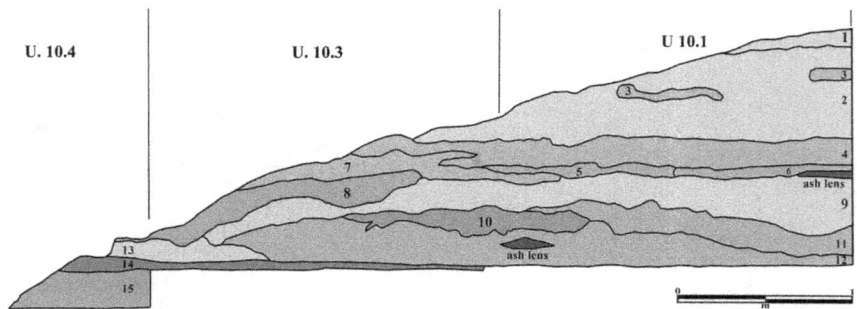

Table 13.1   South Profile of Units 10.1, 10.3, and 10.4

Stratum	Color	Soil Consistency/Interpretation
1	7.5YR 4/3	silty loam; topsoil-plow zone
2	7.5YR 5/3	compact sandy-silty loam mottled with clay chunks
3	7.5YR 4/3	compact sandy silt
4	5YR 4/3	compact clay loam
5	5YR 4/1	mottled sandy clay loam; some organic content
6	7.5YR 4/6	compact sandy clay loam
7	7.5YR 4/3	loosely packed silty sand
8	5YR 5/4	highly compact silty loam
9	7.5YR 4/4	compact sandy loam mottled with clay chunks
10	7.5YR 4/4	moderately compact sand
11	7.5YR 5/3	compact sandy clay loam mottled with clay
12	7.5YR 5/3	moderately compact sandy loam
13	7.5YR 4/4	compact clay loam
14	7.5YR 4/2	loose sandy loam with artifacts; occupation surfaces
15	5YR 4/4	compact clay loam; precultural substrate

temporary occupations dating to the early portion of the Late Formative (50 BC–AD 200) (Janusek 2015; Ohnstad 2007).

Our analyses suggest some preliminary conclusions. Putuni was constructed over a long history and its Late Formative composition differed substantially from its Tiwanaku incarnation. Late Formative 1 Putuni mound occupations pre-dated the construction events that produced the Tiwanaku platform. Stratum 14 is visible for over 40 m along the east side of the Putuni platform, indicating that it was extensive under the Putuni platform. The poorly mixed sediments overlying this Late Formative occupation constitute mound construction fill. The density of the fill deposits and the absence of cultural or organic materials within them indicates that they were deposited either as a single event or as a quick series of events. Judging their stratigraphic position, this took place sometime after early Late Formative 1 and before the Tiwanaku period, and likely during Late Formative 2 (AD 300–500).

These conclusions cannot be generalized to the Putuni mound as a whole. Whatever construction did occur, it is not possible to say whether this altered the entire Putuni mound or simply aggrandized its east portion. Yet even if construction was limited to the east side of the mound, the extent of Stratum 14 points to a substantial labor investment in mound construction between Late Formative and Tiwanaku occupations.

Test Unit 10.1 measured 2 m × 2 m and was opened 10 m west of the west edge of the three-unit trench. This location is atop the flat part of the Putuni mound and away from its eroded eastern slope. In this unit we observed a pattern reminiscent of the trench. The upper 10 cm of the unit produced a small number of Tiwanaku sherds and faunal remains. Below this depth, deposits quickly shifted to sterile deposits of very high density similar to those just to the east. It was impractical to excavate the unit to the depth of Stratum 14, so excavation was discontinued after three arbitrary levels. We hypothesized that this inner part of the mound was characterized by the same kind of earthen platform construction witnessed in the three units to the east.

Putuni South Excavations: Sector 11

Excavations in Sector 11 sought to expose pre-Hispanic occupations and architectural elements in an area of extremely high artifact density. As in much of the Putuni mound, most of the sherds on the surface were of Tiwanaku style, but we observed a significant number of Formative Period sherds and a handful of Inka sherds as well. Excavations included four units **(Figures 13.5 and 13.6)**; 11.1 (2 m × 2 m), 11.2 (2 m × 2 m), 11.3 (1 m × 1 m), and 11.4 (2 m ×

Figure 13.5   Plan of Sector 11 excavations showing notable features.

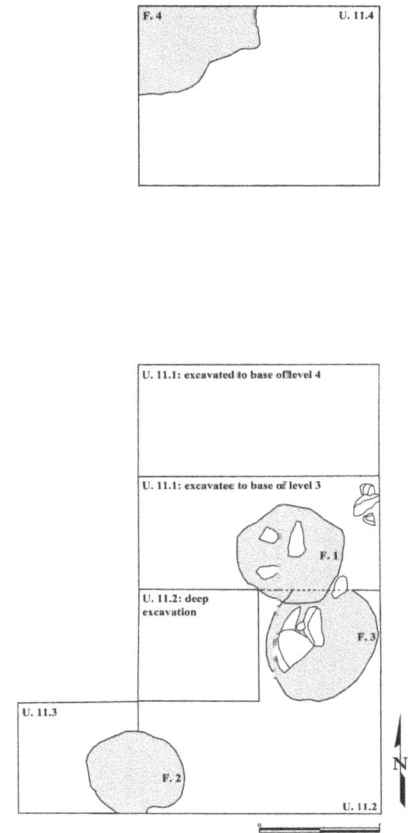

Figure 13.6   View of Sector 11 excavations, facing north.

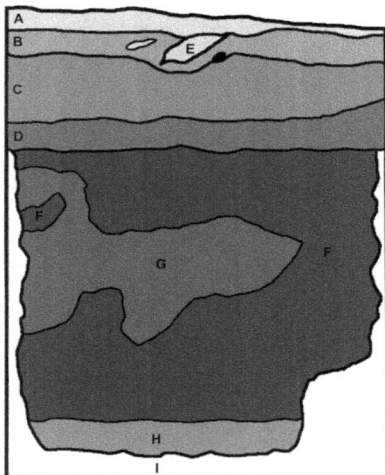

Figure 13.7 Stratigraphic profile of northeast quadrant of Unit 11.2.

2 m). Units 11.1–11.3 were contiguous and yielded Features 1–3. Unit 11.4 was placed 2 meters to the north of Unit 11.1 and it exposed Feature 4. Excavations revealed several Tiwanaku period features, including two refuse pits, a large bell-shaped pit, and a stone-lined tomb.

Stratigraphy in the area was best observed in Unit 11.2 (**Figure 13.7**). Strata A, B, C, and D all contained extremely high densities of artifacts in all units of Sector 11. This undoubtedly is a result, in part, of continued deflation of the surface through plowing and aeolian erosion. Artifacts included high volumes of faunal material and ceramic sherds, which included a number of Tiwanaku polychrome vessel and *incensario* fragments. Strata A and B had been heavily disturbed by later plowing and other activities. Strata C and D appeared less mixed and generally better preserved, but their lack of clear features or surfaces left them difficult to interpret.

The stratigraphic transition from Stratum D to F suggested the presence of a possible surface (**Table 13.2**). Stratum F consisted of a very compact clay loam, and possibly represented a clay floor. The suggestion that the top of Stratum F was an actual surface is supported by two main observations. First, the upper portions of Features 2, 3, and 4 (all subterranean pits of one sort or another) all were first identifiable at the top of Stratum F. Second, a quadrant of Stratum F that contained no feature was excavated in Unit 11.1. This excavation produced culturally sterile clay soil, supporting the notion that the top of Stratum F constituted the original surface of the Putuni mound during its in initial Late Formative or Tiwanaku occupation. Unlike Sector 10, none of the stratigraphy in Sector 11 suggests that this portion of the mound was amplified as a platform.

Table 13.2   East Profile of northeast quadrant of Unit 11.2, featuring Feature 3

Stratum	Color	Soil Consistency / Interpretation
A	7.5YR 4/3	silty loam; topsoil-plow zone
B	7.5YR 5/3	moderately compact sandy-silty loam
C	7.5YR 5/3	moderately compacted sandy loam
D	5YR 5/4	highly compacted orange-brown loam
E	10YR 6/2	loose, soft, sandy ash inclusion
F	7.5YR 6/3	extremely compact clay loam
G	5YR 6/4	moderately compact light brown loam
H	7.5YR 5/4	loosely compacted light brown sand
I	5YR 5/4	tomb floor; highly compacted orange-brown sandy loam

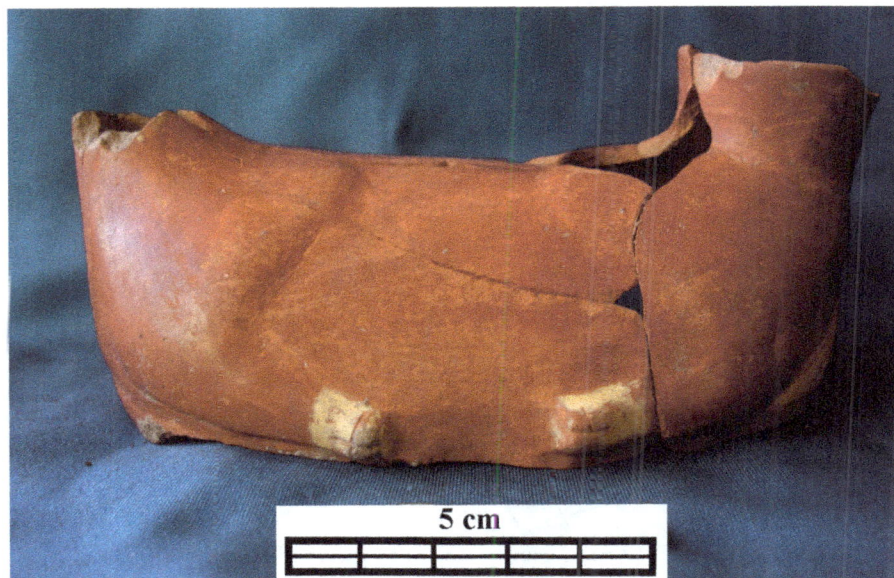

Figure 13.8   Llama effigy vessel deposited in U11.1, Feature 1 (photo by John Janusek).

5 cm

Following, I detail the four principal pit features identified in Sector 11. Feature 1 was an ash/refuse pit, the top of which had been disturbed by plowing. The feature cut through Strata C and D. The pit was located in the southeast corner of Unit 11.1 and intruded just slightly into the northeast corner of Unit 11.2. It was roughly circular in plan and 90 cm in diameter. The disturbed upper portion of the feature was first visible at approximately 22 cm below the surface and reached a maximum depth of 41 cm below the surface. The base of the pit contained a number of unworked stones. We recovered a large number of ceramic sherds from within this pit, including several fragments of a red-slipped llama effigy vessel and a high volume of camelid bone **(Figure 13.8)**. Small fragments of pigment and possible metal were also collected.

Feature 2 was a large bell-shaped pit that first appeared in the southwest corner of Unit 11.2 **(Figure 13.9, Table 13.3)**. Unit 11.3 was initiated as a 1 m × 1 m extension to this unit in order to excavate the feature entirely. The top appeared approximately 20 cm below the surface, in the sloping south portion of Sector 11. In relation to the broader stratigraphy of this sector, this places the origin of the feature at the likely surface between Strata 2 and 3 (or D and F).

Table 13.3   South Profile of Unit 11.2

Stratum	Color	Soil Consistency/Interpretation
1	7.5YR 4/3	silty loam; topsoil—plow zone
2	7.5YR 5/3	compact sandy–silty loam
3	7.5YR 4/3	compact sandy loam; possible occupation surface
Feature 2	10YR 5/2	Sandy ash with carbonized camelid dung

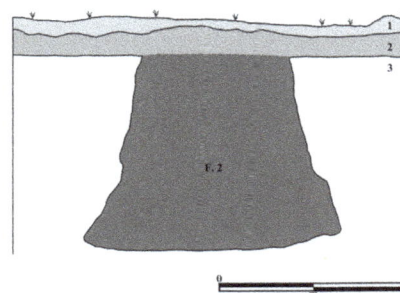

Figure 13.9   South profile of Feature 2 and vicinity. No clear stratigraphy was identified in the feature itself.

Figure 13.10 Trichrome kero found at the base of Feature 2 (photo by John Janusek).

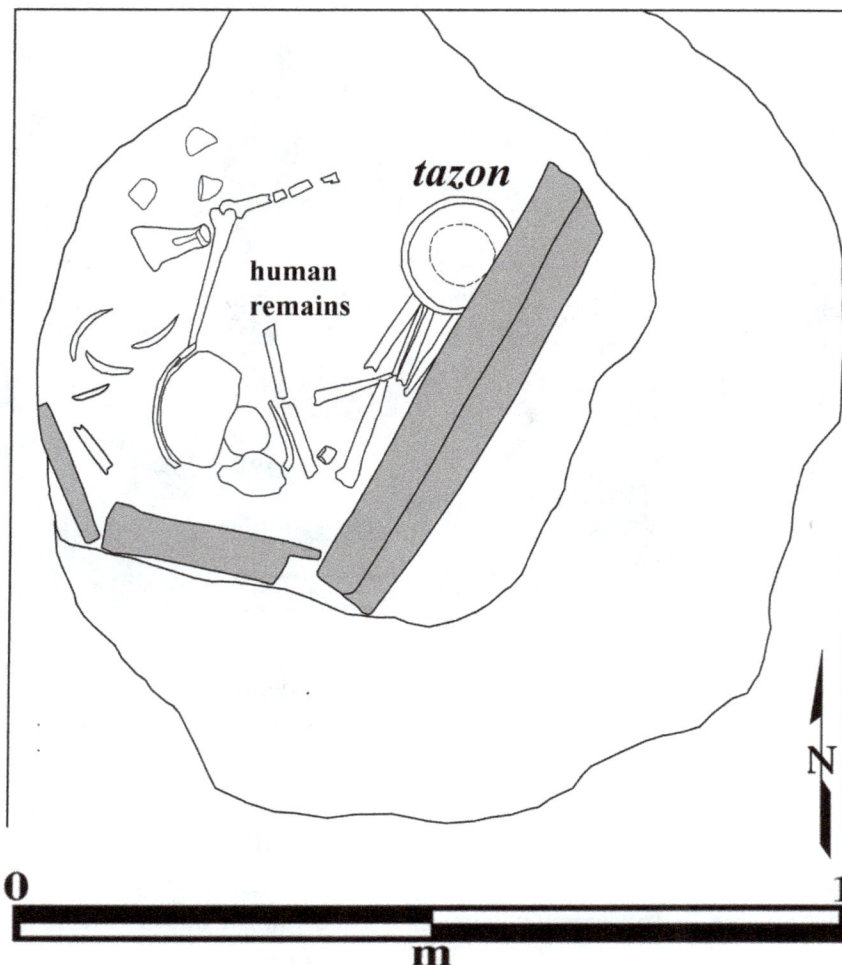

Figure 13.11 Plan of the human burial (Feature 3) excavated in Sector 11.

The pit was approximately 75 cm in diameter at its top and 140 cm at its widest extent close to the base. At its deepest point, it was approximately 120 cm below the surface. It was filled with high volumes of midden, including extremely high densities of Tiwanaku style ceramic sherds and faunal remains. Sherds represented a number of polychrome vessels. We observed no clear stratigraphy in the feature. Heavily mottled soils with high proportions of ash and carbon were mixed throughout the pit fill. A number of large faunal remains rested on the pit's floor, including a deer antler and the skull of an immature llama. Also resting on the floor was an intact *kero* with a perforation in its base **(Figure 13.10)**.

Feature 3 was a stone-lined cist burial that first became visible at the interface between Strata D and F as a patch of gravel fill in the northeast corner of Unit 11.2 **(Figure 13.11)**. The feature was partially overlain by Feature 1. The upper part of the pit feature became visible at about 36–30 cm below the slop-

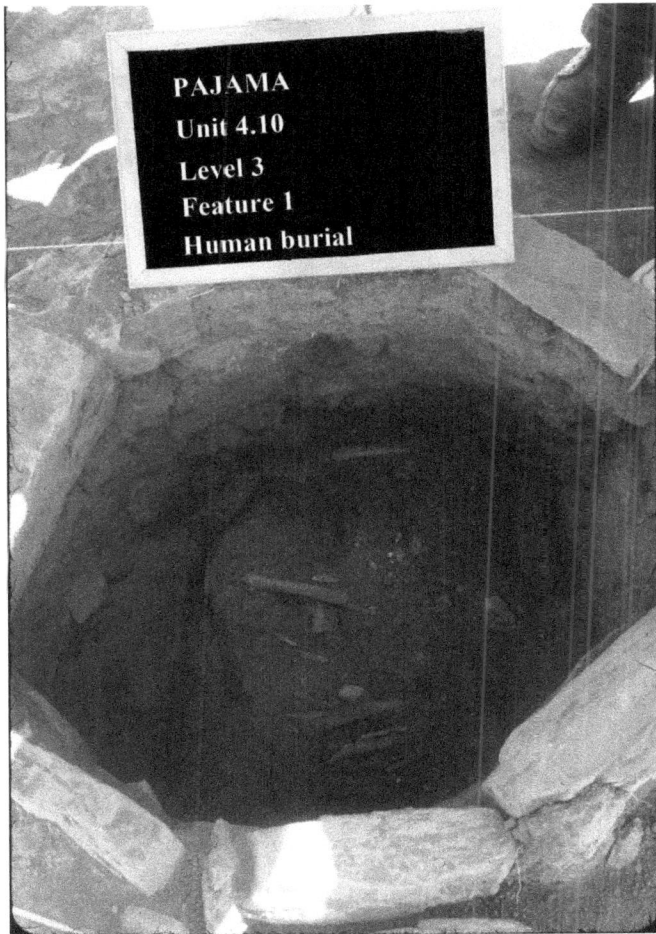

Figure 13.12   View of the burial (Feature 3) excavated in Sector 11. Note the poor condition of the human remains.

ing surface. The cist was circular in plan, about 1 m in diameter, and approximately 140 cm deep. The capstone of this tomb first became visible at about 48 cm below the surface. It had collapsed into the burial and was resting at an oblique vertical angle, which had caused significant damage to the human interment itself. The cist was lined with flat sandstone blocks, but did not have a stone base. The southeast part of the cist included a bench approximately 100 cm below the surface.

The human remains themselves occupied the deep part of the pit below the bench **(Figure 13.12)**. The human remains were very poorly preserved, yet it was clear that several long bones had been articulated at the time of burial. Bioarchaeological analysis indicated that they represented a gracile adult, and thus likely either a young male or an adult female (Blom 2005). The position of the remains suggests that the deceased person was seated in a flexed position, probably facing south or southeast. Several preserved offerings had been placed next to the remains. They included an intact bichrome *tazon* **(Figure 13.13)**, an unbaked clay tube similar to several others found at

Figure 13.13 Tiwanaku-style *tazon* depicting a continuous volue motif accompanied the human remains of Feature 3 (photo by John Janusek).

Figure 13.13 Tiwanaku-style *tazon* depicting a continuous volue motif accompanied the human remains of Feature 3 (photo by John Janusek).

Lukurmata (Janusek 2004:176), and a soft, textured material surrounding the body that likely manifests remnant textiles that enwrapped the flexed person.

Feature 4 was a fire pit in Unit 11.4 located slightly uphill and north of the other units in Sector 11. The feature occupied approximately the same stratigraphic level as Features 2 and 3. Feature 4 occupied a large portion of the NE quadrant of Unit 11.4. The pit was eccentric in shape, but at its greatest width was about 160 cm across in both N–S and E–W dimensions. Its maximum depth was approximately 20 cm. The pit contained abundant ash and midden, yet artifact density was low and included only a few diagnostic Tiwanaku sherds.

Conclusions

Excavations in 2002 first investigated the Putuni mound, Khonkho's second most important after Wankane itself. Excavations indicated that, like Wankane, much of Putuni was a constructed platform. In particular, its central east side (Sector 10) consisted of tightly superimposed strata of dense, deposited construction fill. It remains unclear whether a monumental structure occupied the top of the platform. Excavations on the south edge of the mound revealed middens and features associated with Tiwanaku period occupations. Main features included a couple of refuse pits, a cist burial containing a human interment, and a fire pit. Later excavations in 2005–2006 indicated that these Tiwanaku strata and a thick earlier platform covered successive layers of Late Formative occupations (Janusek 2015; Ohnstad 2007). Platform construction and Tiwanaku occupations covered earlier, thin superimposed residues of temporary, cyclically recurring occupations. Understanding these early occupations, the timing of platform construction—whether Late Formative 2 or Tiwanaku period—and Putuni's ongoing pre-Hispanic transformations should be a priority for future research.

Part V

∽

Project Jach'a Machaca,
Phase One

༄

Chapter 14

Initial Conclusions

John Wayne Janusek

Our initial phase of research established an essential foundation for understanding Khonkho Wankane's long history and shifting importance in the Lake Titicaca Basin. It revealed that Khonkho Wankane spanned a long history of intensive pre-Hispanic occupation beginning in Late Formative 1 (200 BC–AD 300) and continuing through the Early Pacajes Period (or Andean Late Intermediate Period, AD 1100–1450) (Janusek 2013, Zovar 2013). Burials located on the northeast portion of the Wankane platform indicate that human activity continued into the Colonial Period (Ohnstad 2008). Yet Khonkho was a particularly large and complex site during the Late Formative period (200 BC–AD 500). Combined stratigraphic profiles, architectural styles, artifactual assemblages, and a series of radiocarbon dates indicate that Khonkho reached its apogee of regional importance during this period, and particularly during Late Formative 2 (AD 300–500) (Janusek 2011, 2013; Marsh 2012, 2013; Ohnstad 2013; Smith 2009).

Regional survey directed by Carlos Lémuz indicated that throughout its history, Khonkho Wankane constituted a critical focus of shifting settlement relations (chapter 3). Its construction in Late Formative 1 constituted a dramatic departure from Middle Formative settlement patterns, which had clustered around the site of JM-110 just to the west. Beginning with that transformation, Khonkho Wankane became an important center in the region. During the Late Formative, Khonkho was the social and ceremonial center for several other sites in the immediate region, and one of several other interrelated and competing monumental centers in the southern Lake Titicaca Basin. Later excavations reveal that many of Khonkho's immediate sites were only cyclically occupied, raising important questions regarding the role of this incipient urban center. Khonkho Wankane remained an important site during the ensuing Tiwanaku period, but largely as a local settlement dedicated to specialized production and human interment. It was no longer a monumental center with influence across the Lake Titicaca Basin.

Wankane Monumental Complex and its Monoliths

During the Late Formative the site incorporated monumental architecture and included several ceremonial spaces and bounded residential compounds.

Although the site core consisted of two primary and several smaller mounds, Wankane was the primary mound and it incorporated the core monumental complex. The largest space for social gathering and ceremony on Wankane was the Main Plaza. It housed Khonkho's stylistically latest monolith, Tata Kala (chapters 5 and 6). A central basin near its center—now obliterated—drained water from the plaza and surrounding structures into a massive subterranean canal that exited the south edge of Wankane. I hypothesize that it was built early and served as an extensive social and ritual space for most of Khonkho's Late Formative and perhaps even later history.

Several large structures were constructed around the Main Plaza during the Late Formative. The earliest appears to be the South Platform and the bounded structures it housed, the trapezoidal Sunken Temple and Compound 1 (chapters 7 and 8). Attached to the Main Plaza by a wide corridor, the Sunken Temple provided a relatively intimate space for gathering and ritual. Artifactual debris littered its superimposed surfaces and indicates vibrant activities that included commensalism and burning incense or fat in ceramic braziers. Rectangular Compound 1 occupied the east side of the Sunken Temple and incorporated a residential unit centered on a circular structure. With an elaborate paved entrance linking it directly to the Main Plaza, it appears to have been built at approximately the same time as the Sunken Temple. Yet a west wing was later added to the north portion of the compound wall and the west compound wall was dismantled, creating an intimate linkage between the two structures. In light of the unusual stones and precious items recovered in the north section of Compound 1 and its entrance, I hypothesize that this portion of the compound came to serve as a preparation area for rituals staged in the adjacent Sunken Temple. The occupants or landlords of Compound 1, in this scenario, were those responsible for orchestrating those recurring events.

The Dual-Court Complex was constructed toward the end of Late Formative 1 or early in Late Formative 2 (chapter 9). It incorporated the Wankane West Platform, and was oriented east-west on the west side of the Main Plaza. Rather than a single *Kalasasaya*, as Rydén suggested, the complex comprised two courts that were likely built at different times. Entrance to each of the courts from the Main Plaza was far more constricted than entrance into the earlier Sunken Temple, alluding to novel and perhaps more atomized movement flows between ritual spaces at the site. The narrow corridor to the north court incorporated niches with sculpted stone blocks. Furthermore, the floors of the two courts were far cleaner than those of the Sunken Temple, indicating that they provided different sorts of ritual spaces. While it is tempting to envision the relation between the Sunken Temple and Dual-Court Complex as complementary, the former was abandoned and allowed to collapse early in Late Formative 2. The Dual-Court Complex ultimately replaced the Sunken Temple, whether or not that was originally intended.

Khonkho Wankane is best known for its four carved monoliths (chapter 1). The stylistically latest and most robust monolith, the Tatakala, is still located in what we think was its original context, the central Main Plaza (chapter 5). The other three were found *ex situ*. The stylistically earliest of these monoliths, the Portugal, was found smashed into several pieces and buried as a cache just off of the Wankane platform (Portugal 1955). If somewhat speculative, it is a reasonable inference that each of these three originally stood in one of Wankane's other primary ceremonial spaces. Meshing Ohnstad's stylistic seriation with Smith's architectural chronology of the site (2009), I hypothesize that the purposefully destroyed Portugal originally stood within the early trapezoidal Sunken Temple. This temple, recall, was abandoned soon after the construction of the Dual-Court Complex. Possibly, its central material icon was deemed to require ritualized destruction and interment. The Wila Kala and Jinch'un Kala monoliths, which clearly composed as a pair, possibly stood within the paired courts of the new Dual-Court Complex (Janusek and Ohnstad 2018; Ohnstad 2013).

Residential, Mortuary, and Depositional Activities Beyond the Wankane Core

Phase One research at Khonkho Wankane revealed several areas dedicated to residential, mortuary, and depositional activity just off of the Wankane mound as well as platform construction on the adjacent Putuni mound (chapter 13). Excavations in the northeast sector of the Wankane mound—Sector 3—revealed evidence for Late Formative occupation associated with a remnant rectilinear structure (chapter 10). Most other primary remains from Sector 3 consisted of Tiwanaku interments. Excavations at the north edge of the Wankane mound revealed an intricate, multi-room structural complex dating to the Tiwanaku period (chapter 11). Inhabitants of the complex engaged in a specialized practice, whether it involved making ceramic vessels, metal adornments, or something else. This sector also included abundant Tiwanaku period human interments. Deep excavations revealed that the sector was first inhabited during the Late Formative.

Phase one research also initiated investigations on the adjacent Putuni mound north of Wankane. This mound is smaller than Wankane, but as 2001–2002 excavations first demonstrated, much of it was humanly constructed to form a massive platform (Janusek 2015). Excavations on the eroded east edge of the platform (Sector 10) provided an initial window into Putuni mound construction. Platform soil was incredibly dense and intermeshed clay strata dredged from around the mound with bags or baskets of mixed sandy to silty clay loam (chapter 13). Excavations on the sloping south edge of Putuni

(Sector 11) revealed remnants of a Tiwanaku occupation that incorporated a hearth, a bell-shaped storage pit, an ash/refuse pit, a human burial, and arti-factually dense strata of occupation zone and secondary midden. Putuni was constructed as a platform during the Late Formative and harbored dense occupation during the Tiwanaku period.

Conclusions

Our research confirms that Khonkho Wankane was remarkably influential in the southern Lake Titicaca Basin during the Late Formative. Details of the site's incorporation into the expanding Tiwanaku polity are poorly understood. Yet Khonkho Wankane clearly was not Tiwanaku's "second city." Of all of Khonkho's Late Formative ritual spaces, only the north court of the Dual-Court Complex appears to have been employed as ritual space during the Tiwanaku period. Substantial Tiwanaku occupations were located in many deposits beyond the Wankane platform, for example on the north and northwest edges of the Wankane Mound (Sectors 3, 4, and 8) and on the south edge of the Putuni mound (Sector 11). Khonkho Wankane also incorporated Early Pacajes (LIP) occupations, but they tended to be ephemeral and centered on pastoral features at the site. Khonkho Wankane peaked as an incipient urban center (see chapter 1) of regional social encounter and ceremonial convergence during the Late Formative.

Bibliography

Albarracín-Jordan, Juan
  1996   *Tiwanku: Arqueología regional y dinámica seg-
         mentaria.* La Paz, Bolivia: Plural Editores.

Albarracín-Jordan, Juan V. and James E. Mathews
  1990   *Asentamientos Prehispánicos del Valle de Tiwana-
         ku, Vol. 1.* La Paz: CIMA.

Albó, Xavier
  2012   *Tres municipios Andinos camino a la autonomía
         indígena: Jesus de Machaca, Chayanta, Tarabu-
         co.* La Paz: CIPCA.

Alconini Mujica, Sonia
  1991   Algunas reflexiones sobre la formación de la
         arqueología en Bolivia. *Etnología: Boletín del
         Museo Nacional de Etnografía y Folklore* (La
         Paz) 19:57–68.
  1995   *Rito, Símbolo e Historia en la Pirámide de Akap-
         ana, Tiwanaku: Un Análisis de Cerámica Cere-
         monial Prehispánica,* La Paz: Editorial Acción.

Anonymous
  1936   La responsibilidad de Buck: Las ruinas arque-
         ológicas de Konko. Article from an unknown
         Bolivian periodical dated October 13, 1936.

Bandy, Matthew S.
  2001   *Population and History in the Ancient Titicaca
         Basin.* Ph.D. Dissertation, Department of An-
         thropology, University of California, Berkeley.
  2004a Fissioning, Scalar Stress, and Social Evolution
         in Early Village Societies. *American Anthropol-
         ogist* 106(2):322–333.
  2004b Trade and Social Power in the Southern
         Titicaca Basin Formative. In *Foundations of
         Power in the Prehispanic Andes,* C. A. Conlee,
         D. Ogburn, and K. Vaughn, eds., pp. 91–111.
         Washington, D.C.: American Anthropological
         Association.

Bandy, Matthew S. and Christine A. Hastorf, editors
  2005   *Kala Uyuni: An Early Political Center in the
         Southern Lake Titicaca Basin,* pp. 5–12. Contri-
         butions of the Archaeological Research Facil-
         ity, No. 64. University of California Berkeley.
         https://escholarship.org/uc/item/1kp3r778

Barba, Luis
  1990   *Radiografía de un sitio arqueológico.* México, DF:
         Instituto de Investigaciones Antropológicas de
         la Universidad Nacional Autónoma de Méxi-
         co.

Benitez, Leonardo
  2009   Descendants of the Sun: Calendars, Myth
         and the Tiwanaku State. In *Tiwanaku: Papers
         from the 2005 Mayer Center Symposium at the
         Denver Museum of Art,* edited by Margaret
         Young-Sanchez, pp. 49–82. Denver Art Muse-
         um.

Bennett, Wendell C.
  1934   Excavations at Tiahuanaco. *Anthropological
         Papers of the American Museum of Natural His-
         tory,* New York 34:359–494.
  1950   Cultural Unity and Disunity in the Titicaca
         Basin. *American Anthropologist* 16(2):89–98.

Bermann, Marc
  1994   *Lukurmata: Household Archaeology in Prehispan-
         ic Bolivia.* Princeton, NJ: Princeton University
         Press.
  1997   Domestic life and vertical integration in the
         Tiwanaku heartland. In: *Latin American Antiq-
         uity* 8(2):93–112.

Bermann, Marc and Jose Estevez Castillo
  1995 Domestic Artifact Assemblages and Ritual
        Activities in the Bolivian Formative. *Journal of
        Field Archaeology* 22(3):389–398.

Blom, Deborah E.
  2005 Restos Humanos de Khonkho Wankane:
        Inventarios y datos. In *Khonkho Wankane:
        Segundo informe preliminar del Proyecto Jach'a
        Machaca (Investigaciones en 2004 y 2005)*, J.
        W. Janusek and V. Plaza Martinez, eds., pp.
        207–215. Official technical report submitted
        to the Viceministry of Culture and the Na-
        tional Institute of Archaeology, Bolivia.

Browman, David L.
  1972 Asiruni, Pucara-Pokotía, and Pajano: Pre-Ti-
        ahuanaco South Andean Monolitoic Stone
        Styles. Paper presented at the 37th Annual
        Meeting of the Society for American Archae-
        ology, St. Louis, MO.
  1978 The Temple of Chiripa (Lake Titicaca, Boliv-
        ia). *El Hombre y la Cultura Andina, III Congre-
        so Peruano, Vol. 2*, R. Matos, ed., pp. 807–13.
        Lima: Editoral Lasontay.
  1995 Pa-Ajanu: A Formative Titicaca Religious
        Stela Tradition. Paper presented at the 60th
        Annual Meeting of the Society for American
        Archaeology, Minneapolis, MN.
  1997 Pajano: Nexus of Formative Cultures in the
        Titicaca Basin. Paper presented at the XLIX
        International Congress of Americanists, Qui-
        to, Ecuador.

Buck, Fritz
  1937 *El Calendario Maya en la Cultura de Tiahuana-
        cu*. La Paz: Lit. e Imp. Unidas.

Chávez, Sergio and Karen L. Mohr Chávez
  1975 A Carved Stela from Taraco, Puno, Peru,
        and the Definition of an Early Style of Stone
        Sculpture from the Altiplano of Peru and
        Bolivia. *Ñawpa Pacha* 13:45–83.

Chávez, Karen L. Mohr
  1988 The Significance of Chiripa in Lake Titicaca
        Basin Developments. *Expedition* 30:17–26

Chávez, Sergio
  1988 Archaeological Reconnaissance in the Prov-
        ince of Chumbivilcas, South Highland Peru.
        Expedition 30(3):27–38.
  1992 *The Conventionalized Rules in Pucara Pottery
        Technology and Iconography: Implications for
        Socio-Political Developments in the Lake Titica-
        ca Basin*. Ph.D. Dissertation, Department of
        Anthropology, Michigan State University.

Choque Canqui, Roberto
  1993 *Sociedad y Economía Colonial en el Sur Andino*.
        La Paz: Hisbol.

Clark, Anthony J.
  1990. *Seeing Beneath the Soil: Prospection Methods in
        Archaeology*. London: B.T. Batsford.

Fish, S. and S. A. Kowalewski, Eds.
  1990 *The Archaeology of Regions: A Case for
        Full-Coverage Survey*. Washington, D.C.:
        Smithsonian Institution Press.

Frame, Mary
  2001 Blood, Fertility, and Transformation: Interwo-
        ven Themes in the Paracas Necropolis Em-
        broideries. In *Ritual Sacrifice in Ancient Peru*,
        edited by E. P. Benson and A. G. Cook, pp.
        55–92. Austin: University of Texas Press.

Gaffney, Chris and John Gater
  2003 *Revealing the Buried Past: Geophysics for Ar-
        chaeologists*. Stroud, Gloucestershire: Tempus
        Publishing Ltd.

Harris, Edward C.
  1989 *Principles of Archaeological Stratigraphy*. New
        York: Academic Press.

Hastorf, Christine A.
  2003 Community with the Ancestors: Ceremonies
        and Social Memory in the Middle Formative
        at Chiripa, Bolivia. *Journal of Anthropological
        Archaeology* 22:305–332.

Hastorf, Christine A., Matthew S. Bandy, Emily Dean,
David Kojan and William Whitehead
  1996 Guide to field and laboratory operations, Pro-
        yecto Arqueológico Taraco. Report submitted

to the National Direction of Anthropology
and Archaeology (DINAAR), La Paz, Bolivia.

Hastorf, Christine A., editor

1999 *Early Settlement at Chiripa, Bolivia: Research of the Taraco Archaeological Project.* Contibutions of the Archaeological Research Facility, No. 57. University of California, Berkeley. https://escholarship.org/uc/item/4gw9z9mj

Hester, Thomas R., Harry J. Schaffer and
Kenneth L. Feder

1997 *Field Methods in Archaeology,* 6th ed. Mountain View, California: Mayfield Publishing.

Ibarra Grasso, Dick Edgar and Roy Querejazu Lewis

1986 *30.000 Años de Prehistoria en Bolivia.* La Paz, Bolivia: Los Amigos del Libro.

Janusek, John Wayne

2003a Vessels, Time, and Society: Toward a Chronology of Ceramic Style in the Tiwanaku Heartland. En: *Tiwanaku and its Hinterland: Archaeology and Paleoecology of an Andean Civilization, Vol. 2,* A. L. Kolata, ed., pp. 30–92. Washington, D.C.: Smithsonian Institution Press.

2003b The Changing Face of Tiwanaku Residential Life: State and Social Identity in an Andean City. In *Tiwanaku and Its Hinterland: Archaeology and Paleoecology of an Andean Civilization, Vol. 2.* A. L. Kolata, ed., pp. 264–295. Washington, D.C.: Smithsonian Institution Press: 264–295.

2004 *Identity and Power in the Ancient Andes: Tiwanaku Cities through Time.* London: Routledge.

2006 The Changing "Nature" of Tiwanaku Religion and the Rise of an Andean State. *World Archaeology* 38(3):469–92.

2008 *Ancient Tiwanaku.* London: University of Cambridge Press.

Janusek, John Wayne

2009 Centralidad regional, ecología religiosa y complejidad emergente durante el period formatvo en la Cuenca del Lago Titicaca. *Boletín de Arqueología PUCP* 11:23–52.

2011 Contextualizando el sitio de Khonkho Wankane: Objectivos, antecedentes, y resultados preliminaries del Proyecto Jach'a Machaca. *Nuevos Aportes: Revista de Arqueología Boliviana* 5:3–30. http://www.arqueobolivia.com/revistas.php

2013 Jesus de Machaca Before and After Tiwanaku: A Background to Research at Khonkho Wankane and Pukara de Khonkho. In *Advances in Titicaca Basin Archaeology 2,* A. Vranich and A. Levine, eds., pp. 7–22. Los Angeles: Cotsen Institute of Archaeology, University of California.

2015 Incipient Urbanism in the High Andes: Recent Research at Khonkho Wankane, Bolivia. *Journal of Field Archaeology* 40(2):127–142.

Janusek, John Wayne, and Howard E. Earnest

1990 Urban residence and Land Reclamation in Lukurmata: A View from the Core Area. In *Tiwanaku and its Hinterland,* report submitted to the National Science Foundation, Alan L. Kolata, ed., pp. 118–43.

Janusek, John Wayne and Alan L. Kolata

2003 Prehispanic Rural History in the Katari Valley. In *Tiwanaku and Its Hinterland: Archaeology and Paleoecology of an Andean Civilization, Vol. 2,* A. L. Kolata, ed., pp. 129–172. Washington, D.C.: Smithsonian Institution Press.

Janusek, John W. and Arik T. Ohnstad

2019 Stone Stelae of the Southern Basin: A Stylistic Chronology of Ancestral Personages. In *The Southern Andean Iconographic Series,* W. A. Isbell, ed. Los Angeles: Cotsen Institute of Archaeology, University of California, Los Angeles.

Janusek, John Wayne, Arik Ohnstad and
Andrew P. Roddick

2003 Khonkho Wankane and the Rise of the Tiwanaku State. *Antiquity* 77: Web publication: http://antiquity.ac.uk/ProjGall/janusek/janusek.html

Jones, Geoffrey

2001 Geophysical Investigation at the Falling Creek Ironworks, an Early Industrial Site in Virginia. *Archaeological Prospection* 8(4):247–256.

Joukousky, Martha.

1980 *Field Archaeology: Tools and techniques of field work for archaeologist.* Spectrum: New Jersey.

Kolata, Alan L.

1986 The Agricultural Foundations of the Tiwanaku State: A View from the Heartland. *American Antiquity*, 51:748–62.

1987 Research Objectives and Strategies: The 1987 Field Season. In *The Technology and Organization of Agricultural Production in the Tiwanaku State: First Preliminary Report of Proyecto Wila Jawira*, Alan L. Kolata, Charles Stanish, and Oswaldo Rivera, eds., pp. 260–269. Official report submitted to the National Institute of Archaeology (INAR), La Paz.

1993 *Tiwanaku: Portrait of an Andean Civilization.* Cambridge: Blackwell.

Kolata, Alan L., editor

1989 *Arqueología de Lukurmata, vol. 2.* La Paz: Producciones Puma Punku.

Korpisaari, Antii, and and Martii Pärssinen

2011 *Pariti: The Ceremonial Tiwanaku Pottery of an Island in Lake Titicaca.* Helsinki, Finnish Academy of Science and Letters.

Kvamme, Kenneth L.

2001 Current Practices in Archaeogeophysics: Magnetics, Resistivity, Conductivity, and Ground-Penetrating Radar. In *Earth Sciences and Archaeology*, Paul Goldberg, Vance T. Holliday, and C. Reid Ferring, eds., 353–384. New York: Kluwer Academic/Plenum Publishers.

Lémuz Aguirre, Carlos

2001 Patrones de Asentamiento Arqueologico en la Peninsula de Santiago de Huata, Bolivia. Licensiature Thesis, Department of Anthropology and Archaeology, Universidad Mayor de San Andrés, La Paz.

2005 Patrones de asentamiento arqueológico en el área de influencia del sitio de Khonkho Wankane. In *Segundo informe preliminar del Proyecto Arqueológico Jach'a Machaca (excavaciones en 2004–2005)*, J. W. Janusek and V. Plaza Martínez, eds., pp. 5–44. Official technical report submitted to the Viceministry of Culture and the National Institute of Archaeology, Bolivia.

Manzanilla, Linda

1992 *Akapana. Una pirámide en el centro del mundo.* Universidad Nacional Autónoma de México. México, D.F: Instituto de Investigaciones Antropológicas.

Marsh, Erik J.

2012 The Emergence of Tiwanaku: Domestic Practices and Regional Traditions at Khonkho Wankane and Kk'araña. Ph.D. Dissertation, Department of Anthropology, University of California, Santa Barbara.

2013 Excavations of a Late Formative Patio Group at Khonkho Wankane, Bolivia. In *Advances in Titicaca Basin Archaeology 2*, A. Vranich and A. Levine, eds., pp. 45–52. Los Angeles: Cotsen Institute of Archaeology, University of California.

Mathews, W., C. A. I. French, T. Lawrence, D. F. Cutler, and M. K. Jones

1997 Microstratigraphic Traces of Site Formation Processes and Human Activities. *World Archaeology* 29(2):281–308.

McAndrews, Timothy L.

1997 Early Village-Based Society and Long-Term Cultural Evolution in the South-Central Andean Altiplano. Ph.D. dissertation, Department of Anthropology, University of Pittsburgh.

2001 Organización y crecimiento de los sistemas de asentamiento tempranos basados en aldeas en el altiplano Andino del Sur Central. *Textos Antropológicos* 13(1–2):135–146.

Ohnstad, Arik T.

2007 Investigaciones en áreas preiféricas de los montículos de Wankane y Putuni. In *Khonkho e Iruhito: Tercer Informe Preliminar del Proyecto Jach'a Machaca, (Investigaciones en 2006)* John W. Janusek and Victor Plaza Martinez, eds., pp. 141–186. Official technical report submitted to the Viceministry of Culture and the National Institute of Archaeology, Bolivia.

2008 Investigaciones en la Plaza y el Templo Hundido. In *Khonkho Wankane y la Pukara de Khonkho: Cuarto informe preliminar del Proyecto Jach'a Machaca, Investigaciones en 2007*, John W. Janusek and Victor Plaza Martinez, eds., pp. 39–62. Official technical report submitted to the Viceministry of Culture and the National Institute of Archaeology, Bolivia.

2011 La escultura prehispánica de Khonkho Wankane, Jesus de Machaca, Bolivia. *Nuevos Aportes: Revista de Arqueología Boliviana* 5:119–142.

2013 The Stone Stelae of Khonkho Wankane. In *Advances in Titicaca Basin Archaeology 2*, A. Vranich and A. Levine, eds., pp. 53–66. Los Angeles: Cotsen Institute of Archaeology, University of California.

Ohnstad, Arik, and John W. Janusek

2004 Ritual and Iconography at Khonkho Wankane: New Perspectives on the Late Formative in the Southern Lake Titicaca Basin. Paper presented at the 23rd Annual Midwest Conference on Andean and Amazonian Archaeology and Ethnohistory, Urbana, Il.

Petraglia, Michael

1993 The Genesis and Alteration of Archaeological Patterns at Abri Dufaure: An Upper Paleolithic Rockshelter and Slope Site in Southwestern France. In *Formation Processes in Archaeological Contexts*, D. T Nash, P. Goldberg, and M. D. Petraglia, eds., pp. 97–112. Madison, WI: Prehistory Press.

Plaza Martinez, Victor

2007 Excavaciones arqueologicos desarolladas en el Sector 6 (Comuesto 1). In *Khonko e Iruhito: Tercer Informe Preliminar del Proyecto Jach'a Machaca (Investigaciones en 2006)*, John W. Janusek and Victor Plaza Martinez, eds., pp. 20–101. Official technical report submitted to the Viceministry of Culture and the National Institute of Archaeology, Bolivia.

Ponce Sanginés, Carlos

1970 *Las Culturas Wankarani y Chiripa y su Relación con Tiwanaku.* La Paz: Academia Nacional de Ciencias de Bolivia.

1980 *Panorama de la Arqueología Boliviana, 2nd edition.* La Paz: Librería Editorial Juventud.

1981 *Tiwanaku: Espacio, Tiempo, Cultura: Ensayo de síntesis arqueológica.* La Paz: Los Amigos del Libro.

1989 *Arqueología de Lukurmata, vol. 1.* La Paz: Producciones Puma Punku.

1990 *Descripción Sumaria del Templete Semisubterráneo de Tiwanaku*, 6th ed. La Paz: Librería Editorial Juventud.

1995 *Tiwanaku: 200 Años de Investigaciones Arqueológicas.* La Paz: Producciones CIMA.

Portugal Ortiz, Max

1981 Expansion del Estilo Escultorico Pa-Ajanu. *Arte y Arqueología* 7:149–158.

1988 Informe de la prospección a Pacajes. *Arqueología Boliviana* 3:109–117.

1992 Aspectos de la cultura Chiripa. *Textos Antropológicos* 3:9–26.

1998 *Escultura Prehispanic Boliviana.* La Paz: Universidad Mayor de San Andrés.

Portugal Zamora, Maks

1936 Breve estudio acerca de las ruinas de Huancane. La Paz: La Razon

1937 Estudio sintético sobre el ultimo descrubimiento arquológico en Huancane-Khonko. *Revista de Bolivia* 10(2).

1941 Las Ruinas de Jesus de Machaca. *Revista Geográfica Americana* 16:291–300.

1955 El Misterio de las Tumbas de Wanqani. *Khana* 11–12:51–67.

1988 Aspectos generales sobre Tiwanaku del area circundante al Lago Titicaca (sector Bolivia). *Arqueología Boliviana* 3:15–26.

Posnansky, Arthur

1945 *Tihuanacu: The Cradle of American Man, Vol. I,* New York: J.J. Augustin.

Renfrew, Colin and Paul Bahn

1991 *Archaeology: Theories, Methods and Practice.* New York: Thames and Hudson.

Rivera Casanovas, Claudia S.

2003 Ch'iji Jawira: A Case of Ceramic Specialization in the Tiwanaku Urban Periphery. In *Tiwanaku and Its Hinterland: Archaeology and Paleoecology of an Andean Civilization, Vol. 2,* A. L. Kolata, ed., pp. 296–315. Washington, D.C.: Smithsonian Institution Press.

Rosen, Arlene Miller

1993 Microartifacts as a reflection of cultural factors in site formation. In *Formation Processes in Archaeological Context,* D. T Nash, P. Goldberg, and M. D. Petraglia, eds., pp. 141–148. Madison, WI: Prehistory Press.

Roskams, Steve

2001 *Excavation (Cambridge Manuals in Archaeology).* Cambridge University Press.

Rowe, John H. and Catherine T. Brandel

1969–1970 Pucara Style Pottery Designs. *Ñawpa Pacha* 7–8:1–16.

Rydén, Stig

1947 *Archaeological Researches in the Highlands of Bolivia.* Göteborg: Elanders Boktryckeri Aktiebolag.

Sagárnaga Meneses, J. A.

1987 *Fritz Buck: un hombre, una colección.* La Paz: Los Amigos del Libro.

Schiffer, Michael B.

1996 *Formation Processes of the Archaeological Record.* Salt Lake City: University of Utah Press.

Smith, Scott C.

2009 Venerable Geographies: Spatial Dynamics, Religion, and Political Economy in the Prehistoric Lake Titicaca Basin, Bolivia. Ph.D. Dissertation, Department of Anthropology, University of California, Riverside.

2013 Late Formative Period Spatial Organization at Khonkho Wankane, Bolivia. In *Advances in Titicaca Basin Archaeology 2,* A. Vranich and A. Levine, eds., pp. 23–44. Los Angeles: Cotsen Institute of Archaeology, University of California, Los Angeles.

Smith, Scott C., and Maribel Pérez Arias

2014 From Bodies to Bones: Death and Mobility in the Lake Titicaca Basin, Bolivia. *Antiquity* 89(343):106–121.

SNC (Secretario Nacional de Cultura de Bolivia).

1997 *Reglamento de excavaciones arqueológicas en Bolivia.* La Paz, Prefectura del Departamento de La Paz.

Stanish, C.

1989 Tamaño y complejidad de los asentamientos nucleares de Tiwanaku. In *Arqueología de Lukurmata vol. 2,* A. L. Kolata, ed., pp. 41–58. La Paz, Bolivia: Producciones Puma Punku.

2003 *Ancient Titicaca: The Evolution of Social Complexity in Southern Peru and Northern Bolivia.* Los Angeles: University of California Press.

Stanish, Charles, Edmundo de la Vega M.,

Lee Steadman, Cecilia Chávez Justo,

Kirk Lawrence Frye, Luperio Onofre Mamani,

Matthew T. Seddon and Percy Calisaya Chuquimia

1997 *Archaeological Survey in the Juli-Desaguadero Region of the Lake Titicaca Basin, Southern Peru.* Chicago: Field Museum of Natural History.

Steadman, Lee

1995 Excavations at Camata: An Early Ceramic Chronology for the Western Titicaca Basin. Ph.D. Dissertation, Department of Anthropology, University of California, Berkeley.

Stein, Julie K.

1992   Organic matter in archaeological contexts. In *Soils in Archaeology: Landscape Evolution and Human Occupation*, V. T. Holliday, ed., pp. 193–216. Washington, D.C.: Smithsonian Institution Press.

Thierry, G. E., Marie-Agnes Courty, Wendy Matthews and Julia Wattez

1993   Sedimentary Formation Processes of Occupation Surfaces. In *Formation Processes in Archaeological Context*, D. T Nash, P. Goldberg, and M. D. Petraglia, eds., pp. 149–164. Madison, WI: Prehistory Press.

Uhle, Max

1895   Field report submitted to the Department of Archaeology and Paleontology of the University of Pennsylvania, based on travel and investigation conducted in Bolivia in 1894 and 1895. Philadelphia: Penn Museum official report.

Vellard, Jean

1955   Las Ruinas de Khonkho Wancane. *Revista del Museo Nacional de Antropologia y Arqueologia, Lima* 2(2):51–56.

1963   *Civilisations des Andes*. Paris: Gallimard.

Vranich, Alexei

2009   The Development of the Ritual Core of Tiwanaku. In *Tiwanaku: Papers from the 2005 Mayer Center Symposium at the Denver Museum of Art*, edited by Margaret Young-Sanchez, pp. 11–34. Denver Art Museum.

Waters, Michael R.

1992   *Principles of Geoarchaeology: An American Perspective*. Tucson: University of Arizona.

Williams, Patrick R., Deborah E. Blom, Nicole Couture, Chris Dayton, John W. Janusek and Ben Vining

2003   Visualizing the Urban and Monumental Components of the Tiwanaku State: New Perspectives from Geophysics in the Andean Altiplano. Paper presented at the 22nd Annual Northeast Conference of Andean Archaeology and Ethnohistory, Harvard University, Cambridge.

Williams, Patrick R., Nicole Couture, Deborah Blom, John W. Janusek, Benjamin Vining and Chris Dayton

2004   Ground-Based Remote Sensing and Early State Development in the South-Central Andes. In *Proceedings of the International Conference of Remote Sensing Archaeology*, 149–157. Beijing: Joint Laboratory of Remote Sensing Archaeology, Chinese Academy of Sciences.

Williams, Patrick R., Nicole Couture and Deborah E. Blom

2007   Urban Structure at Tiwanaku: Geophysical Investigations in the Andean Altiplano. In *Remote Sensing in Archaeology*, J. Wiseman and F. El-Baz (eds.), pp. 423–441. New York: Springer.

Zovar, Jennifer M.

2006   Excavaciones en Sector 7, Compuesto K3. In *Segundo informe preliminar del Proyecto Archaeólogico Jach'a Machaca: Excavaciones en 2004–2005*, John W. Janusek and Victor Plaza Martinez, eds., pp. 142–160. Official technical report submitted to the Bolivian Viceministry of Culture and the National Institute of Archaeology, Bolivia.

2012   Post-Collapse Constructions of Community, Memory, and Identity: An Archaeological Analysis of Late Intermediate Period Community Formation in Bolivia's Desaguadero Valley. Ph.D. Dissertation, Department of Anthropology, Vanderbilt University.

2013   Pukara de Khonkho: Preliminary Analysis of a Pacajes Hilltop Settlement. In *Advances in Titicaca Basin Archaeology 2*, A. Vranich and A. Levine, eds., pp. 67–78. Los Angeles: Cotsen Institute of Archaeology, University of California.